BAKER & TAYLOR

Called to Serve

Called to Serve

A History of Nuns in America

Margaret M. McGuinness

NEW YORK UNIVERSITY PRESS

New York and London

NEW YORK UNIVERSITY PRESS
New York and London
www.nyupress.org

References to Internet websites (URLs) were accurate at the time of writing.
Neither the author nor New York University Press is responsible for URLs that
may have expired or changed since the manuscript was prepared.

Library of Congress Cataloging-in-Publication Data
McGuinness, Margaret M.
Called to serve : a history of nuns in America / Margaret M. McGuinness.
p. cm.
Includes bibliographical references and index.
ISBN 978-0-8147-9556-9 (cl : alk. paper) — ISBN 978-0-8147-2472-9 (e-book) — ISBN 978-
0-8147-8926-1 (e-book)
1. Nuns—United States—History. 2. Monasticism and religious orders for women—United
States—History. 3. Monastic and religious life of women—United States—History. 4.
United States—Church history. I. Title.
BX4220.U6M34 2013
271'.90073—dc23   2012038065

New York University Press books are printed on acid-free paper, and their binding materials
are chosen for strength and durability. We strive to use environmentally responsible suppliers
and materials to the greatest extent possible in publishing our books.

Manufactured in the United States of America
10 9 8 7 6 5 4 3 2 1

To Bill, Will, Sarah, and Erin, with love

Contents

Acknowledgments

IT IS A PLEASURE to remember and thank all those who helped to make this book a reality. Administrators at La Salle University in Philadelphia, especially Brother President Michael McGinniss, FSC, Joseph R. Marbach, provost, and Dean Thomas Keagy have been consistently supportive of this project. In addition, I am thankful for a research leave that I received from the University's Leaves and Grants Committee during the fall of 2010, which allowed me some uninterrupted time to think and write about women religious. The staff at La Salle University's Connelly Library was unfailingly gracious and pleasant as they tracked down some rather obscure sources. I am particularly grateful to Stephen Breedlove for his ability to find every book and article I requested. Yvonne Macolly, administrative assistant in the Religion department, makes my life easier in many ways, and her presence on the second floor of McShain Hall has been a blessing.

A number of people read chapters or portions of chapters and offered constructive comments while saving me from a number of embarrassing errors. Joseph Mannard, Anne Butler, Kathleen Sprows Cummings, Barbra Mann Wall, Carol K. Coburn, Eileen Flanagan, and Regina Siegfried, ASC, all fine commentators on the history of women religious in their own right, took time away from their work to critique, support, and encourage. Ellen Pierce, James O'Toole, Regina Bechtle, SC, Patricia Byrne, CSJ, Anne Francis Campbell, OLM, Mada-anne Gell, VHM, Karen Kennelly, CSJ, Joseph Chinnici, OFM, and Cait Kokolous helped me to understand some of the subtleties involved in trying to portray American women religious as accurately as possible. Judith Metz, SC, Mary Ellen Gleason, SC, Peter Schmid, Tom Felton, Anne Schwelm, M. Alan Wurth, ASC, and Patricia Anne, OSC helped to find photographs that accurately represented women religious in the United States. A number of archivists, too numerous to name, worked with me to find a suitable photograph for the book's cover. I am especially grateful to Janet Welsh, OP, who enlisted Dominican archivists far and wide to assist in my search for just the right picture. Any errors, of course, are mine alone.

During the past several years I have had long conversations with friends and colleagues about the history of sisters and nuns in the United States. Many of these have taken place at the meetings of the Conference on the History of Women Religious. Having the opportunity to engage with those who either write about women religious or serve as community archivists so that others can tell the story is something to which I very much look forward. It is my hope that this organization remains active for many, many years.

My good friend and mentor, Margaret Mary Reher, read the entire manuscript and talked about it with me on many occasions. Mary Ann Biller has been cheering me on since she hired me to join the faculty of Cabrini College in 1985. Marge's and Mary Ann's own knowledge of this area, along with their keen eye for detail and wonderful sense of humor, led to many great conversations—not that we have ever needed an excuse to get together—and ultimately, I think, a better manuscript. Shirley Dixon, Ruby Remley, Carol Serotta, and Marilyn Johnson planned lunches and dinners and helped me to remember that there are other aspects of life that do not revolve around research and writing. Marjorie Allen, Kevin Harty, Alice Hoersch, MarySheila McDonald, Brother Emery Mollenhauer, FSC, Pidge Molyneaux, Gail Ramshaw, Michael Roszkowski, and Margot Soven were part of many lively conversations about women religious that took place on La Salle's campus—mostly in the Faculty Dining Room.

Jennifer Hammer is a fine editor, and any thanks I may express do not do justice to the wonderful work she does for authors at NYU Press. She responded to emails promptly, answered any and all questions, offered perceptive comments and criticisms, and supported and encouraged this work from the beginning. All authors should have the wonderful experience I have had working with her, and I thank her from the bottom of my heart.

Finally, I want to thank two very special groups of people. The first is the Class of 1971 from St. Mary Academy Bay View in Riverside, Rhode Island. In July 2011, many of us from that class came together to celebrate our fortieth reunion. The night before the reunion, I sat with Kate Fielder, Beth Dolan Whitehead, and Jane DiPetro Gallagher and enjoyed the feeling one gets when the years begin to melt away. As about sixty of us caught up with each other the following day—there's a lot to talk about after forty years—it became clear to me that women religious played a vital role in our formative years. The Sisters of Mercy, some of us remembered, not only required us to read books that are banned in many schools today, they tested us on them. In addition to teaching algebra, chemistry, history, and English, they told us in no uncertain terms that women could govern, lead, and research as well as men, and we had better get busy and make something of ourselves. Perhaps more important was their insistence that we understand the world around us and be especially concerned about those living on the margins of society. Although my classmates have gone in many different directions since we received our diplomas, I think that many of us took those lessons to heart. In that spirit, I especially thank Jane Carey, a teacher who became a friend, for mentoring me in many, many ways.

The second group is significantly smaller, but they have made my world a much better place for the past twenty-eight years. Bill, Will, Sarah, and Erin Shipley help to define who I am. Time spent with Will and Sarah is always a delight, and I am glad I stopped working on this book long enough to celebrate with them as they began a life together. Erin read the entire manuscript and helped me to think about questions undergraduate students might raise about women religious. I suspect she will write her own book someday, and I hope to be the first to read it. Bill also read the entire manuscript and saved me from several errors. He and I have spent many years together, and with any luck, there will be many more. This book is dedicated to them, with love.

Introduction

SISTER MARY SCULLION, RSM, a member of the Sisters of Mercy, began working with Philadelphia's homeless and mentally ill men and women in 1978 at the age of twenty-five, leading her, she once reflected, to "the most profound experience [she] ever had of God."[1] As her ministry to this population grew into a lifetime commitment, Sister Mary was arrested at least twice for distributing food to those homeless seeking shelter in Philadelphia's 30th Street train station, and although never convicted, she spent several nights in jail. On another occasion, Sister Mary, along with some men and women who had been denied admittance to the city's overcrowded shelters, occupied the basement of the Municipal Services Building, "the hub of city offices and services."[2] These public demonstrations, combined with other activities such as leading protestors into Philadelphia City Council meetings and badgering then Mayor Edward G. Rendell to increase city allocations for services for the homeless and mentally ill, drew cheers from some and angry comments from others. Rendell once remarked that "Sister Mary Scullion is Philadelphia's Joan of Arc because so many people want to burn her at the stake."[3]

All women religious, often called nuns or sisters by the general public, take vows of poverty, chastity, and obedience, but Sisters of Mercy also vow to care for the poor, sick, and ignorant. Project H.O.M.E., which Sister Mary cofounded with Joan Dawson McConnon, a lay activist and volunteer working with the homeless, in 1989, helped her to live this fourth vow by seeking solutions to the problem of homelessness.[4] The approximately 56,000 women religious serving the Catholic Church in the United States at the beginning of the twenty-first century, like Sister Mary Scullion, constitute the most recent in a long line of sisters and nuns whose commitment to their faith led them to choose a life of service to those in need.

The history of women religious is intricately connected to the story of the church in the United States. The small group of Catholics who sailed from England on two ships, the *Ark* and the *Dove*, in 1633 certainly did not imagine the large number of parishes, schools, hospitals, and social service agencies that would comprise the twenty-first century Catholic Church in the United States. Their calling to a life of service led many communities to involve themselves in these "traditional ministries." American sisters have worked as parochial school teachers, nurses and hospital administrators, and social workers, and served on the staff of orphanages and residences for senior citizens. Others, however, have undertaken a journey leading in a different direction, including ministering to those suffering from Hansen's disease (leprosy) on a remote Hawaiian island, teaching on Indian reservations, marching in civil rights demonstrations, and advocating for the abolition of the death penalty.

This book tells the story of those women religious who have been serving their church and its people since 1727. Although Catholic sisters could have chosen other ways to work with those in need that did not involve entering a religious community, their faith directed them to minister in institutions identified as Catholic. Portions of every sister's day were dedicated to prayer and meditation; it was her relationship with God that gave meaning to what she did. In addition, sisters embraced a specific lifestyle governed by a rule that often restricted many activities, including visiting with family, going out at night, and eating in public places. Despite a strictly legislated lifestyle, they contributed to the growth and development of the church in the United States, and were often the visible manifestation of Catholicism for Americans of all religious beliefs.

A Long Line of Foremothers

As early as the fourth century, women and men chose to set themselves apart from the temptations of the world in order to achieve a deeper relationship with God. Sometimes they lived alone as hermits, but other times they formed a community with like-minded Christians desiring to share an experience of the holy. This style of living and praying became known as monasticism, from the Greek word *monos*, alone.[5] Both men and women believed they were called to monastic life, and by the end of the fourth century approximately seven thousand monks and nuns were living in Egypt.[6]

Female monasticism migrated from the Middle East to Europe by the middle of the fifth century, but communities of women grew more slowly than their male counterparts. Historians suggest two possible reasons for the rather slow growth of women's monastic groups: first, convents for women tended to be founded by members of the upper classes for their families and friends, leaving few options for those from lower socioeconomic groups desiring to enter religious life; and second, the Viking invasions of the sixth and seventh centuries destroyed or damaged many of the European houses of women religious, and it was difficult to finance the rebuilding of these institutions. Women who wanted to dedicate their lives to prayer and meditation were given the option of either remaining in their own homes or finding a way to attach themselves to a male monastic community.[7]

Distinctive clothing, called habits, was originally intended to distinguish women religious from the upper classes in European society, but later became a "visual symbol of consecration and practical physical protection."[8] Ecclesiastical legislation mandated that women religious wear a habit as early as the Fourth Council of Constance (869–870), and the Fourth Lateran Council (1215) decreed excommunication—expulsion from membership in the church—for all nuns not dressed as religious.[9] One knew the congregation to which a nun belonged by the habit she wore.

By the end of the twelfth century, the number of European houses for women religious, known as convents, had significantly increased.[10] Between 1070 and 1170, for instance, houses in northwestern England, some containing as many as one hundred women, quadrupled.[11] These institutions usually developed rather informally. At times, a group of women followed a hermit, emulating his lifestyle until he worked out a way for them to live and pray together; at other times, they established a house in close proximity to a male monastery and constructed a lifestyle modeled on that of the monks. Nuns—as these women came to be called—began to wear a veil and ring to symbolize a spiritual marriage with Christ. They lived a life of strict claustration or cloister—nuns did not leave the monastery grounds—and dedicated themselves to prayer and devotional exercises. In order to remain as far away from the temptations of the world as possible, a grille separated convent residents from their visitors; even priests hearing confessions had no direct contact with them. Turntables allowed the women to pass gifts and necessities back and forth with their visitors.[12]

In 1298, Pope Boniface VIII (1294–1303) issued the papal bull, or proclamation, *Periculoso*, which required nuns to be cloistered, because, according to the pontiff, men were constantly tempted by women, and consequently unable to stop themselves from committing rape. Nuns living outside of an enclosed convent, Boniface VIII reasoned, were in danger of being sexually assaulted. As a result of this papal bull, women called to religious life had very little opportunity to serve those in need. Those women not interested in a traditional contemplative life that called for devoting oneself to prayer within the confines of a cloister had no formal place in the institutional church.

This situation began to change in 1532, when Angela Merici (1474–1540), who was sixty years old at the time, formed a "company of virgins" to serve wherever needed. Because Merici placed the community under the patronage of St. Ursula, the women who answered Merici's call became known as Ursulines. They lived in their own homes, did not wear distinctive clothing, took no vows, and were required to support themselves. The ministry of the Ursulines was to "give charity where charity was needed," and they quickly became involved in the care of orphan girls. By 1544, when the new community was approved by Pope Paul III (1534–1549), one hundred and fifty women were affiliated with it. Critics expressed their disapproval of women religious ministering outside of the confines of the cloister, but the Ursulines remained the only option for women who chose not to marry or enter an enclosed convent.[13] In 1568, Milan Cardinal Charles Borromeo requested twelve Ursulines to teach catechism in his diocese. He attempted to silence the negative voices by permitting the women to live together in a community under the authority of a local bishop beginning in 1580. They were expected to perform works of charity, many of which were related to education, and spend part of the day in prayer. One contemporary described them by saying, "They frequented the Sacraments and the exercises of Christian doctrine; they assisted the poor, visited the sick, and devoted themselves to all the other works of piety which their age and their sex allowed."[14]

At the Council of Trent (1545–1563), called to respond to the Protestant Reformation, *Periculoso* was inserted into canon law, which governs the Catholic Church, and the requirement concerning women religious and strict enclosure began to be reiterated and enforced.[15] In order to adhere to the Tridentine decrees, Ursuline communities were eventually forced to adopt a cloistered lifestyle. They were able to continue teaching, however, as long as their schools were located within the convent walls and they maintained a daily schedule of prayer. Purists worried about what they considered a compromise, but "early modern society was getting serious about educating its girls, and there was no one around who could do it as well as these women."[16] By the middle of the seventeenth century, almost every French town boasted a convent of teaching nuns.

In the middle decades of the seventeenth century, Vincent de Paul (1581–1660) and Louise de Marillac (1591–1660) worked together in France to recruit women interested in serving the poor. Those responding to this call lived together in a community while they taught religious education to children, nursed the sick, and supported themselves through manual labor. Louise and Vincent were not interested in forming another cloistered community of nuns—they sought women willing to roll up their sleeves and move among those in need of their services—but *Periculoso* clearly stated that female religious communities were to be enclosed. Vincent de Paul's solution to this requirement was to allow members of the community, known as the Daughters of Charity, to take what are called simple vows. Cloistered nuns took solemn vows for life, but simple or private vows were renewed annually. In the official language of the Catholic Church, nuns took solemn vows, and simple vows defined one as a "secular sister." The Daughters of Charity "adopted the characteristics of nuns, living communally, performing set devotions, obeying a rule and a superior—all of which made them, in a sense, half-nuns."[17] Although the community did not receive official recognition from the Vatican until the late nineteenth century, they were credited with serving the needs of "civil society and of the church's apostolate."[18] Women entering religious life now had the option of becoming either a cloistered nun or a sister who served those in need through education, hospital work, or direct contact with the poor.

The young women responding to Vincent de Paul's call began a ministry that originally called for them simply to visit the poor in French towns and villages. Under the direction of Louise de Marillac, they were taught skills that allowed them to add teaching and nursing to their list of ministries. Impressed with their dedication to the poor, civic and religious leaders invited the women to open small schools and staff hospitals. As their numbers increased, the Daughters of Charity became more organized and developed a rule, or constitution, which governed how the community would lead a common life. Unlike contemplative nuns, members of this community did not practice strict enclosure. Their cloister, according to Vincent de Paul, was to be the streets of the city.[19]

The Ursulines and the Daughters of Charity helped to begin what became a pattern for women called to serve God and others by ministering to those in need. By the end of the seventeenth century, every French town with a population greater than five thousand contained a poor house administered by communities of sisters, including the Sisters of Providence, Filles de la Sagesse (Daughters of Wisdom), and Sisters of Saint Thomas de Villeneuve. Other traditionally cloistered communities followed the example set by the Ursulines and modified their rules so that they could care for the poor and sick within the confines of their enclosure.[20]

The need for women religious willing to work outside of the cloister was so great that some of these new communities found themselves involved in several ministries. Founded in 1650 in France, the Sisters of Saint Joseph dedicated themselves to teaching and assisting the poor, but often cared for the sick as well. This pattern was repeated in the United States, where it was not unusual to find a religious community that administered schools, hospitals, and a variety of institutions devoted to the care of women, children, and the elderly. When the Catholic Church in the United States entered a period of rapid growth in the nineteenth century as a result of European immigration, its leaders discovered that many of the newcomers required a host of services. Women religious staffed the extensive network of parochial schools that stretched throughout the country, staffed and administered health care facilities, and cared for children, working women, and the elderly in various charitable settings. Because they earned a very small salary, bishops and other clerical leaders were able to expand services provided by the church without worrying about personnel costs. Sisters ministering in these areas not only carried out the mission of Catholicism, they also influenced the larger society. Religious communities administering orphanages and children's homes, for instance, were involved in discussions concerning public policy related to the welfare of minors. Had women religious not been available and willing to serve wherever and whenever they were needed, the story of U.S. Catholicism—and indeed, of the nation itself—would be very different.

From Europe to the United States

There were no women religious ministering in the thirteen colonies prior to the ratification of the Constitution. By the time Jamestown, Virginia, was settled in 1607, England had been officially Protestant for about fifty years, and Catholic women called to religious life, including those in the colonies, had no choice but to enter a convent located in one of the more tolerant European countries. Several female colonists entered one of these convents, including the Carmelite monastery in Hoogstraten, located in the Belgian province of Antwerp, and later returned to the new nation to establish the first congregation in the former British colonies—the Carmelite community of Port Tobacco, Maryland—in 1790. During the next century, these Carmelites were joined by a host of other congregations of women religious.[21] Some sisters left their homes in Ireland, France, Italy,

Poland, and Germany to begin ministering in a land where they were unfamiliar with the language and customs; others entered communities that were founded by U.S. Catholic women responding to the "signs of the times."

The work of women religious in the United States began in 1727 in New Orleans—French territory at the time—when twelve Ursulines left France to begin a ministry of health care in that city. When the sisters realized that the residents of New Orleans also needed a school dedicated to the education of girls and young women, as well as a plan to catechize the city's African population, slave and free, they expanded their work to include both teaching and a ministry to the area's black residents. In the aftermath of the American Revolution, other European religious communities heeded the requests of bishops and priests and sent members to a new nation that, despite the relatively small number of Catholic citizens, needed their services. French members of the Society of the Sacred Heart of Jesus, Sisters of Mercy from Ireland, Missionary Sisters of the Sacred Heart of Jesus, who were founded in Italy, and Polish Felician Sisters, were among those communities that developed ministries of teaching, health care, and social service in the United States during the nineteenth and twentieth centuries.

European congregations were joined by communities of women religious founded in the United States. In the early nineteenth century, for instance, the Sisters of Charity of St. Joseph and the Sisters of Loretto at the Foot of the Cross worked with urban Catholics as well as those living on what was known as the frontier, those regions where Anglo-Europeans found themselves feeling uncomfortable with both the surrounding topography and indigenous cultures. In the early twentieth century, Mary Josephine Rogers's Maryknoll Sisters and the Sisters of Our Lady of Christian Doctrine founded by Marion Gurney, established congregations dedicated to specific issues facing the Catholic Church during the early twentieth century, focusing on the need for foreign missionaries and for women dedicated to assisting Catholics immigrants as they adjusted to a new country.

Writing the History of American Catholic Sisters

The history of Catholic women religious in the United States offered in this book steers clear of the "great man"—or, in this case, "great woman" or "great sister"—approach to history in favor of what might be called a collective study. It is, of course, impossible to include every community of women religious that has ever ministered in the United States in one volume; there are too many, especially if the branches of some of the larger groups, such as Franciscans, Dominicans, and Benedictines, are counted separately. In addition to including those congregations with which most Catholics are familiar, such as the Sisters of Charity, Sisters of Mercy, and Sisters of St. Joseph, I have tried to make sure that others, such as the Sisters of Our Lady of Christian Doctrine, Sisters of the Good Shepherd, the Holy Spirit Adoration Sisters—also known as the Pink Sisters because of their rose-colored habits—and Adorers of the Blood of Christ also become part of the story.

A collective history of women religious in the United States demonstrates that with the exception of celebrating Mass or administrating the sacraments, sisters were more actively involved in the everyday lives of Catholics than priests. In the late nineteenth century, for instance, a large urban parish might have four priests living in the rectory, but the convent probably housed at least sixteen sisters. Children and parents experienced sister-teachers in parochial schools and academies, but Catholics interacted with them in a variety of other settings as well. Hospital patients, immigrants seeking work, and unemployed men eating in soup kitchens all came into contact with women religious. Sisters also worked with wounded Union and Confederate troops during the Civil War, Native Americans on reservations, and inmates on death row. For many, they were and are the face of the U.S. Catholic Church.

Writing about Catholic sisters collectively is not meant to minimize the fact that there were many communities of women religious from which a potential entrant could choose. In order to learn about the congregation she was entering, a candidate usually spent about six months as a postulant, and at least one year as a novice. Since a young woman leaving home for her new life as a sister or nun was expected to embrace the community as family and take on an identity as a religious, most congregations conferred a new name on a sister to symbolize her entrance into a new life. Although there were similarities among congregations, "these women identified themselves not as generic 'sisters' but as 'daughters of St. Joseph,' 'children of the Immaculate Heart,' or 'daughters of St. Francis.'" Religious vows, Sister Assisium McEvoy, a Sister of St. Joseph explained, might seem the same to an outsider, but "every community does not observe them the same way."[22] Even congregations sharing the same ministry, such as teaching, did not often come together to share information prior to the middle of the twentieth century. "The average teaching sister was unlikely to 'ever see the inside of a school of another religious community or exchange a thought with a Sister of a different habit.'"[23] Despite the separation among communities, women religious did help each other out in unusual circumstances. When a new community arrived in a city or town, for instance, they often received assistance from sisters already living and working in the area.

In order to write this history of Catholic sisters in the United States, I developed a framework that concentrates on their work, or ministry. This book is about what sisters did as much as who they were. A number of bishops, including Philadelphia's Cardinal Dennis Dougherty (1918–1951), have claimed the title "God's Bricklayer" because of the number of churches, schools, and hospitals erected during their administrations, but sisters were often the ones responsible for establishing, staffing, and administering those institutions. Although they often—but not always—enjoyed the hierarchy's moral support, religious communities usually raised the funds needed to build and maintain many of the edifices that served hundreds of thousands of Catholic immigrants and their children. In addition to staffing thousands of parochial schools for very little compensation, women religious established private academies, colleges, hospitals, orphanages, and settlement houses, as well as convents, motherhouses, and centers to train those entering religious life.

When viewed from the perspective of their collective work, the accomplishments of women religious are impressive. Not every woman entering a religious community, however, was remarkable or holy; sometimes they were not even good teachers, nurses, social workers, or missionaries. In addition, until the 1960s women religious often supported the prevailing societal structures in the United States. Prior to the passage of civil rights legislation, for instance, southern hospitals, schools, and colleges were segregated. Sisters working directly with the poor did not often question the economic system that kept people in poverty. Religious communities devoted to foreign mission work usually combined the Gospel message with western values.

Chapter 1 focuses on the early history of women religious in the United States. The story began in 1727, when the twelve French Ursulines arrived in New Orleans, and is continued in the former English colonies by the four Carmelite nuns who settled in Port Tobacco, Maryland, in 1790. The establishment of the Sisters of Charity of St. Joseph, now known as the Daughters of Charity, by Elizabeth Ann Seton in 1808, helped Archbishop John Carroll (1789–1815) begin to create a network of American Catholic institutions. Along with establishing schools, the sisters quickly found themselves nursing those stricken in epidemics and caring for orphaned children. Their willingness to serve the church and its people in a variety of ways created a precedent followed by other communities of women religious. By the end of the 1820s, eight congregations of women were ministering throughout the United States, including the Oblate Sisters of Providence, an African American community working with black Catholics.

The second chapter, "Service to a Growing Catholic Community," focuses on the ways in which women religious in the antebellum period established a network of institutions wherever they were needed. Religious communities from France, Ireland, and Germany joined their American counterparts as they followed Catholics settling throughout the country, even when it meant living and working under less than ideal conditions. Their distinctive style of dress identified them clearly as Catholic women religious, and made them an easy target for Protestants concerned about what they perceived as a growing "popish" presence in the nation.

Chapter 3 is the first of three chapters focusing on a specific ministry of women religious. In this chapter, the subject is teaching sisters. Most Catholics—and indeed most Americans—primarily think of teachers when they talk about women religious, and there is good reason for this. Sisters have been educating American Catholic youth since the Ursulines began teaching young girls within three months of their arrival in New Orleans. Most congregations of women religious originally focused on the education of girls and young women, but as the parochial school system expanded during the nineteenth century, many of them adapted their rule to offer instruction to both sexes. When young Catholic women began to desire an education that extended beyond high school, sisters established colleges as an alternative to secular universities. In the 1960s, changes in the Catholic Church, American society, and the lives of women religious led to a decrease both in the number of parochial schools and the sisters who worked in them. Women religious remained committed to educating those in need, however, and expanded their educational ministry to include work in prison literacy programs, English classes for immigrants, and early intervention programs for at risk children.

In addition to teaching, sisters developed an extensive network of health care institutions; this is the subject of chapter 4. Along with the nursing care provided by the Ursulines in New Orleans, Elizabeth Seton's Sisters of Charity found themselves involved in health care within fifteen years of their founding. Religious communities not only established hospitals, but willingly offered their services during the many epidemics that swept through American cities in the nineteenth and early twentieth centuries. During the Civil War, sisters from both the North and the South ministered to the wounded and dying, earning them the respect of medical and government leaders. Women religious also founded hospitals in remote locations, such as mining towns, and offered health care to all those in need, including recent immigrants who neither spoke nor understood English and distrusted doctors and hospitals. Religious congregations involved in health care ministry worked to keep abreast of new developments in medicine and technology, but were also affected by changes in health care policy that sometimes led to the closing and merging of hospitals, increased bureaucracy (and paperwork), and spiraling costs.

Although sisters tend to be identified with either teaching or nursing, chapter 5 focuses on women religious called to other ministries. A concern for the welfare of Catholic children led some congregations to open orphanages, which were, at least in some instances, a logical extension of educational and health care ministries. Their work in schools and hospitals heightened sisters' awareness of the numbers of children whose parents were unable or unwilling to care for them. Work with children caused some communities to develop ministries designed to help mothers care for their children, and others to assist young single women in finding a safe job and living situation in urban areas. Still others, notably the Sisters of the Good Shepherd, focused on "troubled" women and attempted to provide them with the skills needed to set them on the right path.

Other religious communities did very little teaching or nursing and used their talents to reach those in need in somewhat nontraditional ways. Several congregations established social settlements—or settlement houses—in the late nineteenth and early twentieth centuries to offer material, educational, and spiritual sustenance to Catholic immigrants struggling to assimilate into a new country and culture. In addition, European sisters sometimes journeyed to the United States to minister to a particular ethnic group. The Missionary Sisters of the Sacred Heart of Jesus (better known as the Cabrini Sisters) arrived in New York City in 1889 to begin work with the city's Italian immigrants. Several communities willingly sent sisters to rural America, including the Alaskan territory, to minister to Native Americans, while others defied traditional stereotypes and worked with African Americans. Those called to be missionaries found themselves joining communities that believed the Gospel was best exemplified by living among people on the distant continents of Africa and Asia.

Although most American women religious served in active ministries such as teaching or health care, some answered a call to a life centered on prayer. The contemplative communities scattered throughout the United States—both in the middle of large cities and in remote rural areas—are the subject of chapter 6. Contrary to some public perceptions, contemplative women religious, all of whom are cloistered, have always believed that a ministry of prayer is an essential way to support both the church and the world's people. The Poor Clares, Carmelites, and Pink Sisters are an integral part of the history of women religious in the United States. Like other Americans, contemplative nuns have adapted to societal and cultural changes, and begun to incorporate technology into their ministry, enabling people to request prayers via websites and email.

Chapter 7 details the changes in the lives and work of women religious during the second half of the twentieth century. There had never been a sufficient number of sisters to staff all the institutions in need of their services, and this situation was exacerbated when growing numbers of Catholic children, combined with the need for new schools in suburban parishes, placed an increasing demand on communities to supply sisters for teaching positions, even if they had not completed their own education. In the 1950s, the Sister Formation Conference not only helped congregations find ways for their young members to complete their undergraduate degrees before assigning them to a classroom, it also paved the way for further changes that took place in religious life during the 1960s and 1970s. The Second Vatican Council (1962–1965) did not solicit the opinions of women, lay or religious, as its participants drafted documents related to the Catholic Church in the modern world. Several of the Council documents, including a decree on the renewal of religious life, were of special interest to American sisters because they called them to adapt to the twentieth century in the same way that their founders had read the "signs of the times" when their communities were first established. As a result of the Council's mandate, some sisters decided that the events of the twentieth century were calling them to support the civil rights movement, and they traveled to Selma, Alabama, to support those marching for voting rights; others worked to end racism by ministering in inner-city black communities.

Entering a religious community in the 1950s meant becoming part of a culture that had remained virtually unchanged for several hundred years. The changes taking place in both the Catholic Church and American society led to efforts to bring religious communities into the modern world. As women religious examined their place in the contemporary world, many concluded that they no longer needed to dress in a style more suited to sixteenth-century Europe than the United States of the late twentieth century. In addition, a number of communities abolished many of the rules that kept sisters separated from friends and family, including censorship of mail, restrictions on traveling, and the requirement that they live in traditional convents. Church leaders did not always support these changes, and conflicts sometimes developed between religious communities and local bishops. The drastic decrease in the number of sisters in the middle decades of the twentieth century led to further changes. Not only did fewer women hear a call to religious life, but many communities saw members leave for a variety of reasons, including a general dissatisfaction with the Catholic Church and a desire to marry.

The eighth and final chapter focuses on the work of women religious since the 1970s. As an historian, I am reluctant to comment on the future of sisters in the United States, but it is important to document the role they have played in issues of social justice, such as the abolition of the death penalty, ecology and environmental responsibility, and standing with the poor throughout the world. The early years of the twenty-first century have seen women religious demonstrate a keen understanding of both Catholic social teaching with its emphasis on the dignity of the human person, and the vision of those who first established religious communities. It has not been unusual for sisters to lobby members of Congress, attend shareholder meetings in order to advocate for corporate responsibility, or remind government and business leaders of the importance of placing the needs of the poor and dispossessed before all others.

Women Religious in the Twenty-First Century

There are far fewer women religious in the United States in the twenty-first century than there were one hundred years ago. According to Georgetown University's Center for Applied Research in the Apostolate (CARA), there were 55,944 women religious in the United States in 2010, down from 179,954 in 1965.[24] The result of this decrease is that there were not as many sisters available to staff schools, hospitals, and social service institutions, and some communities either closed these institutions or turned them over to other groups. Webster University in St. Louis, Missouri, for instance, was founded in 1915 by the Sisters of Loretto. Originally known as Loretto College, it was one of the first Catholic women's colleges west of the Mississippi River. The school's name was changed to Webster College in 1924, and it was operated by the Sisters of Loretto until 1967, when the congregation transferred ownership to a lay board of directors. Today, Webster University is a private nondenominational school.

As the numbers of sisters have decreased, the average age of women religious has increased. In 2003, 4 percent of those responding to a CARA survey reported that they had "very seriously" considered entering a religious community; by 2008 that number had dropped to less than 1 percent.[25] The fact that the average age of American sisters in that year was over seventy—in some communities the average age was over eighty—meant that difficult decisions had to be made about ministries, property, and the care of aging sisters. Even contemplative nuns had to adjust their schedules to reflect the reality of aging. During the 1980s, the Carmelite community in Hudson, Wisconsin, changed the schedule of prayer that had been a part of the congregation's life for several centuries. The nuns still came together to pray four times during the day, but they ceased gathering together in the chapel at midnight because of health issues. Although their lives remained centered on prayer, one member of the community was assigned to maintain the webpage, "fielding questions about the monastery and responding to an average of fifteen prayer requests a day."[26]

Many communities have worked diligently to ensure that those working in their institutions understand the importance of making decisions that are aligned with the community's mission. They created Offices of Mission Integration and developed sophisticated orientation programs to educate employees—Catholic and non-Catholic—about the vision and history of their congregations. Recognizing the importance of keeping their spirit alive, a number of congregations have initiated associate programs, consisting of women and men supportive of the sisters and their work. Some associates focus primarily on communal prayer; others help raise money to support the congregation and its ministries. Still other associate programs function as lay partners, and members commit to incorporating the mission and ministry of the community in their own lives and work.

It is impossible to know what the future holds for women religious in the United States. Associate programs and mission integration offices keep the legacy alive, but do not bring in new members. Some communities will most likely fade away and others will merge. At least a few congregations are thriving, and may continue to flourish for at least several more decades. Whatever the future holds for religious life, sisters will continue to minister to those in need; in doing so, they remain the face of Catholicism for many Americans.

1

Organizing to Serve

THE LIVES OF Jerusha Booth Barber and her husband, Episcopal priest Virgil Barber, changed dramatically when they decided that the Catholic Church was indeed the true path to salvation. In February 1817, Jerusha and Virgil, parents of five children, received their First Communion from Father Benedict Fenwick, who would be named Bishop of Boston in 1825.[1] Virgil, of course, now had to find another career; as a Catholic he could no longer serve a Protestant parish. With Fenwick's encouragement, Barber announced that he intended to begin a course of study that would lead to his ordination as a Catholic priest. Shortly after making this decision, the Barber family moved to Washington, D.C., where Baltimore Archbishop Leonard Neale (1815–1817) "pronounced the separation of Mr. and Mrs. Barber," essentially granting the couple an annulment. Virgil then left to study for the priesthood in Rome, and Jerusha entered the Visitation Convent in Georgetown.[2] She struggled with her husband's decision, but eventually concluded that it was God's will. Toward the end of Jerusha's life, when her youngest daughter reportedly asked why she had allowed Virgil to study for the priesthood, she replied, "I felt . . . that I must make the sacrifice to God; and that if I would refuse He would deprive me of my husband and children both in this world and the next."[3]

Jerusha had a far more difficult time adapting to a celibate, single life than her husband, finding it hard to live separately from Virgil and at least some of her children. Shortly after beginning her religious training in Georgetown, Jerusha left the community for a few months because she thought she was pregnant, returning to the convent when it was clear she was not going to have another child. Josephine, who was only ten months old when her parents decided to enter religious life, was too young to live in a convent, and was cared for by Fenwick's mother. The three daughters remaining with Jerusha had to be fed, educated, and clothed, placing a considerable burden on a religious community with limited financial resources.

The Barbers encountered numerous difficulties as they attempted to raise five children—all of whom entered religious life—and embrace their

Portrait of Elizabeth Seton. She apparently gave a portrait of herself to the Filicchi family. They had it redone to portray her wearing the black cap and habit of the Sisters of Charity. Courtesy of Sisters of Charity of Cincinnati.

vocations. One of the more serious challenges involved determining who was responsible for financially supporting the children, especially the four girls housed at the Georgetown Visitation convent. The community's spiritual director, Father Joseph Picot de Clorivière, believed that since Virgil Barber had entered the Jesuits, responsibility for the young women's financial upkeep rested on that community. He apparently told Jerusha, now called Sister Mary Augustine, that the Jesuits should place her husband in a paying job and allow him to contribute to the children's support.[4] Baltimore Archbishop Ambrose Maréchal (1817–1826) seemed to share de Clorivière's views, writing to the Archbishop of Quebec: "The Jesuit father [Fenwick] who converted Mr. Barber and his family has certainly done a good work. But the device of his confrères in relieving themselves of the onerous burden that was the consequence thereof is by no means deserving of praise. It is yet an unsolvable problem to me how they could have succeeded in putting my poor Visitandines to the expense of entertaining and feeding five persons."[5] Despite these issues, on February 23, 1820, Jerusha Barber pronounced her vows as a Visitandine; her husband took his vows as a member of the Society of Jesus on the same day.

According to her youngest daughter, Sister Josephine Barber, who later entered the Visitation community, taking vows as a woman religious did not prevent Jerusha Barber from loving and worrying about her children. Sister Josephine later reflected on what she had known of her mother's life as a woman religious when she was a child: "I know nothing more of this part of Sister M. Augustine's life," she wrote, "except that she continued to suffer inexpressibly on account of her children; feeling them to be a burden on the community in its state of poverty, and knowing the opposition of some of the Sisters to their [the children] remaining, we were necessarily poorly clad; and she had told me that many a time she has sat up nearly half the night patching the children's clothes . . . and knitting stockings for them."[6] Sister Mary Augustine played an important role in developing the academy administered by the community in Georgetown, as well as helping to establish convents in Kaskaskia, Illinois (1833), and St. Louis, Missouri (1844), until her death in 1860.

Although there are other cases of married couples converting to Catholicism and entering the priesthood and religious life, Sister Mary Augustine Barber's biography is not representative of the history of women religious in the United States. Her story is important, however, because it reminds us that American religious communities—both those transplanted from Europe and those founded in the United States—were confronted with situations and challenges unique to a country that had recently severed its ties with England. The creation and development of a civil government without a monarch, combined with the ratification of the Constitution and the Bill of Rights, whose provisions included religious freedom and the separation of church and state, meant that the Catholic Church was able to increase both in size and significance as immigrants began to leave Europe for the United States. Priests were few and far between, and lay Catholics often had neither the resources nor the education to create the complex network of institutions needed to minister to this population. But Jerusha Barber and thousands of other women religious took responsibility for this work, and their willingness to make great sacrifices to provide education, health care, and social services to those in need is an important part of the church's story in the United States.

Catholic Sisters in the New World

The history of women religious in the United States does not begin with the thirteen English colonies, but in the territory of Louisiana. The first French colonists settled in 1699 in Biloxi, Mississippi, but New Orleans, founded in 1718, quickly evolved into the territory's principal settlement. Within five years of its founding, Commissioner Jacques Delachaise expressed a desire for French women religious willing to help establish some sort of order in the city. Citing the poor condition of the public hospital, Delachaise hoped the sisters would have some training as nurses. In addition to administering the hospital, they could care for orphans and perhaps try to reform the prostitutes who had found their way to the colony. Because they were primarily involved in nursing, Delachaise hoped the Filles de la Charité (Daughters of Charity) would respond to his pleas for assistance. The women were in high demand in their native France, however, and had no desire to undertake a new mission in Louisiana. Leaders of the Ursuline community were intrigued by the proposal of French colonists and investors, and agreed to send six sisters to Louisiana. Most would be involved in hospital work; one would have responsibility for teaching.[7]

The country's leaders believed the Ursulines' ministry of teaching was helping to win back those who had left the church during the Reformation, and was preventing France from drifting further toward Protestantism. As we have seen, the Council of Trent reiterated the rules governing women religious, and decreed that nuns were to remain cloistered unless they received special dispensation from a bishop. In addition to the traditional vows of poverty, chastity, and obedience, the Ursulines took a fourth vow to provide Christian education, which allowed them to open their convents to students on a daily basis.[8] In 1639, a widow from Alençon, Mme. de la Peltrie, recruited three other French Ursulines, including Marie Guyart (1599–1672), whose religious name was Marie de l'Incarnation, to serve the Canadian missions.[9] Upon arrival in the "new world," the missionaries attempted to keep "the rule of enclosure." In the rough world of French Canada the traditional sturdy walls were replaced by cedar fences, but the sisters continued to follow a lifestyle governed by the cloister. The only time Marie de l'Incarnation ever left the enclosed convent was to flee from a fire in 1650.[10]

The original plan called for the women to teach the native people catechism, and Marie de l'Incarnation hoped that young native women would be called to enter the community. Native parents often abandoned their daughters when they left for the winter hunt, and some of these girls sought shelter among the Ursulines, who "competed for the humble task of scrubbing off the grease with which the Indians warded off the cold and the lice that fed on it."[11] They cared for their charges while instructing French novices in the languages of the native groups. The daughters of

French settlers originally lived, ate, and studied with the native girls, but financial hardships eventually required the Ursulines to bring in more and more young women whose families could afford to pay tuition, room, and board.

Marie de l'Incarnation eventually concluded that the education of French girls was at least as important as converting the native peoples to Catholicism. The work of her community, she believed, was as vital as that of the women religious responsible for the sick in Quebec's hospital. "Great care is taken in this country," she wrote, "with the instruction of the French girls, and I can assure you that if there were no Ursulines they would be in continual danger for their salvation."[12] By the time of her death in 1667, Marie de l'Incarnation had concluded that the lifestyle of native women was incompatible with Ursuline life, writing, "They cannot endure the cloister for they have a melancholy nature and their habits of liberty augment it."[13] She continued to insist, however, that the primary mission of the community was twofold: to convert native people—who would help spread Christianity when they returned to their villages to marry and start a family—and to ensure that French Canadian women were able to transmit Catholicism to their children. Despite her commitment to both phases of this mission, the rule of enclosure prevented the Ursulines from leaving their convent to minister among the people, and forced them to focus their attention primarily on the wives and daughters of European colonial settlers.

The Ursulines who arrived in New Orleans in 1727, like their sisters who settled in Canada, were enthusiastic about the opportunity to serve as missionaries in a place far from the world of eighteenth-century Europe. Marie Tranchepain (1680?–1733), superior for the Ursulines traveling to Louisiana, agreed to a contract that required the community to serve in areas outside their usual ministries because she was convinced they were called to this new mission by a higher power. Although the women were told that their primary responsibility was not teaching but nursing—the convent was located adjacent to the hospital so the rule of enclosure would not be violated—Tranchepain and her eleven sisters, six more than were called for in the original contract, were involved in a ministry of education almost from the beginning, and managed to avoid hospital work for nearly seven years.

The colonists were apparently as eager for teachers as they were for nurses. Tranchepain explained that "All the inhabitants try their best to make us feel the joy which they experience to have us for the education of their children."[14] Within three months of establishing a convent in the Crescent City, the first boarding students arrived, and they were soon joined by day students, including African Americans and Native Americans who attended catechism classes.[15] Six additional Ursulines joined the original twelve in New Orleans between 1727 and 1736. Four died and four others either returned to France or left religious life, but by 1757, twenty women religious were ministering in the city. When the Natchez Indians launched a surprise attack on a military outpost and settlement at Fort Rosalie, killing most of the men stationed there, the Ursulines willingly expanded their ministry and took in thirty girls who had been orphaned as a result of the battle.[16]

Although the women offered catechetical instruction to African and Native Americans, the Ursulines owned slaves. Unlike other slaveholders in the American South, however, all slaves were kept within their nuclear families. This policy may have been viewed by some as more enlightened or humane than the actions of other slaveholders, but the sisters made no effort to work toward the abolition of slavery in the eighteenth and early nineteenth centuries. They owned as many slaves as they thought necessary to maintain their school, and are not known to have spoken against the evils of a system that held human beings in bondage.[17] Women religious owning slaves did not surprise many American Catholics of this era. Pope Gregory XVI (1831–1846) condemned the slave trade in 1838, but never spoke against slavery itself, and no American Catholic bishop outwardly supported the abolition of slavery prior to the Civil War. Catholics tended to endorse the practices of the region in which they lived; New Orleans residents would have been shocked—and angry—if the Ursulines had worked for the abolition of what has been called the "peculiar institution."[18]

When the United States acquired New Orleans from France as part of the Louisiana Purchase in 1803, the Ursulines came under the jurisdiction of Bishop John Carroll (1789–1815), whose vast diocese was defined as "all the faithful living in communion with the Catholic Church . . . so long as they are subject to the government of the Republic, whether they dwell in the provinces of the Federated America, or in the neighboring regions."[19] Not only were the sisters afraid of losing their property as a result of Louisiana becoming part of the United States, they worried that their work might be hindered by a government whose attitude toward established religion was very different from what they had experienced in Catholic France prior to the 1789 revolution. On November 1, 1803, superior Mother Thérèse de St. Xavier Farjon wrote to Carroll expressing her concern, and the bishop forwarded her letter to Secretary of State James Madison. After showing Carroll's letter to President Thomas Jefferson, Madison was able to assure the bishop of the president's desire to promote educational and charitable activities in the newly acquired territory.

Several months later the community wrote directly to Jefferson, explaining that they were not concerned about loss of property to protect their material goods and assets, but because of their work with the poor. "It is then less their own cause which they plead than that of the public," they told the president. "It is, in fact, the cause of the orphan and the destitute child. It is, moreover, the cause of a multitude of wretched beings snatched from the horrors of vice and infamy, in order to be, by the petitioners, brought up in the path of religion and virtue, and formed to become happy and useful citizens."[20] The people described as "wretched beings" were African American girls the Ursulines had taught for a number of years. Jefferson assured Mother Thérèse that she had no cause for worry, writing: "Whatever diversity of shade may appear in the religious opinions of our fellow citizens, the charitable objects of your institution cannot be indifferent to any; and its furtherance of wholesome purposes by training up its young members in the way they should go, cannot fail to insure it the patronage of the government it is under. Be assured it will meet with all the protection my office can give it."[21]

When the annexation of Louisiana brought the New Orleans Ursulines into the United States, they joined two other communities of women religious, the Carmelites and the Visitandines, ministering to Catholics in the new republic. During the next thirty years, the demands placed on these women religious were eased a bit by the addition of new communities founded in the United States as well as by European congregations willing to send sisters to minister in a foreign country.[22]

An Old Church in a New Country

Benjamin Franklin thought it was noteworthy enough to record John Carroll's 1785 appointment as Superior of the Mission in the thirteen United States of America. "The Pope's Nuncio, called" Franklin, who was living in Paris, wrote, "and acquainted me that the Pope had, on my Recommendation, appointed Mr. John Carroll, Superior of the Catholic Clergy in America."[23] One of Carroll's first official acts in his new position was to submit a "report on the state of religion in the united provinces of federated

America."[24] His description of the Catholic Church in the United States may have caused European ecclesiastical leaders to wonder how it could survive in the new country. There were 15,800 Catholics living in Maryland, 3,000 of whom, according to Carroll, were slaves. Seven thousand Catholics lived in Pennsylvania, and only 200 could be found in Virginia. About 1,500 lived in New York, and Carroll had heard that a number of French Canadian Catholics had settled in the Mississippi valley. Twenty-one priests, nineteen in Maryland and two in Pennsylvania, were responsible for ministering to the entire country.[25] The report did not mention women religious; there were not yet any living or working in the former British colonies.

A great supporter of the American experiment—his cousin Charles was a signer of the Declaration of Independence—Carroll worried that Catholics in the United States neither understood nor practiced their faith properly. Immigrants, "who pour in upon us in large numbers from various European countries," did not seem overly interested in the tenets of Catholic belief and practice.[26] He was also concerned about his small flock of Catholics, who might be easily swayed by a Protestant majority. One solution to both problems was a system of religious education that did not reside solely with the overworked clergy: "since the children [and presumably the slaves] are busy with constant chores and can be with the priest only rarely, most of them usually are uninstructed in the faith and very lax in morals."[27] If Catholicism was going to become a vibrant force on the country's landscape, Carroll needed to develop a network of leaders and institutions compatible with American republicanism.

Convinced that the United States needed a bishop to supervise and discipline clergy, ordain priests, and confirm children and adults, clerics petitioned Pope Pius VI (1775–1799) to create a diocese in the United States. The pope granted their request on July 12, 1788, and on May 18, 1789 John Carroll was elected first bishop of the United States.[28] As bishop, Carroll was charged with continuing his work developing the American Catholic Church, including the establishment of churches, schools, and hospitals, along with finding the personnel to staff these institutions.

Prior to the American Revolution, a young Catholic woman called to religious life had to make the difficult decision to leave her home and family and enter a convent on the European continent. Religious houses in England had been prohibited since Henry VIII ordered them suppressed between 1536 and 1541. Convents for Englishwomen began to appear on the European continent in 1599, when one was opened in Belgium. In addition to women from England, thirty-six Catholic women from Maryland entered convents in either Belgium or France during the colonial period.[29] Ann Teresa Matthews (1732–1800) left Charles County, Maryland, and entered a cloistered Carmelite convent in Hoogstraeten (Belgium); she was professed, or received into the congregation, in 1755 as Sister Bernardina at the age of twenty-three. When the American Revolution ended and travel resumed between the United States and Europe, Mother Bernardina—a title conferred upon her when she was named superior—was joined by two of her nieces, Susanna (Sister Mary Eleanora of St. Francis Xavier) and Ann Teresa (Sister Mary Aloysia of the Blessed Trinity), who were both professed in 1784.[30] Those Catholics anxious for women religious to open a convent in the United States urged the Carmelites to return to their country. Rev. Ignatius Matthews, brother of Mother Bernardina, supported this idea, writing to his sister that "Now is your time to found in this country for Peace is declared and Religion is free."[31] When the revolutions sweeping Europe in 1789 made the future of European religious life uncertain, the nuns' confessor at Hoogstraeten, Father Charles Neale, suggested that the women return home with him and establish a convent at Port Tobacco, Maryland.

On April 19, 1790, not long after the ratification of the U.S. Constitution, the three American women, along with Mother Clare Joseph Dickenson, a native of London who was a member of the Hoogstraeten community, accompanied Neale on a journey to found a convent in the United States. The nuns wore silk dresses so as not to attract the attention of any non-Catholics who might harass or insult the women. Their ship dropped anchor in New York on July 2, and the women left for Maryland immediately.[32] They arrived on July 10, settling on property in Port Tobacco that had been purchased for them. On October 15, 1790, the feast of St. Teresa of Avila, they dedicated their convent.[33] Elizabeth Carberry, who was forty-seven years old, became the community's first postulant—a woman in the process of determining that she has a vocation to religious life—that same year. Early living conditions were less than ideal; the nuns' cells (bedrooms) were not protected from the weather and the women sometimes had to shake snow off of their beds on winter mornings.[34]

These four women—the first women religious in the former English colonies—were part of a religious order whose origins can be traced to the great mystic, Teresa of Avila (1515–1582), who, along with several other women, established the first foundation of the Discalced (Barefoot) Carmelites in 1593.[35] Like all women religious, Carmelites take vows of poverty,

chastity, and obedience, but—unlike active communities—they are cloistered and do not work outside their convent. Despite their life of prayer
and contemplation, the community quickly became known among Maryland Catholics, attracting eleven members during its first ten years in the
United States.[36] Of the fifty-three women entering Carmelite religious life
between 1790 and 1850, forty-one were from Maryland.[37]

Carroll was less than enthusiastic about Charles Neale's plan for a
cloistered community in the United States; he needed teachers, not nuns
whose primary ministry was prayer. "The miniscule Catholic population
of this burgeoning pioneer land was in dire need of women religious to
provide active ministries of charity and education. Instead, it got contemplative nuns who devote their lives to the prayer ministry."[38] As early as
1788, the bishop's friend, John Thorpe, writing from Rome, advised Carroll to discourage the community from settling in the United States, and
warned him against turning them into teachers. "If the Carmelites become
school teachers," he told his friend Carroll, "[a]fter some time you will
have neither good Teresians nor good school mistresses."[39] Carroll himself
expressed concern in a letter to another friend, Charles Plowden, as early
as 1778: "Mr. Chas. Neale of Antwerp is eager to introduce Teresians (Carmelites). I wish rather for Ursulines."[40] His cousin, Ann Louise Hill, who
remained in the Hoogstraeten convent, took a different position, informing Carroll of her delight that a convent would be established in the United
States: "It is the subject of great joy to hear our holy Faith and religion
flourishes so much in my native country . . . I am glad our holy order is the
first."[41]

It is easy to see why Carroll hoped for women religious engaged in active ministry to settle in the United States. The first American diocese encompassed the entire country until it was divided in 1808, and the dioceses
of Boston, New York, Philadelphia, and Bardstown, Kentucky, and the
Archdiocese of Baltimore were created. It was difficult for bishops to offer those Catholics spreading throughout the growing country the opportunity to attend Mass, receive the sacraments, or gain a clear knowledge
of the doctrines of their faith. Communities of women religious willing to
provide education, health care, and social services were the answer, Carroll
thought, to manifesting a Catholic presence in the United States.[42]

Despite the Carmelites' cloistered lifestyle, Carroll hoped to persuade
them to open a school for girls, and asked the Vatican to consider modi-
fying the community's rule to give the women an opportunity to teach.
In 1792, he reported to Cardinal Leonardo Antonelli that the enclosed

Carmelites seemed to exert a positive influence on the nation's Catholics, writing: "Their example, a novelty in this country, has aroused many to serious thoughts on divine things." But, he continued, "They would be far more useful if . . . they undertook the education of girls."[43] Antonelli replied, "While they are not to be urged to undertake the care of young girls against their rule, they should be exhorted not to refuse this work which will be so pleasing to God and which is badly needed."[44] Carroll reported Antonelli's response to Mother Bernadina Matthews, and asked her to consider his request, but Charles Neale informed Carroll that the nuns were not willing to become a teaching order. They simply desired to continue to fulfill their ministry of praying for the Catholic Church and the American mission.[45] Carroll understood, but even after the nuns had been in the country ten years, he wished they would change their mind. "They have multiplied themselves considerably, and give much edification by their retirement and total seclusion from the world," he wrote to Charles Plowden in 1800, "and I do not doubt the efficacy of their prayers in drawing down blessings on us all; but they will not concern themselves in the business of female education, tho the late Pope, soon after their arrival, recommended it earnestly to them."[46]

The Carmelites remained faithful to their rule demanding strict enclosure until 1830, when diminishing financial resources and a convent in dire need of repair led Archbishop James Whitfield (1828–1834) to suggest that they move to either Baltimore or the District of Columbia, where they could support themselves by teaching.[47] The nuns agreed, and a cornerstone was laid for a monastery in Baltimore on September 29, 1830. The move proved difficult for both the nuns and their Port Tobacco neighbors, who missed the opportunity to attend Mass in the Carmelites' chapel on a regular basis. Like many Americans living below the Mason-Dixon Line, the Carmelites held slaves who were brought to the convent as a part of the dowry—or entrance fee—of some community members. The nuns could not afford to free their slaves when they moved from the farm to the city, but allowed them to choose their own masters, and took whatever price the buyer was willing to pay.[48]

The nuns' teaching ministry was short-lived; it was simply too difficult to teach and remain faithful to the rule of enclosure. Classrooms, for instance, had to be outside the cloister, but only teachers and students could enter them. In addition, in order to ensure that the nuns focused primarily on their ministry of prayer, they were forbidden to talk about the school or their students inside the convent, even during recreation.[49] These difficulties notwithstanding, the school was successful enough to support the community, attracting the daughters of the wealthy southern elite. The Carmelites administered the academy for twenty years, until a new archbishop, Francis Patrick Kenrick (1851–1863), decided that they should return to their primary apostolate of prayer within a contemplative lifestyle.

One other European religious community attempted to build a foundation in the United States during the late eighteenth century. The French Revolution and subsequent Reign of Terror caused the departure of many priests and women religious from what had been a Catholic country. Mother Marie de la Marche, Sister Celeste le Blond de la Rochefoucault, and Sister Luc, members of the cloistered Poor Clares, were expelled from their convent in Tours at the beginning of the Reign of Terror in 1792. They traveled in disguise to Harve de Grace and boarded a ship bound for Charleston, South Carolina, arriving in that city on January 11, 1793. Because they could not communicate with the city's residents—the Poor Clares did not speak English—the nuns decided to relocate to Baltimore. After an unsuccessful attempt to open a school, they moved to New Orleans and lived for two years with the Ursuline community in that city— now under Spanish rule—supported by a small stipend from the King of Spain. They decided to return to France, but when their ship stopped in Havana, a priest they met convinced them to return to Baltimore. In 1798, the three women opened the Georgetown Academy for Young Ladies in Washington, D.C.[50]

A community such as the Poor Clares was of no more help to John Carroll than the Carmelites. Founded by Clare of Assisi (1194–1253), friend of Francis of Assisi (1181/1182–1226), in 1212, the Poor Clares emphasized a life of poverty and serving those in need. As a cloistered community, the nuns were expected to interact with convent visitors through a grille, and were not to leave the enclosure except for "necessary and good purposes," including "charity work outside of the convent."[51] In 1250, Innocent IV (1243–1254) warned the nuns that they were not to imitate their Franciscan brothers and wander the countryside begging.[52]

The three Poor Clares attempting to minister in the United States were hindered by their inability to speak English. They struggled to support their school, at one time selling "Excellent Waters for the cure of almost all kinds of Sore Eyes . . . [and] Salves for the cure of different sorts of sores, hurts, wounds, etc."[53] When Leonard Neale, a priest ministering in Philadelphia, was named coadjutor Bishop of Baltimore, he convinced three women, Alice Lalor, Maria Sharpe, and Maria McDermott, to travel with him and assist the Poor Clares in their educational efforts.[54] The three "pious ladies" originally lived with the nuns, but Neale eventually purchased a separate residence for them.[55] When Mother Marie de la Marche died in 1804, the two remaining Poor Clares decided to return to France and the two pious ladies—Sharpe had died in 1802—assumed complete charge of the school that had been purchased by Neale. In addition to teaching, the women lived together in an informal religious community; they were not associated with a particular order, but set aside time for prayer, meditation, and other devotional activities.[56]

Leonard Neale—and perhaps the women as well—realized that the life of extreme poverty to which the Poor Clares were committed was not conducive to teaching young women, and began to consider other communities with a rule that was more appropriate for a ministry of education. A copy of the rule of the Order of the Visitation was discovered among the books left behind by the Poor Clares, and the women began to follow the lifestyle of this community. One commentator, however, gives Neale a much more direct role in the decision, writing: "After long and mature deliberation aided by unceasing prayer to the Almighty . . . the bishop determined to introduce the Institutions of the Visitation, founded by St. Francis de Sales, as best suited to the spirit of the age and the peculiar duties proposed for their secular occupation."[57]

The Visitation community originated when Jeanne de Chantal (1572–1641), a widow with seven children, became friendly with Francis de Sales (1567–1622) as a result of her work among the poor. When Francis de Sales presented her with an idea for a religious community combining a contemplative lifestyle with charitable work, she "responded by enclosing herself with two companions in a house . . . while keeping herself free to attend to the needs of her family and friends."[58] Others soon followed her example. The bishop of Lyons, France, required the women to take formal religious vows beginning in 1615, which led the various groups to become more institutionalized.[59] Although de Sales envisioned a religious community working with the sick poor, the Vatican would only approve a cloistered community. As a result, the congregation supported itself by administering boarding schools. By the beginning of the nineteenth century, convents of the Order of the Visitation existed in every major French city. Maryland Jesuits, all of whom were educated in France, were very familiar with the Visitandines.[60]

One of Leonard Neale's first communications with the Vatican after being named Archbishop of Baltimore upon John Carroll's death in

December 1815 requested that the women living in community in Georgetown be approved as a convent of the Order of Visitation. Permission was
quickly granted, and on December 28, 1816, the first three sisters made
vows of poverty, chastity, and obedience. Alice Lalor, now Sister Teresa,
was appointed superior; her assistant was Sister Frances McDermott, and
Sister Agnes Brent was named Mistress of Novices. On January 6, 1817,
nineteen other sisters took first vows; most of them took final vows later
that month.[61]

Since there were no Visitandines in the United States, Neale wrote to
a French convent in 1817 asking for help and information. Mother Teresa
Lalor and her community essentially had to learn to live as members of
the congregation with which they were now affiliated. They did not even
know how they were supposed to dress, and had been wearing a modified
Carmelite habit.[62] In his letter, the Archbishop reported that thirty-five
sisters were living in the Georgetown community, and asked the French
nuns to send someone "who would lead them on to a perfect compliance
with each minute point of the Institute."[63] Neale's request was circulated
throughout Visitation houses, and the Paris convent sent books containing
the community's rule and constitutions, as well as forty silver crosses and a
doll clothed as a Visitandine.[64]

Young American women were attracted to the Order of the Visitation,
and at the same time, Visitation Academy—now Georgetown Visitation—
was growing into one of the country's premier Catholic academies for
girls. When the community's spiritual director, Sulpician priest Michael
Wheeler, SS, asked for Visitandines from Europe to come to America and
work with the Georgetown community in 1828, the convent strengthened
the bond with its European roots. Four years later in 1832, the women established their second convent in Mobile, Alabama.[65]

The Beginnings of American Women Religious

John Carroll's wish for a community of women religious dedicated to serving the Catholic Church through active ministry began to be realized when
Elizabeth Ann Bayley Seton (1774–1821) moved to Maryland and formed
an American religious congregation. Raised in New York City as a devout
Episcopalian, Seton's earliest memory was connected to the question of
salvation and the afterlife. She remembered, "At 4 years of age sitting alone
on a step of the door looking at the clouds while my little sister Catherine

2 years old lay in her coffin they asked me did I not cry when little Kitty was dead?—no because Kitty is gone up to heaven I wish I could go too with Mama."[66] After attending "Madame Pompelion's" school, where she received an education appropriate for young women of her social class, she married William Seton at the age of nineteen, and had five children. In 1798, her father-in-law died, and the couple became responsible for William's seven younger half-siblings, ranging from seven to eighteen years of age.[67]

The family's financial holdings suffered a substantial loss when William Seton's business failed in 1801. Shortly after losing his livelihood, Seton contracted tuberculosis and Elizabeth took him to Italy in 1803 in the hope that he would regain his health. Her husband died shortly after their arrival, but while Elizabeth and her daughter were in Italy her friendship with the family of one of William Seton's business partners, Antonio Filicchi, along with an exposure to Italian Catholic culture, caused her to think about the tenets of Catholicism, especially the Eucharist. In a journal Seton kept for Amabilia Filicchi, she wrote of attending a service at her Episcopal church, "Yet I got in a side pew which turned my face towards the Catholic Church in the next street, and found myself twenty times speaking to the blessed Sacrament *there* instead of looking at the naked altar where I was."[68]

In January 1805, Elizabeth Seton made the decision to convert to Catholicism; her two main reasons were a belief in the Real Presence of Christ in the Eucharist and the conviction that an Episcopal bishop could not truly absolve sins. She described her feelings at attending a service at St. Peter's Church on Barclay Street in Manhattan: "—when I turned the corner of the street it is in, here my God I go said I, *heart all to you*—entering it, how that heart died away as it were in silence before the little tabernacle and the great Crucifixion over it—Ah My God here let me rest said I—and down the head on the bosom and the knees on the bench."[69]

As a widow and a recent convert, Seton was faced with the challenge of supporting a growing family without the support network offered by Protestant churches. Father Louis Dubourg, president of St. Mary's College in Baltimore, encouraged her to open a school for girls in that city.[70] Seton and her young children left New York for Baltimore in 1808, and she opened a school on Paca Street. On March 25, 1809, Seton "took vows of poverty, chastity, and obedience and thereafter became known as Mother Seton"; she was permitted to keep her children with her until they became adults.[71] Mother Seton experienced great joy as a result of entering religious life; it was all she hoped it would be, she wrote her friend Julia Scott, expressing "the joy of [her] soul at the prospect of being able to assist the

Poor [*sic*], visit the sick, comfort the sorrowful, clothe little innocents, and teach them to love God."[72]

On June 1 of that year, Seton and four other women, including Cecilia O'Conway and Maria Murphy, both from Philadelphia, formed themselves into the Sisters of Charity of St. Joseph; later that month they moved to Emmitsburg, Maryland.[73] John Carroll explained that the women's relocation to rural Maryland would expedite the formation of a religious community dedicated to "the purpose of training piously disposed females to the duties of a perfect life, particularly with a view of enabling them to aid the poor by their work and industry, to nurse the sick and perform for them all kinds of necessary attention and care. Their undertaking," he concluded, "embraces other objects, too long to be detailed."[74]

Carroll's positive assessment of the move to Emmitsburg notwithstanding, the conditions the women found in their new home were primitive, to say the least. "They had been forewarned that they would 'find pebbles for beads, tin cups to drink out of and plates of pewter,' and were instructed 'to cultivate plenty of carrots' for coffee." Only the sick were provided with cots for sleeping; the others placed mats on the floor. The sleeping quarters were in the garret of the house, and the poor condition of the roof required that the sisters shovel snow out of this area during the winter months, like the Carmelites had in Port Tobacco.[75] Despite a less than ideal living situation, eighteen sisters were residing at St. Joseph's in Emmitsburg by 1813. Some women, of course, tried to live in the community and decided they were not called to religious life. Others, including Cecilia O'Conway, who first joined Seton in Baltimore, preferred the life of a cloistered nun to an active ministry. Shortly after Mother Seton's death, O'Conway left Emmitsburg and entered an enclosed community. Like her friend John Carroll, Elizabeth Seton doubted the necessity for cloistered nuns in the United States. "[T]his is not a country my dear one," she wrote O'Conway, "for Solitude and Silence, but of warfare and crucifixion."[76]

Mother Seton and her sisters taught day and boarding students at St. Joseph's Academy in Emmitsburg, and provided religious education to Catholics living in the surrounding community. She hoped the congregation would eventually expand and be able to serve those in need whenever and wherever possible. "If I was a man," the future saint wrote to her son, William, in 1818, "all the world would not stop me, I would go straight in [St. Francis] Xavier's footsteps."[77] The sisters believed teaching should be their primary ministry, followed by nursing and the care of orphans, but they were willing to be flexible and adapt their work to meet the needs of the growing church in the United States.[78] In 1814, they were asked to administer St. Joseph's Orphanage in Philadelphia, and three years later they were invited to minister in the Diocese of New York. The sisters began working in Baltimore in 1821—the year of Seton's death—and eleven years later they were able to send women to Boston.[79] By 1830, the Sisters of Charity of St. Joseph were conducting schools, hospitals, and orphanages all along the East Coast and in Cincinnati, St. Louis, and New Orleans.[80]

Prior to her conversion, Elizabeth Seton had been active in New York charitable circles—she and her sister-in-law had even been referred to as the Protestant Sisters of Charity—and along with Joanna Graham Bethune and Isabella Graham, she devoted a good deal of time and energy to the Society for the Relief of Poor Widows with Small Children. As a Sister of Charity, she continued this type of work even as she depended on financial assistance from family and friends to help the small community rent a building for their school and hire a servant. Her service to the poor as a woman religious, however, was performed in a very different context from Protestant women's benevolent societies. Most of the charitable work conducted under the auspices of the Catholic Church at the turn of the nineteenth century was carried out by women religious, not laywomen. Catholic laywomen were not expected to establish and raise money for orphanages and hospitals; that work was assigned to women religious.[81]

Protestant reformers often attacked women religious because they believed Catholic sisters were in direct opposition to the belief that "the well-being of the community depended upon American women assuming responsibilities in their proper domain—the home."[82] Not only did sisters reject the role women were expected to play in building the country, but their ministry of educating and caring for children threatened to "replace American mothers as the moral and cultural arbiters of the nation."[83] The home, maintained Protestant reformers such as Catharine Beecher, was the place where women were able to have a voice in society. Women religious involved in education and child care were viewed as competitors in the struggle for influencing the next generation of Americans.[84] Catholic moralists did not completely disagree, claiming that most Catholic women were called to be wives and mothers and participate in the important task of instilling values in the nation's children. Religious life, however, was superior to the married state; virginity was a higher calling than motherhood. As women who were "brides of Christ" *and* involved in teaching, caring for orphans, and nursing, sisters were gifted with a "maternity of the spirit," and played an important role in helping to create good Catholics and good Americans.[85]

Growing Sisterhoods

The first three communities of women religious to establish permanent ministries in the new nation—the Carmelites, Visitandines, and Sisters of Charity—were centered on Baltimore and its environs. Included in that city's Catholic population were a group of Santo Domingan refugees from the 1793 revolution in what are now Haiti and the Dominican Republic. These French-speaking Catholics were joined by those fleeing the French Revolution, including priests from the Order of St. Sulpice, known as Sulpicians, who arrived in Baltimore between 1791 and 1793. Dedicated to the education of clergy, the Sulpicians established both St. Mary's Seminary and St. Mary's College. They began offering catechism classes for black Santo Domingan Catholics in 1796, and in 1827 Father James Joubert was assigned to this ministry.[86]

During the course of his work in Baltimore, Joubert met two African American women, Elizabeth Lange and Marie Balas, who had established a school for black children in Baltimore. "Both of them told me," Joubert wrote, "that for more than ten years they wished to consecrate themselves to God for this good work, waiting patiently that in His own infinite goodness He would show them a way of giving themselves to Him." After meeting Lange and Balas, Joubert was convinced that the formation of an African American community of women religious should take precedence over all his other plans.[87] On June 13, 1828, Rosine Boegue, an émigré from the Caribbean, joined Lange and Balais in the novitiate; that same day the three opened their School for Colored Girls with eleven boarders and nine day students. Along with Marie Therese Almaide Duchemin, they were professed on July 2, 1829.[88] The congregation was approved by Baltimore Archbishop James Whitfield in 1829, and recognized by Rome in October 1831.[89] At a time when many Americans were opposed to the education of African Americans, the community's primary ministry was the *"Christian education of young girls of colour [sic]."*[90]

The Oblate School for Colored Girls—the name was later changed to St. Frances Academy—was the first Roman Catholic school for African Americans in the Archdiocese of Baltimore. Located in a row house, the faculty, boarders, and day students, along with three orphans, lived and worked under one roof.[91] St. Frances was conducted on the traditional model developed by other communities of American women religious. The sisters accepted boarders and day students and provided an education designed to prepare young women to be faithful Catholics and good wives and mothers, but the community's rule referred to their students as "persons of the lower order" and members of a "humble and naturally dutiful class of society." In addition to instruction in Catholic doctrine, students studied reading, writing, geography, English, arithmetic, music, bead work, French, sewing, and embroidery, but were also taught to wash and iron.[92] This particular course of instruction may have been implemented to prepare students for their station in life; it was not inconceivable that some of them would find work as domestic servants.[93] Joubert believed girls attending the school would "either become mothers of families, or be introduced as servants, into decent houses," but the sisters tried to ensure that the education their students received "was on a par with other schools of the time."[94]

It was clear, however, that the Oblates were viewed as different from and possibly inferior to their sisters in other religious communities. When the community was suddenly forced to vacate their property in April 1829, they had difficulty finding a new location for their convent and school. According to Joubert, houses that met their needs were available, but "several refused absolutely to let us have them, when they were informed that it was for a school, and still more a school for colored children."[95] In 1835, Sulpician Father Louis Deluol, Superior of St. Mary's Seminary, asked that two Oblates assume responsibility for housekeeping at the school. Lange agreed to provide sisters for the task, but informed Deluol that they were to live as women religious and be treated with the respect accorded to their vocation. "We do not conceal the difficulty of our situation [a]s persons of color and religious at the same time," she wrote Deluol, "and we wish to conciliate these two qualities in such a manner as not to appear too arrogant on the one hand and on the other, not to miss the respect which is due to the state we have embraced and the holy habit which we have the honor to wear."[96] Slaves lived and worked on the seminary's grounds and Lange wanted to be clear that her sisters were not part of that community. To ensure that the women lived in accordance with their rule, the Oblates were not to have any more interaction with other servants and visitors than necessary.[97] Deluol replied that he was happy to accept the conditions stipulated by Lange, explaining, "You write the paper . . . under which you will come and I shall sign it."[98]

The Oblate Sisters of Providence never received the financial support from ecclesiastical leaders enjoyed by the other three religious communities in Maryland and Washington, D.C. When the Carmelites relocated to Baltimore in 1830, for instance, Archbishop Whitfield helped them secure accommodations that supported their cloistered lifestyle. After finding what he described as "a most beautiful garden, with a brick house, in a very respectable part of the city," Whitfield personally donated $100 toward the $6,250 needed to purchase the property.[99] The Oblates, on the other hand, counted many friends, but few financial benefactors among the American clergy. Some church leaders were decidedly unfriendly—or at best indifferent—toward the struggling community. Samuel Eccleston, who succeeded Whitfield as Archbishop in 1834, was from a family of slaveholders, and almost immediately demonstrated his indifference toward the African American women religious ministering within his archdiocese. His official proclamation of Whitfield's death stipulated that three of the four religious communities, "the Nuns of Mount Carmel in Baltimore, those of the Visitation at Georgetown, and the Sisters of Charity," were "to offer three communions each, for . . . [the repose of Whitfield's soul]." The Oblate sisters were not mentioned in Eccleston's statement.[100]

When their primary clerical advocate, James Hector Joubert, died in 1843, the Oblates began a four-year struggle both to maintain their ministries and to develop their spiritual lives. Without Joubert, it was difficult for Mass to be offered in their chapel on a regular basis; when a priest arrived to celebrate the liturgy on October 8, 1843—the feast of St. Benedict the Moor—it marked the first time the sisters had been able to attend Mass in their chapel since September 12.[101] Neither Eccleston nor Deluol seemed very concerned that the community was without a spiritual director. Ecclesiastical indifference was followed by restrictions prohibiting the acceptance of new community members and limiting the number of Masses celebrated in the convent chapel to once a month. These difficulties were resolved when John Neumann, newly appointed superior of the Redemptorist priests in the United States, assigned Father Thaddeus Anwander "to take charge of the Oblate Sisters, then in a very bad condition of abandonment," in 1847. Eccleston initially refused to endorse Anwander's appointment as spiritual director of the community, but changed his mind after the priest knelt and asked for permission to work with the sisters.[102] The community persevered, but never had more than twenty members at any time prior to 1860.

Unlike other religious communities, the Oblates were not able to easily expand their ministries to other parts of the country. In general, bishops were constantly seeking women religious willing to minister within their dioceses, but the Oblates often "virtually pleaded with prelates to allow them to establish missions in their jurisdictions."[103] While attempting to establish a school in the area governed by Cincinnati Archbishop John Baptist Purcell in 1857, Sister Gertrude Thomas informed the prelate of her community's desire to send members to Ohio, telling him that she was "waiting for your own arrangements whatever they may be and if possible . . . [would] acquiesce to your good pleasure in every respect as far as lies in my power [sic]."[104] No Oblate mission was established in Cincinnati.

Beyond Baltimore

By the early nineteenth century, Catholic tobacco farmers had exhausted the soil in southern Maryland and began moving to Kentucky in search of more fertile land. As a result, more Catholics were soon living within the environs of the city of Bardstown than any other city on what was then considered the frontier. Bardstown's first bishop, Benedict Flaget, assumed responsibility for a vast territory, which included Kentucky, Tennessee, and Ohio, as well as an area bordered on the north by the Great Lakes and the Tennessee border on the south. The Allegheny Mountains served as the diocese's eastern edge, and the Mississippi River marked its western boundary. Although Catholics settled throughout the diocese, clergy were few and far between. Six priests were ministering in Kentucky, and three others were responsible for the remainder of the vast region. Almost as soon as he arrived in Bardstown, Flaget announced three priorities for the growing Catholic Church on the frontier that echoed those set by John Carroll in 1789: first, a seminary; second, a cathedral; and third, the establishment of a community of women religious.[105]

Sisters of Loretto. Three years after Elizabeth Seton founded the first sisterhood in the United States, and less than a year after Flaget announced his priorities for the diocese, the Sisters of Loretto at the Foot of the Cross were founded when Mary Rhodes, Christina Stuart, and Ann Havern were accepted by Reverend Charles Nerinckx.[106] When the community began on April 25, 1812, its primary work was defined as the education of young girls and the care of orphans. Between 1814 and 1818, the sisters administered Gethsemani School, which also served as an orphanage. The sisters founded Bethlehem Academy in Breckinridge County in 1823. In that same year, they expanded their ministry beyond the borders of Kentucky, establishing a foundation in Perry County, Missouri.[107]

Sisters of Charity of Nazareth. When Bishop Flaget arrived in Bardstown, he was accompanied by Sulpician priest John Baptist David.[108]

David hoped to found a community of women religious that would minister among rural congregations in pairs, returning to the motherhouse to participate in retreats and other aspects of community life. In December 1812, Teresa Carico and Elizabeth Wells, described in the community's annals as "two young women of the country, poor and illiterate but of good repute," became the first to enter the Sisters of Charity of Nazareth. They were joined by Catherine Spalding on January 21, 1813.[109]

David and Flaget, both French Sulpicians, had been influenced by the life and work of Vincent de Paul, and chose the model of religious life developed by the French saint. The new community's ministry was defined as teaching and "works of mercy . . . especially those that can contribute to aid the work of the mission," which included "manufacturing all the clothing worn by the seminarians." The sisters' early works of mercy involved assisting several elderly men and women living and working on the property where the convent was located. When three additional young women joined the group, there were enough members to elect nineteen-year-old Catherine Spalding as superior.[110] Although the community shared a rule with the Sisters of Charity in Emmitsburg, they remained two separate foundations. David explored the possibility of joining with the Maryland sisters, but decided the Kentucky group should remain independent when he realized a merger would require him to surrender control of the community.[111]

The Sisters of Charity of Nazareth first opened a one-room school at St. Thomas Farm near Bardstown to serve the area's poor children; the school was named Nazareth Academy after its move to the town by the same name in 1822. They later founded Bethlehem Academy (Bardstown) in 1819, and two years later opened St. Vincent's Academy in Union County. The community's rapid growth—it increased from 3 to 145 members during the first generation—allowed the sisters to expand their ministry of education and service. In 1831, Mother Catherine Spalding, along with three other sisters, opened Presentation Academy in Louisville. One year later, there were enough sisters to establish an orphanage in the same city. In 1842, at the request of Bishop Richard Miles, the community sent sisters to Nashville, Tennessee, where they founded a school for girls and a hospital.[112]

Dominicans. Dominic de Guzman established a monastery for women in Prouille, France, in 1206, about six years before he founded the male Order of Preachers in 1216.[113] Prouille and other early communities became the foundation of the Second Order of St. Dominic, a cloistered congregation of women religious.[114] Father Samuel Wilson, a Dominican priest ministering in Kentucky, was responsible for establishing the Dominican sisters in the United States, the third community of women religious founded on what was then considered the frontier.

Cincinnati Bishop Edward Fenwick, OP (1822–1832), who was a member of the Dominican order, planned to request an English women's religious community to send members to the United States, but Wilson convinced him that it was more practical to establish an indigenous American community of Dominicans, one whose members were not required to live within a cloister. On February 28, 1822, Wilson preached a sermon designed to call women to religious life, and nine came forward and expressed their desire to enter a community. Four women received the religious habit on April 7 of that year. Sister Angela Sansbury was named the first superior, and under her leadership St. Mary Magdalen Academy (later St. Catharine's) was founded in 1823.[115]

The Kentucky Dominicans were not supposed to live a life that was strictly cloistered, but they were governed by a rule designed for contemplative communities. In addition to rising at midnight for prayers, for example, they were expected to pray at regular intervals throughout the day. At the same time, they lived an active life—teaching, tending to the fields and grounds, and selling their linen and wool to support themselves.[116] By 1830, despite years of hard work, they were experiencing financial difficulties. Father Raphael Muños, the community's spiritual director, did not support the idea of women religious performing manual labor (e.g., farming and carpentry), and advocated that the group disband, but the sisters resisted. Father Stephen Montgomery, Muños's successor, was more sympathetic to the community's situation and by 1833, with his assistance, the sisters had repaid their debt. Since women joining the Kentucky Dominicans sometimes brought their slaves with them, the sisters were able to spend less time on the farm than in the classroom.[117] Financial hardship notwithstanding, the community was strong enough to open a second convent in Somerset, Ohio, in 1830. Throughout the nineteenth century, a number of Dominican communities—with both European and American roots—were established in the United States.[118]

Sisters of Charity of Our Lady of Mercy. A fourth religious community was founded in 1829 by John England (1820–1842), Bishop of Charleston, South Carolina, when four women he had met in Baltimore, Mary and Honora O'Gorman, Mary Teresa Barry, and Mary E. Burke, constituted the founding members of the Sisters of Charity of Our Lady of Mercy.

Appointed bishop in 1820, England was responsible for as many as five thousand Catholics residing in North Carolina, South Carolina, and Georgia. He informed the Vatican of the new community, writing: "In Charleston four nuns are living a religious life under a rule which I drew up for them. . . . [T]hey desire to take simple vows each year and to dedicate themselves to teaching young girls, in instructing the negro slaves in faith and morals, and for caring for the sick and infirm."[119] England deliberately chose not to invite the Sisters of Charity to Charleston because he feared it would mean giving up control over the women religious serving in the diocese, but he modeled the new congregation on the Emmitsburg community. "I do not," he wrote, "wish to make my institutions depend on Superiors over whom I have neither control [n]or influence. Hence I shall try what can, within the diocese, be done upon the same principle." The decision to establish a religious community in South Carolina allowed England to mold the group according to his own vision and philosophy.[120]

Although five more women joined the community in 1830, their work was hindered by a lack of financial resources. For the first couple of years, the sisters were so poor they had difficulty caring for orphans because they were unable to provide them with the necessary food and shelter. When Julia Datty joined the community at age 66, however, their financial situation brightened considerably. A native of Haiti, Datty administered a school in Charleston for many years, acquiring a reputation for academic excellence. Her entrance into the community increased the number of students—day and boarding—in the school the sisters had established. At the same time, young women were expressing an interest in the Sisters of Charity of Our Lady of Mercy, and the community's membership increased to fourteen by 1834.[121]

The bishop was clear that the community should work with the poor—white and black. In 1835, England opened a school for free African American children; seminarians taught the boys and the girls were instructed by the Sisters of Charity of Our Lady of Mercy. After some of the city's leading citizens protested the existence of a school for blacks, it was closed, but reopened in 1841. In addition to working with Charleston's free blacks, the sisters also cared for the sick in their homes and temporary hospitals, and performed all of the housekeeping tasks at the diocesan seminary.[122]

The small community found itself in difficulty when John England died in 1842 because he had never written a constitution that provided a governance structure for the sisters. Until a replacement was named, only community members who had taken vows for five years remained "under vows." Others were unable to renew their vows until England's successor, Ignatius Reynolds (1843–1855), provided them with a constitution in 1844 that was based on the original rule drafted by England, and the rule of the "Sisters of Charity in America."[123] When the first community elections were held in 1844, Sister Teresa Barry, one of the original members, was elected mother superior.[124]

Looking Forward

By 1830, women religious were rapidly becoming a part of the Catholic religious landscape in the United States. They were working with the daughters of the wealthy in academies such as Georgetown Visitation, ministering to the Catholic and non-Catholic poor in Charleston, South Carolina, and spending their days praying for Catholics in the United States and throughout the world. Women religious reflected the Catholic Church, which in turn reflected the larger society. The Oblate Sisters of Providence suffered as a result of prejudice and racism, and other communities shared the financial struggles of Americans attempting to create a better life for themselves and their families in a society increasingly dependent on the vicissitudes of the marketplace.

Communities such as Elizabeth Seton's Sisters of Charity of St. Joseph adapted a European rule to meet the needs of women religious ministering in the United States. Others, such as the Visitandines, tried their best to work within a lifestyle determined by forces unfamiliar with the American way of life. With the exception of contemplative communities, all of them served where and when they were needed if resources allowed, sending sisters to distant cities and towns as the Catholic population spread throughout the country.

The number of women religious working in the United States at the end of the 1820s, however, was not sufficient to meet the demands of what has been described as an immigrant church. In the 1830s, an influx of European Catholics, many of them desperately poor, began to dramatically increase the size of the church. Bishops were called upon to provide assistance for these new Americans, but the number of women religious was not adequate to establish the schools, hospitals, orphanages, and other institutions needed to serve the newcomers. In addition, the demographics of Catholicism had changed. It was no longer a church centered below the Mason-Dixon Line, but reached almost everywhere Americans were settling, including remote frontier outposts.

Church leaders would turn to European communities to help increase the numbers of women religious ministering in the Catholic community. At the same time, American women with a call to religious life would help swell the ranks of communities either founded in Europe or originating in the United States. The work begun by women religious prior to 1830 set the tone and the pattern for those ministering to Catholics throughout the nineteenth and twentieth centuries. The early communities laid a foundation that successive generations would build upon as they played their role in the growth and development of the Catholic Church in the United States.

2

Service to a Growing Catholic Community

WHEN ANNE-THÉRÈSE GUERIN'S parents celebrated her birth in the French village of Etables-sur-Mer in 1798, they never expected that their beloved daughter would find fulfillment as a woman religious in rural Indiana. Anne-Thérèse was convinced that she was called to religious life from an early age, but family responsibilities, including caring for her mother and maintaining the household, prevented her from entering the French order of the Sisters of Providence of Ruillé-sur-Loir until 1823 at the age of twenty-five. Given the name Sister Mary Theodore, she was assigned to teach, but also spent time visiting the sick and the poor. The course of Sister Theodore's life would change considerably in 1839, when Simon Bruté, the bishop of Vincennes, Indiana, sent Reverend Célestine de la Hailandière to France to persuade a religious community that they were needed to minister to the Irish, French, and German Catholics settling in the diocese.[1] Bruté needed sisters to teach, care for the sick, and provide religious instruction and sacramental preparation to those unable to attend a Catholic school. While in France, Hailandière learned that Bruté had died and he had been named bishop of the vast diocese. He asked the Sisters of Providence for help, and the superior general suggested Sister Theodore who, in her opinion, was the best person to lead a group of sisters to the United States. "We have only one Sister capable of making the foundation," she wrote. "If she consents, we shall send you Sisters next summer."[2] Sister Theodore accepted her appointment as superior of the group, and in 1840 she and five other sisters departed France for a new land.

Mother Theodore—she received the title after being appointed superior—and her companions traveled by stagecoach, steamboat, canal boat, and train before finally reaching Indiana. Accustomed to the cosmopolitan world of nineteenth-century France, she noticed the rugged, unsettled world that comprised her new home. Describing the sisters' stagecoach ride to Vincennes, she wrote: "we entered a thick forest where we saw the most singular kind of road that could be imagined. It was formed of logs, of trees that had been felled to clear the way and then were brought together as though to form a raft. Where some of these logs had become rotten, there were large holes. The coach jolted so terrible as to cause large bumps in one's head. This day, indeed, we danced without a fiddle all afternoon."[3]

The sisters' initial experience in their new city was challenging, to say the least. After settling in the household of the Sisters of Charity and putting on the habits they had not worn during their journey, the sisters requested to be taken to the cathedral, only to discover it was not quite the kind of edifice with which they were familiar. "Our barn at Soulaines is better ornamented and more neatly kept," Mother Theodore explained. "I could not resist this last shock and wept bitterly, which relieved me somewhat. . . . The Bishop's seat is an old red chair which even our peasants would not have in what they consider a nice room. . . . I can say nothing of the town except that I doubt whether it will ever grow much on account of its position. . . . It is said there are four thousand inhabitants, but I think they would have hard work to find that number."[4] On October 22, 1840 the sisters arrived at St. Mary-of-the-Woods, where they found several postulants waiting for them. Unconvinced that such a solitary place was suitable for both a novitiate to house and educate postulants and novices and an academy, Mother Theodore expressed her worries—and commented on the American character—to those involved in the work. "All have given reasons [for establishing the academy at St. Mary-of-the Woods]," she wrote, "that are not entirely satisfactory [to me]; yet I dare not disregard them. The spirit of this country is so different from ours that one ought to be acquainted with it before condemning those who know more about it than we do; so I await the issue before passing judgment in a positive manner. If we cannot do any good here, you know our agreement, we will return to our own country."[5] Despite her reservations, the community opened an academy for girls, now St. Mary-of-the-Woods College, later that year.

Bishop Hailandière's strong opinions on the way the Sisters of Providence should live and work did not always coincide with those of Mother Theodore. He challenged her authority on numerous occasions, and opened two convents while she was in France that he expected to fall outside her jurisdiction. Because sisters living in those residences would be under the authority of Haliandière rather than Mother Theodore, the community would be divided into two, but the sisters themselves refused to live in those convents established by the bishop.[6] The relationship between Haliandière and Mother Theodore grew from bad to worse as the bishop demanded complete authority over the community. During one particularly contentious disagreement in 1847, the superior was locked in the bishop's residence until she agreed to carry out his orders. A day later, Mother Theodore was removed "as superior, released . . . from religious vows," and those sisters who agreed with her were threatened with excommunication.[7] After deciding that her disagreements with the bishop were insurmountable, Mother Theodore prepared to relocate the community to Detroit because the bishop there was anxious to gain the sisters' services. At the last moment she received word that Haliendière had been replaced by John Bazin. As a result, Mother Theodore and her sisters remained in the diocese, and by her death in 1856, they had established twelve schools in Indiana and Illinois, two orphanages, one for girls and one for boys, and pharmacies where those in need could receive medicine.

Mother Saint Theodore Guerin—she was canonized in 2006—came to consider herself a true Hoosier. In 1844, she wrote about returning from a fund-raising trip in Europe to the country she now called home: "The farther north we went, the lower became the temperature and the bleaker the landscape. . . . The severe change was sweet to me, for it meant I was nearing home. Finally, on the fifth day, with inexpressible joy I saw once more my Indiana. This land was no longer for me the land of exile; it was the portion of my inheritance, and I hope to dwell in it all the days of my life."[8]

The increasing number of American Catholics—by 1850 they comprised the largest religious denomination in the country—demanded an increase in the numbers of women religious. Sisters contributed to this growing church during the first half of the nineteenth century by meeting the many and varied needs of the country's rather diverse Catholic population. In some cases, women raised in a European environment found themselves adapting to a very different way of life in a strange land. Mother Guerin and her companions were part of an ever growing number of communities, both European and American, who rose to the challenge of helping to build and nurture an institution and its people.

An Immigrant Church

The arrival of large numbers of immigrants to the United States in the nineteenth century altered the traditional look of Catholicism. The Catholic Church had been a presence in Europe for many centuries, but it was "culturally quite homogeneous, with the native culture clearly the dominant force in the church."[9] In the United States, however, Catholicism somehow had to incorporate people from many countries and cultures into one church. Men and women from Ireland had been settling in the United States since the colonial era, but between 1820 and 1840 more than 260,000 Irish left their homeland for a new life in America. These numbers increased even further when the potato crops in Ireland failed; over one million people left that country between 1846 and 1851. German Catholics also constituted a sizeable immigrant group; about 1,500,000 settled in the United States prior to 1860.[10] Although many Irish and German immigrants were Catholic, they had little in common with each other except for a shared religious tradition.

Many, if not most, immigrants were poor and uneducated, and church leaders were challenged to find ways to meet their basic needs—food and medical care, for instance—while providing the necessary tools, such as an adequate education, to help them succeed in their new home. The precarious financial position of the institutional Catholic Church meant that bishops often found themselves with neither the money nor the personnel to provide the necessary services for new arrivals. Women religious offered one way for church leaders to increase the number of schools, hospitals, and charitable institutions despite limited resources.

It is difficult to determine why women religious volunteered to leave the comforts of home for a country many viewed as lacking in even the basic amenities of life. Nineteenth-century sisters "believed their good work would be recognized in the hereafter by an all-knowing God, they made little or no effort to preserve records of their comings and goings or the reasons for them."[11] One sister whose story survives was Alice Nolan, who left Dublin for New Orleans to enter a Dominican community. The young woman reflected on what she was about to undertake at the beginning of her ocean voyage. Leaving St. Mary's, the school she had come to love, was a way of repaying the sisters for all they had done. "My only sustenance in this heartfelt struggle," the future Sister Columba wrote in her diary, "[is] the conviction that a high duty calls me hence."[12] Whether longing to be missionaries or enticed by a cleric's description of the needs facing Catholics in the United States, women religious from several countries willingly embarked on a dangerous and risky journey to a country that seemed primitive by the standards of their homelands.

Close political and diplomatic ties between the United States and Catholic France led American bishops to recruit women religious from French communities. Appointed Bishop of Louisiana in 1812, Louis Dubourg

(1812–1825) needed sisters willing to labor in a vast diocese whose boundaries stretched from the Mississippi River to the Rocky Mountains and from Canada to the Gulf of Mexico, including the former Spanish colony of Florida. On a fund-raising trip to Europe in 1817, the bishop met members of the Society of the Sacred Heart of Jesus, a religious community founded by Madeleine Sophie Barat in 1801. Mother Rose Philippine Duchesne (1769–1852), who entered the Society shortly after the French Revolution, was a fervent admirer of Canadian missionary Marie de l'Incarnation, and hoped Dubourg had come to plead for sisters willing to work in his huge diocese.[13] Although Mother Barat had not intended to send anyone to America, she reportedly told Duchesne, "If the Bishop asks for us to go to Louisiana, Philippine, I will take it as an indication of God's will."[14] The next day Dubourg requested sisters, and after pleading with Mother Barat for permission, Mother Duchesne left France with four other members of the community, arriving in St. Louis on August 21, 1818.[15] The Society was a quasi-cloistered community; sisters taught within the confines of the convent, but entertained visitors and traveled on business. Mother Barat gave those bound for America permission to leave the convent grounds "if the superiors judge it useful for the glory of God."[16]

After several unsuccessful attempts to find the sisters suitable housing in St. Louis, Dubourg settled the small community in St. Charles, Missouri, where they immediately opened a free school for area children. The women were astounded at their students' inability to read and write or understand basic tenets of Catholicism, but claimed their young charges learned quickly, boasting, "it was astonishing to see these same children, after four months' tuition, singing Benediction and many of the familiar hymns, and having made a good beginning in other subjects."[17] Because they enrolled only three paying boarding students, the community had difficulty maintaining the school, and eventually moved to Florissant, Missouri, closer to St. Louis. In 1826, they were finally able to open a house in St. Louis.

Several years later, St. Louis Bishop Joseph Rosati (the diocese had been divided between St. Louis and New Orleans in 1826) invited the Sisters of St. Joseph—another French community—to work in his diocese. The six sisters who arrived in the city in 1836 began work immediately. Three opened a school in a French Canadian parish in Cahokia, Illinois, and the others stayed in St. Louis until they could establish themselves in Carondelet, about five miles south of the city. By 1846, the sisters were administering three institutions in St. Louis, including a school for "Catholic colored girls," which soon closed as a result of racist views held by the city's residents.[18]

Members of a religious community whose members were dispersed among several parishes or towns often discovered that their experiences were anything but identical. The Sisters of St. Joseph in Cahokia worked with a group of highly devout parishioners, who with their priest . . ., had provided a set of buildings in the center of the village that the sisters could use for a convent and school."[19] Those who began a ministry in Carondolet, however, were lodged in a two-room cabin empty of furniture except for a cot, table, and two chairs. After sharing a supper of bread and cheese with the sisters on their first night in town, the parish priest informed them that he could barely afford to feed himself and they could expect no support from him.[20]

The Sisters of St. Joseph of Carondolet were aided considerably by the 1839 decision of the Missouri state legislature to appropriate $2,000 annually toward St. Joseph's Institute for the Deaf, which was administered by the community.[21] After Missouri educational leaders attempted unsuccessfully to establish a state school for the deaf, Rosati urged legislators to consider funding St. Joseph's Institute, which boasted a growing enrollment and reputation.[22] The community's financial situation improved further when civic leaders in Carondolet offered the sisters a stipend to provide an education for the town's girls. State and local funding proved a tremendous help to a community struggling to support its members and its students, and allowed the sisters to begin to expand their outreach. New ministries led to growth; in the 1850s 104 women from the United States joined the Carondolet community, decreasing their dependence on European sisters.[23]

Ireland was also viewed as prime recruiting territory for women religious. In addition to the fact that a great number of communities were located throughout the country, those sisters willing to move to the United States did not struggle with the difficulty of learning a new language. Between 1812 and 1881, sixteen communities of Irish women religious established permanent foundations in America.[24] Three Ursulines left Ireland for New York City in 1812, constituting the first religious group of Irish women religious in the United States. Jesuit priest Anthony Kholmann provided them with a convent and the sisters opened a school, but were forced to return to Ireland within three years because they were unable to attract postulants to their community.

Mary Frances Clarke left Dublin with four other women in July 1833. The five women first met as Franciscan tertiaries, which meant that their rule had been adapted to allow them to live in the world. They made promises, but did not take vows, and lived together in a spirit of community while operating a school. When Father Patrick Costello visited Ireland, he met Clarke and invited her group to work in Philadelphia, where, he assured her, there was a great need for Catholic educators. The women agreed, and even though Costello never met them in Philadelphia—it is not clear what actually happened to him—they began conducting classes in the city, taking in sewing to support themselves. In November 1833 the women took vows, forming themselves as the Sisters of Charity of the Blessed Virgin Mary (BVM). They ministered in Philadelphia until 1843, when they were recruited by Bishop Mathias Loras (1837–1858) for the Diocese of Dubuque, Iowa.[25]

An Irish community that grew into a significant American foundation, the Sisters of Mercy (RSM), arrived in Pittsburgh, Pennsylvania, in 1843 under the leadership of Mother Frances Warde. The seven sisters wore secular clothes on their voyage from Dublin to the United States, and after they had recovered from initial bouts of seasickness, visited passengers traveling in second class and steerage. Arriving in New York City, they traveled by train to Philadelphia, and then to Chambersburg, Pennsylvania, where the tracks ended. The sisters completed the remainder of their journey by stagecoach, reaching their destination on December 20, five days before Christmas. One year later an unidentified sister remembered how they had felt arriving in a new country during the Christmas season: "Our sense of loneliness was keen, but we did not allow our feelings to get the better of us. To feel that we were doing God's will was our great consolation."[26] After working in Pittsburgh for three years, six members of that city's community, along with a novice and a postulant, expanded their ministry to New York City.[27]

German Catholics hoped parochial schools staffed by women religious from their native land would help preserve their heritage. In 1847, six School Sisters of Notre Dame (SSND), led by foundress Mother Theresa Gerhardinger, left Bavaria for St. Mary's, Pennsylvania, to minister to a rural German community. Mother Caroline Freiss, who would be appointed superior of the sisters in the United States, described her first impressions of New York City: "New habits and strange customs! Pigs on the street, chickens in front of people's houses, women smoking tobacco, . . . wearing hats and veils driving vehicles, . . . houses and streets illuminated by gas, heating by hot air pipes, very frequent fire alarms."[28] Manhattan's sights and sounds were clearly very different from the Bavaria they had left behind.

Like their Irish and French counterparts, the women were shocked at the rugged conditions they found in the United States. One chronicler of the community wrote of her journey to St. Mary's: "Picture these weary travelers seated in an open wagon, exposed to an August sun and drenching rains and thunderstorms, tormented by mosquitos at night and by the fear of wild animals which still roamed the forest! Finally, having reached a clearing over which log houses were scattered, they asked their escort when they would arrive at St. Mary's. 'We are already in the heart of the city,' he answered."[29]

Religious communities from France, Ireland, and Germany joined those founded in the United States as they followed Catholics settling throughout the country and its territories. Establishing convents in urban centers such as Pittsburgh and New York, and traveling to outposts like St. Mary's and Carondolet, they staffed and administered schools and hospitals, and attempted to assist those in need. Despite hailing from different cultures and communities, some experiences were shared by almost all women religious in the antebellum period.

Sisters in a New Nation

A common theme that runs through the history of women's religious communities in the United States during the first half of the nineteenth century concerns the harsh conditions under which they worked. Mother Philippine Duchesne compared the work of the Society of the Sacred Heart of Jesus in Missouri with that of the Jesuits ministering in Siberia. The lack of domestic help available to the community also troubled her. "As we have no servant," she wrote, "we have frequently to gather wood in the forest."[30] A number of Sisters of Mercy working in Pittsburgh and the surrounding area suffered from the long hours they spent teaching and preparing for class with little space or time for recreation. Bishop Michael O'Connor (1843–1860) was so worried about the sisters' health that he gratefully accepted an offer of land forty miles outside the city on which a school and convent could be built. Both O'Connor and the sisters hoped that more land and fresh air—away from the industrial smog of Pittsburgh—would provide an opportunity for more exercise and healthier living.[31] Some hazardous conditions were the result of women religious performing jobs others would not. When Sisters of Mercy accepted typhus patients at their Pittsburgh hospital in 1848, all of the sister nurses except one died from the deadly disease.[32]

Religious communities founded in the United States experienced the same difficulties as their European counterparts. The Sisters of Charity of Nazareth, founded in Kentucky, "had barely enough to sustain life and no wealthy ladies to provide their favorites with extra food, better clothing, or expensive medicines."[33] The Dominican Sisters ministering in Kentucky performed the work of male pioneers as they "labored in the fields; planted a kitchen garden in front of their cabin; gathered brush and rolled stumps and logs to clear the land for plowing and planted the food crops."[34] Limited financial resources often meant that sisters did not eat well unless they were able to grow their own food. A normal meal for the Sisters of Charity of Nazareth, for instance, consisted of "corn bread, middling (a dish made from coarse grain), and sage tea."[35]

Hard work combined with extreme poverty created difficult situations for women religious. When several Pittsburgh Sisters of Mercy accepted an invitation to minister in Chicago, their new convent was a small, one-story, unpainted building in poor condition. The poverty faced by the women was "extreme and they often had to depend on the generosity of the people for mere necessities."[36] The Sisters of Charity of Nazareth, according to community legend, usually walked barefoot to church to save wear and tear on a valuable commodity, putting their shoes on before entering the building.[37] Vows of poverty allowed priests and bishops, often with limited monetary resources themselves, to justify providing women religious with less than ideal living conditions.[38]

Religious communities recruited to minister in the United States often suffered from the climate changes they experienced in their adopted country. As early as 1818, Mother Rose Philippine Duchesne reported to the motherhouse in France how the community was adapting to the New Orleans climate. "The doctor insisted on our buying dresses of lightweight material," she wrote. "They are black cotton with a single thread of white; the [lay] sisters have dark purple dresses, nearly black."[39] A habit designed for a French climate and lifestyle was simply not practical in the United States. The solution to the humid summers and frigid winters was not always found in a simple change of clothing. "The Sisters of Mercy, who arrived in Pittsburgh in December 1843, shivered in the cold and snow, while the Dominicans from Cabra in Dublin, who settled in New Orleans in 1860, suffered each year from the 'scorching sun,' the unrelenting humidity, and the 'pertinacious mosquitoes.'" When combined with inadequate living conditions and days of back-breaking work, the weather sometimes contributed to the deaths of women religious; this was the case when three

Sisters of Mercy, recently arrived in Pittsburgh, died during the course of one week.[40] Writing to the Louis Mission Society in 1858, Mother Caroline Freiss noted the effects of climate on the School Sisters of Notre Dame. "Though intense the heat—the sisters frequently are obliged to change their coiffure three or four times a day—mosquitoes have been the source of still greater sufferings. . . . There are many opportunities to practice mortification. One is constantly bathed in perspiration and tortured by thirst."[41] Difficulties caused by climate continued throughout the nineteenth and into the twentieth centuries. Toward the end of the nineteenth century, a Benedictine sister living in South Dakota froze to death as she tried to get to the convent from the laundry shed. She was only "yards from the convent door."[42]

In addition to adjusting to strange geographies and climates, European sisters quickly discovered the difficulties involved in maintaining traditional rules and customs in the United States. One rule common to many communities, for instance, required sisters to chant matins and lauds at midnight and to take turns praying in the community's chapel throughout the night, practices very difficult for those involved in active work. Many women concluded that it was impossible to establish an effective ministry while adhering to a rule of canon (church) law requiring women religious to be cloistered; sisters could not even attend Mass at the parish church without the bishop's permission, and sometimes had to supervise children on the school playground from the windows.[43] It often proved difficult to build a convent that was physically separated from the world. Writing from St. Charles, Missouri, in 1818, Mother Duchesne explained, "As to enclosure, there is not a wall within a thousand miles of here; and wooden fences keep out animals, but not men. Our enclosure consists in remaining at home."[44] When Bishop Dubourg encouraged members of the Society of the Sacred Heart of Jesus to adapt the community's rule to reflect the situation in the United States, the sisters insisted on seeking approval from the motherhouse in France. Mother Barat assured them that it was appropriate to make adjustments based on specific circumstances.[45]

When religious communities founded in the United States based their rule on those found in Europe, it often led to a proposed lifestyle that was impossible to follow. Reverend Charles Nerinckx, founder of the Sisters of Loretto (Kentucky), devised a rule that was not only unrealistic, but dangerous to the health and well-being of women living and working on the frontier. In addition to teaching and caring for orphans, community members were expected to perform heavy labor on the farm, wear clothing inappropriate for the climate, go without shoes for much of the year, and follow a Spartan diet. At least one priest complained about the community's harsh rule to Bishop Benedict Flaget, but Nerinckx refused to adapt it to the conditions under which they lived and even proposed recruiting European sisters "to teach the young [American] women the rudiments of religious life."[46] Writing to St. Louis Bishop Joseph Rosati in 1824, Nerinckx claimed that he understood that changes in the community's rule were about to be implemented. "I will not oppose it to avoid dissensions," he wrote, "but I do not wish to share in it."[47]

After Nerinckx's death in 1824, Flaget consulted with several priests and bishops and decided to revise certain components of the sisters' rule. The bishop was particularly concerned with the provisions requiring the sisters to go barefoot and to sleep in their clothes followed by praying in an oratory open to the wind. Both these rules, Flaget believed, made members of the community susceptible to tuberculosis. "Indeed, in the space of eleven years we have lost twenty-four religious, and not one of them has reached the age of thirty years. Besides of the eighty religious of the same family, that we have in Kentucky, there are at present thirty-eight who have bad health and who are perhaps not yet four years in vows. . . . All these deaths and other illnesses so multiplied, do they not prove . . . that the rules are too austere?"[48]

European women religious were sometimes startled by the differences between American society and the one they had left behind. The Sisters of Providence were surprised—to say the least—when Bishop de la Hailandière, who had visited their convent in France attired in clothes befitting his office, "appeared dressed like any other man of the Indiana woods, sunburnt, dusty, and with dry mud on his clothes." Priests dressed in the flat collar and string tie worn by laymen on the frontier rather than clerical garb, caused one sister to remark that the men had exchanged the "joyous grace of France" for the "chilly manner of the Americans."[49]

Communities also wrestled with the issue of class, noting how unaccustomed many Americans were to differentiating among people of diverse economic status. Writing to her superior in France, Mother Theodore Guerin described the different views on servants held by the French sisters and their American postulants. "When dinner time came," Guerin wrote, "there was my washerwoman sitting down at table with us. I was so indiscreet as to say it would be better for her not to take her dinner with the Community. I wish you could have seen the change in the countenances of our American postulants! . . . The mere name of 'servant' makes them revolt, and they throw down whatever they have in their hands and start off at once."[50]

Humorous incidents sometimes resulted when women religious encountered people who did not understand sisters' place in church and society. Shortly after the end of the Civil War, Sisters of St. Joseph traveling from San Diego, California, to Tucson, Arizona, spent the night at a ranch willing to offer them hospitality. According to Sister Monica Taggart: "There were several ranchmen there from the neighboring stations, but no women. . . . After dinner they became sociable. We retired to the stable . . . and they followed. Some proposed marriage to us, saying we would do better by accepting the offer than by going to Tucson, for we would all be massacred by the Indians. The simplicity and earnestness with which they spoke put indignation out of the question, as it was evident that they meant no insult, but our good."[51] Not only did European women religious need to assimilate into American culture, but non-Catholics, who had no experience with celibate women religious, had to gain an understanding of sisters and their call to serve those in need.

Growth of Ministries

Once women religious were established in a particular diocese, they often attracted the attention of other bishops in need of their ministries. It did not take the Sisters of Mercy long, for instance, to expand throughout the country. Three years after their 1843 arrival in Pittsburgh, the community began work in New York City. In the same year, they were asked by William Quarter, Chicago's first bishop (1844–1848), to help minister to Catholics living in the young city. Mother Frances Warde agreed, and brought one professed sister, two novices, and two postulants to the city in 1846. The journey from Pittsburgh to Chicago was not easy, and the sisters traveled by boat up the Ohio River to Beaver, Pennsylvania; they then took a stagecoach for fifty miles until they reached Poland, Ohio, where they stayed the night before chartering a coach to Cleveland. From there, the sisters boarded the SS *Oregon*, which carried the Sisters to Detroit. The next leg of their journey consisted of a second stagecoach ride to St. Joseph's, Michigan, where they finally boarded a steamboat for Chicago.[52] Upon arriving in the city, the sisters taught boys and girls, and opened St. Xavier Academy for girls. In addition, they established a night school to teach adults how to read, and a home for young women looking for work.

They also visited the sick confined to their homes, as well as the jail and the almshouse, on a regular basis.[53]

The Pittsburgh Sisters of Mercy replicated their ministries in a number of other cities. In 1848, they were invited to Loretto, Pennsylvania, and sent four sisters to serve the residents of that area. Three years later they accepted an invitation to work in Providence, Rhode Island, despite high levels of anti-Catholic activity in that city. Even though they wore secular clothes when appearing in public, the sisters were insulted by people in the street and their convent windows were smashed. Such displays did not deter young Rhode Island women from joining the community; within a year the Providence sisters could boast that they had received twenty-two new members. Success in Providence led to invitations in 1852 from Hartford and New Haven, Connecticut. That same year, the sisters were invited to Washington, D.C., to care for the sick; three years later they were asked to teach in Baltimore. In 1859, church leaders in Vicksburg, Mississippi, requested the Baltimore convent to send sisters willing to work in the Deep South. Within the course of sixteen years, the Sisters of Mercy grew from a small foundation in Pittsburgh to one ministering in six states and the District of Columbia.[54]

The Sisters of Mercy were not the only women religious to expand their ministries during this era. In 1849, a group of Sisters of Notre Dame de Namur left Cincinnati for Lowell, Massachusetts, where they opened the state's only parochial school. Reverend Timothy O'Brien, the pastor of St. Mary's parish, agreed to provide a house for the community and an annual stipend of $120 for each sister teaching in the school, and the generosity of the parishioners helped defray other expenses. The sisters repaid the parish's kindness in several ways, including caring for children whose mothers worked in the mills and feeding unemployed men. Their work attracted young women interested in religious life; in 1853, two of them left Lowell and traveled to Cincinnati to enter the community's novitiate.[55]

About ten years after their first foundation was established at St. Thomas Farm in Nelson County, Kentucky, the Sisters of Charity of Nazareth moved their motherhouse and academy to Nazareth, near Bardstown. The community's rapid growth—it increased from 3 to 145 members during the first generation—allowed the sisters to expand their ministry of education and service. In 1831, they were invited to open an orphanage and Presentation Academy in Louisville. When the first Bishop of Nashville, Richard Miles, OP, invited Mother Catherine Spalding to send sisters to Tennessee, she accepted, and in 1842 six sisters opened St. Mary's Academy in that city.

Although the Sisters of Charity of Nazareth did not spread as far or as quickly as the Sisters of Mercy, within several decades of their founding they had moved beyond a small log cabin in the Kentucky woods to staffing and administering schools and orphanages throughout Kentucky and Tennessee.[56]

In their quest for women religious willing to work in a variety of settings, church leaders often promised more than they could deliver. "Bishops and priests, desperate to convince mother superiors to release sisters for frontier work, invariably described a modest, but well-situated and clean convent that would be waiting for the mission teachers and nurses."[57] When the Montreal Sisters of the Holy Names of Jesus and Mary responded to the requests of two biological brothers, Francis and Augustine Blanchet, Vicar Apostolic of the Oregon Territory and Bishop of Walla Walla, Washington, respectively, they agreed to supply sisters to a very large area containing few Catholics. After leaving Montreal, the women embarked on a long journey that took them to Fort Vancouver, Washington, via New York, the Isthmus of Panama, and San Francisco.[58] Upon arriving at their destination, the sisters were greeted by Mother Joseph, a Sister of Providence, who had arrived in the territory three years earlier. Sisters arriving in rural areas, however, usually found no one to greet them, and often waited until a stranger took pity on them and helped them find either the bishop's residence or, failing that, a place to at least spend the night. The Sisters of the Holy Names experienced this situation when they left Fort Vancouver for Portland, and found their "convent"—a former hotel—bolted shut to prevent people from sleeping there. Further investigation revealed that the building was unfurnished, and the women slept on the floor for three nights, using their luggage for pillows. Meals were eaten kneeling around benches because there were no tables or chairs.[59]

Experiences of other communities mirrored that of the Sisters of the Holy Names. When two Dominican sisters waiting at a train station finally saw the man who was to drive them to their convent, they wondered what had happened to the promised welcome—complete with public greetings by the mayor and a judge—celebrating their arrival. Their driver explained that he was both the mayor and the judge; a ride to their destination was not quite the official welcome the sisters were expecting.[60] When describing conditions in their new Iowa convent, Franciscan Sisters of Perpetual Adoration reported that even though they had been assured that "everything in our future home was neat and tidy," in fact, "the stove had no pipes, the living room floor was bare, there were no mattresses for the beds, [only] the spiders were plentiful."[61]

Sisters of Providence arriving at St. Ignatius, Montana, from Montreal, 1873. Left to right: Sisters Mary Julian, Jane de Chantal, Odile Gignac. Courtesy of Sisters of Providence Archives, Seattle, Washington.

As women religious settled throughout the United States in response to requests from church leaders, they manifested a visible Catholic presence to a nation that defined itself as inherently Protestant. The schools, hospitals, and orphanages built and staffed by sisters not only contributed to the growth and development of their church—a church "beginning from scratch"—but reminded others of the perceived threat posed by Catholicism to the American principles of liberty and democracy.[62] The distinctive dress and lifestyle of these women made them an easy target for those hoping to drive Catholicism back across the Atlantic Ocean.

Sisters and Know-Nothings

The American Revolution and subsequent ratification of the Constitution and Bill of Rights laid the groundwork for religious freedom, but the United States was very much a Protestant nation in the early decades of the nineteenth century. Disdain for foreigners was so strong that a national political party was organized around an anti-Catholic and anti-immigrant platform. The American Party, commonly called the Know-Nothing Party because of its members' tendency to claim they "knew nothing" when questioned about the group's platform, claimed victories in several state and municipal elections before fading away in the growing controversy over slavery.[63] These elected party officials and their supporters played a role in the controversy surrounding convents and women religious in antebellum America; they were joined by other groups worried about the negative impact an old religion might have on a new nation.

Non-Catholic Americans were not sure what to make of women religious, who were celibate, lived in community, dressed distinctively, and seemed very different from the traditional nineteenth-century Protestant woman. On the one hand, a cursory look at sisters indicated a "restrictive private existence (more restrictive, perhaps, than that for any other women in America)." On the other hand, they played a greater role in education, health care, and social services than the majority of American women.[64] For Protestants concerned about the minions of the Roman Pope flocking to the shores of their young democracy, this seeming contradiction, when added to the very visible presence of sisters in America's cities and towns, led some to conclude that stamping out convents and their residents was a first step toward curtailing the growth of the country's Catholic population. In 1856, for example, petitions presented to the Maryland state legislature claimed convents were "detrimental to the 'positive welfare of society' because they 'cut off so many from their social duty and a sphere of usefulness.'"[65] Sisters were failing to fulfill the ultimate calling for women in the nineteenth century: to be good wives and mothers.

Recognizing that their habits readily identified them, sisters often dressed in secular clothes when traveling or appearing in public. When eight Visitandines (Visitation sisters) left Baltimore in 1848 to establish a female academy in Wheeling, West Virginia, they did not wear clothes traditionally prescribed by the community. Instead, they pulled together outfits "from their small store of outmoded, cast-off postulants' clothes" and arranged "as best they could their black forehead binder to resemble hair."[66] Their plan worked during the journey, but after establishing their school the sisters still had to contend with anti-Catholic attacks. Sister Magdalen Patterson, who accompanied the school's boarding students on their daily walk, was often verbally attacked by members of the Know-Nothing Party; she once declared she "would rather sit on the stove than take those girls through the city."[67]

Perhaps the most virulent attack on a convent in the United States took place in Charlestown, Massachusetts, in 1834. Reverend John Thayer, a convert to Catholicism from Congregationalism, first suggested establishing a convent in Boston in 1790, at a time when there was only one other in the United States: the Carmelites in Port Tobacco, Maryland. On a visit to Ireland, Thayer became acquainted with the Ryan family, and discovered that Mary and Catherine Ryan were interested in immigrating to Boston to help found the proposed convent. Thayer arranged for the women, along with two others, to train at the Ursuline convent in Trois Rivières, Canada, but died before he could accompany them on their journey. The priest left his rather substantial estate—valued at over $10,000—to the Ursulines.[68] By 1820, the Ryans, along with their sister Margaret, and cousin, Catherine Molineaux, had taken vows and were prepared to open a school in Boston under the direction of Bishop Jean Cheverus (1808–1823). Located next to the Cathedral of the Holy Cross, the school soon boasted about one hundred pupils, many of them poor and the daughters of Irish immigrants.[69]

The Ursulines supported the school and themselves with the money left to them by Thayer and his successor, Father Francois Matignon. When the original sisters were stricken with tuberculosis and Cheverus was recalled to France in 1823, however, Ursulines from Quebec City consented to assume control of the school.[70] The new superior, Madame St. George, the former Mary Anne Moffatt, "helped transform a day school offering the rudiments of education to Boston's poor immigrants into Charlestown's elegant and flourishing academy, enrolling the daughters of the Boston elite, mainly Harvard-educated Unitarians."[71] Under the supervision of Madame St. George, and with the encouragement of Bishop Benedict Fenwick (1825–1846), by 1830 thirty students between the ages of six and fourteen were enrolled at the school.[72]

Rebecca Reed, a convert to Catholicism, spent some time at the Charlestown academy as either a student or a postulant.[73] After an apparently unhappy experience living with the Ursulines, Reed, encouraged by Reverend William Croswell, an Episcopalian priest, published *Six Months in a Convent*. Her narrative, describing "stark austerities experienced by a convert from Protestantism among the Ursuline sisters," did nothing to quell the suspicions of non-Catholic Bostonians concerned about events taking place behind the convent's walls.[74] The success of *Six Months in a Convent* sent Reed on a lecture tour to promote the book. Her appearance in Boston fueled the strong anti-Catholic sentiment found in some of the city's neighborhoods.

The events culminating in the burning of the convent began in 1834, when Sister Mary John (Elizabeth Harrison), an overworked music teacher—she sometimes offered as many as fourteen lessons a day—left the convent and asked the sisters' Protestant neighbor, Edward Cutter, to take her away from the convent to a student's family home in Cambridge. When the sisters discovered she was missing, they summoned Fenwick, who, after meeting with the Ursulines, left for Cambridge hoping to convince Sister Mary John to return to the convent. She refused to speak with the bishop, and after several attempts Fenwick left without Sister Mary John. The next morning, Thomas Harrison, Sister Mary John's brother, agreed to try and persuade his sister to return to the Charlestown convent. Harrison was unsuccessful, but he did convince her to meet with Fenwick later that evening. During the bishop's conversation with Sister Mary John, she agreed to return to her community. According to Fenwick's diary, "The Ladies of the Convent receive[d] her with raptures of Joy."[75]

The Ursuline sisters and Fenwick agreed that Sister Mary John had left the convent because she was suffering from some sort of "nervous excitement or fever." Apparently, she did not remember leaving the community, and after her return "[s]he [could] scarcely believe what she has been told of her leaving the Convent."[76] Despite her continued recovery, Charlestown's residents were recounting the story of an "escaped nun" to anyone who would listen. When elements of Rebecca Reed's earlier account of life in the convent were incorporated into the story, citizens grew outraged at what they believed was taking place in their town. Shortly after Sister Mary John's return, Cutter visited the convent to alert Sister St. George to the growing sentiment against the women and their home. The superior was decidedly less than friendly, and implied Cutter was involved with the group opposed to the convent, saying, "You may fetch your mob, the Bishop has twenty thousand of the *vilest* Irish, who might pull down your houses over your heads—and you may read your riot act till your throats are sore, and you cannot quell them—you . . . will have your houses torn down over your heads."[77]

Neither the superior's threat nor the visitors' report that they had met with Sister Mary John and found no evidence she was being held against her will quieted the growing sentiment against the sisters and their school. Tensions increased when prominent Protestant evangelist Lyman Beecher preached three anti-Catholic sermons throughout the city. In an attempt to raise money for Lane Theological Seminary in Cincinnati, Beecher proclaimed the need for an educated Protestant ministry because "the Roman Catholics of Europe seem to be seeking an asylum for the contentions and revolutions of the old world and a site for the palace of the Pope and the Romish Church in the Great Valley of the Mississippi."[78] The following day, town leaders toured the convent for about three hours, and "'examined from the highest apartment to the cellar—looking into bureaus, and even paint boxes,' searching for imprisoned nuns or their bodies."[79] During the course of their investigation, they spent some time with Sister Mary John, who assured them of her intention to remain with the Ursulines.[80]

Later that evening, an angry mob gathered outside the convent demanding to see Sister Mary John. When informed by the superior that she had already met with investigators but would be available to talk with them the following day, the crowd seemed a bit calmer. After several conversations with Sister St. George, however, they began throwing stones and bricks, eventually setting fire to the building. The Ursulines and their students escaped unharmed, but the sisters were unable to reestablish the school and eventually returned to Canada.[81]

Following their departure, women religious remained an insignificant presence in the Boston diocese until 1849 when the Sisters of Notre Dame de Namur opened their parish school in Lowell. Several years after they began working in that city, a mob attempted to force the sisters to abandon their work. The convent's annalist reported how frightened the sisters were: "Then gathering their few belongings, they bundled them together and each sister was allotted her portion to carry, should they be compelled to flee. A watch was set in the church tower, and one peal of the church bell was to let priests, sisters and people know the godless band was upon them." After waiting for several days, the mob appeared, and the sisters and their defenders were ready for them. "When just within sight of St. Patrick's [Church,] [the mob was] attacked by some strong armed Irish men and women [acting on the side of the nuns]. . . . The march became a melee, and the street was completely filled with the motley crowd. They reached the bridge that spans the canal just within sight of the convent. There was a splash and a ringing cheer—A sinewy matron unable to restrain her indignation had seized one of the leaders of the gang, and flung him over the railing."[82] A potential tragedy had been averted, but members of the Protestant community remained suspicious of women religious, agreeing with Unitarian clergyman George Burnap, who, in a 1853 lecture at Harvard University, bemoaned the fact that "a convent had risen in the sight of Harvard Yard."[83]

Other cities also experienced outbursts directed against women religious. Several months after its founding in 1835, the *Baltimore Literary and Religious Magazine* claimed "[a]n outrage . . . was probably committed" in the city's Carmelite monastery. According to the article, six members of a Protestant Methodist Episcopal congregation had heard cries for help emanating from the fourth floor of the convent, leading the editor to suggest that the women were being held against their will. Four years later, when Sister Isabella Neale left the convent and asked neighbors for help, she triggered three nights of rioting in front of the building. The response of Baltimore civic leaders, including the mayor, the City Guards, and several judges, eventually calmed the crowd and prevented direct attacks on either the convent or its residents. In an attempt to restore order, a committee inspected the building and interviewed the nuns, all of whom expressed their desire to remain in the convent. When physicians certified that Sister Isabella was suffering from mental illness, describing her as a "perfect maniac," the rioters were appeased. A tragedy such as the destruction of the Charlestown convent had been avoided.[84]

The 1836 publication of Maria Monk's *Awful Disclosures of the Hotel Dieu Monastery in Montreal*, an almost fully fictitious account of a young woman held captive in a Canadian convent, continued to focus attention on this very visible group within the Catholic population. Described as "[e]qual parts of pornographic depiction of priest and nun couplings and purple prose," Monk's narrative included stories of nuns burying illegitimate children, secret doors from the convent to priests' bedrooms, and rituals that bordered on the satanic.[85] The "former nun" was later proven a fraud—her own mother claimed her daughter had never been a resident at the Hotel Dieu—and Monk died in poverty and obscurity in 1839. Her book was a huge success, however, and led to investigations of other convents as well as several additional published exposés of convent life.[86]

Women religious remained a mystery to many Americans throughout the nineteenth and twentieth centuries. Because they set themselves apart by their dress, lifestyle, and commitment to a particular ministry, they were sometimes viewed as a threat, especially by those fearing a takeover of the country by the Roman Catholic Church. Although often frightened by anti-Catholic attacks directed at their convents and schools, sisters continued to work with those in need of their services, including non-Catholics, as they contributed to the development of the Catholic Church in the United States.

Slavery, Race, and Women Religious

By the outbreak of the Civil War, women religious had created a network of schools, hospitals, and orphanages that encompassed much of the United States. Although some Protestants remained suspicious and even hostile toward them, young women were not deterred from entering religious life. In 1835, less than a thousand women religious were living and working in the United States; by 1861 that number had increased to almost five thousand out of a total Catholic population of 3,103,000. One estimate suggests at least sixty communities of sisters had been established by the same year.[87]

Many Americans, including Catholics, assumed that sisters had little or no knowledge of or interest in issues being debated throughout the country, but women religious were involved in all the controversies in which Americans were embroiled during the antebellum era, including slavery and race. Records of the Sisters of Charity of Nazareth indicate that two slaves, Abe and Teresa, a young woman "scarcely grown," had been brought to the community by early members. When they moved to new quarters in 1822, eleven sisters, ten novices, one postulant, and two African American slaves had to find places to sleep in the outbuildings surrounding the school and dormitory. "[T]heir mistresses had to depend on their loyalty and cooperative sharing in the cooking, washing, sewing, and labor in the garden and fields."[88]

As the community expanded, the sisters continued to participate in the institution of slavery. In 1840, Mother Catherine Spalding described the purchase of slaves. "We also, in the course of the year," she wrote, "bought five negro men; two women; two girls, and two boys. This year the price of property was high throughout the country; of course we paid high prices for all they bought; the prices of hire were also very high; and the Council [the community's governing board] decided it was better to buy servants for the farm, etc., than pay so much for hire and then often get bad ones."[89] Mother Catherine used the word servants—many Catholic slaveholders referred to their slaves by this term—but she meant slaves, and hoped the eleven men, women, and children could be trained to do work that would support the community's ministries.

A community historian familiar with the writings of Mother Catherine describes her relationship with slaves as "mother" and "mistress" of servants, and notes there is no evidence of slaves being punished or running away. "Slaves were viewed much like children, to be cared for materially and spiritually, assigned tasks, supervised, and then trusted, rewarded, or penalized according to performance."[90] In addition, the sisters apparently did not attempt to teach the slaves living with them to either read or write. They did instruct them in the basic tenets of Catholicism, served as baptismal sponsors, and prepared children for First Communion. Although they did not separate spouses, the sisters occasionally placed parents and children in different houses of the community. The women also participated in the selling of slaves; in at least one instance a slave woman was sold to her husband's owner, presumably so the two could live together.[91]

Mother Catherine and the Sisters of Charity of Nazareth held views on slavery supported by Catholic ecclesiastical leaders. Many bishops shared the views of those in the North, who claimed to dislike the institution but saw no easy way to end the buying and selling of human beings. Women religious holding slaves were exhorted to treat them well and instruct them in the beliefs of Catholicism. Sisters native to the South, including Mother Catherine, "simply did not see the radical injustice of slavery." During the twentieth and twenty-first centuries, members of her community have wrestled with this difficult chapter in their story as they honor their history while recognizing their congregation's complicity in the story of racism in the United States.[92]

The tepid attitude of the Catholic Church toward the abolition of slavery did not prevent African American Catholic women from choosing to enter religious life, but the reluctance of most communities to accept women of color led to the establishment of separate religious communities. New Orleans residents Henriette Delille (1813–1862), Juliette Gaudin, and Josephine Charles, who had been lay members of the Ladies Congregation of the Children of Mary organized by the Ursulines, formed themselves into a quasi-religious community in 1836, but continued to live at home. The women took private vows six years later, and Father Etienne Rousselon, their spiritual advisor, leased a house where they could begin to live in community. They began a novitiate with the Society of the Sacred Heart of Jesus in 1851. The new community, known as the Sisters of the Holy Family, opened a school, orphanage, and home for the aged, catechized slaves, taught free children of color, and in 1853 agreed to provide nursing care to black and white cholera patients.[93]

Although the Sisters of the Holy Family were comprised of African American women, there is evidence that they owned at least a few slaves, and after the Civil War the sisters decided to admit former slaves into the community.[94] In 1872, New Orleans church leaders, who had been less than enthusiastic about recognizing an African American community, finally allowed the women to wear a habit and publicly identify themselves as women religious. The Sisters of St. Joseph living in New Orleans protested this decision, but the community held firm. Sister Bernard Deggs explained, "No one would think that [we were] anything if we were not dressed in this holy habit."[95] In the same year, the first former slaves to be admitted to the community made vows of poverty, chastity, and obedience.

The Sisters, Servants of the Immaculate Heart of Mary (IHM) was founded by Redemptorist Father Louis Florent Gillet and M. Theresa Maxis Duchemin in 1845 in Monroe, Michigan. Sister Theresa Maxis—her father was a white British soldier and her mother a biracial San Domingan woman—had grown up in Baltimore, and was one of the charter members of the Oblate Sisters of Providence.[96] By 1843, she was superior of the financially struggling community that had been "reduced to taking in wash and mending to feed themselves and the few orphans left in the house." Two years later, Sister Theresa Maxis Duchemin announced to the Oblate community her decision to leave for Michigan and, with Gillet's help and support, establish a new community of women religious.[97]

Sister Theresa Maxis was considered African American in antebellum Baltimore, but by the time of her arrival in Monroe, Michigan, she was viewed as white by all except those few that were aware of her family history and origins, including an Oblate who left the community with her to help establish the new group.[98] Gillet, Sister Theresa, and two other women worked together to develop a rule for the community. At a ceremony held in the local Catholic Church, the two former Oblates renewed their vows, and one young woman, who had completed her postulancy, was clothed as a novice.[99]

In 1857, Detroit Bishop Peter Lefevere appointed Reverend Edward Joos spiritual director of the community. At the time, it was not unusual for religious communities of women to have two superiors, a sister and a priest. Priest superiors "exercised extensive powers over the life of the community: the constitutions gave him the right to impose corrections, confirm elections, and even to appoint or remove a sister superior."[100] Religious congregations also ultimately answered either to the Vatican or, as was the case with the Sisters, Servants of the Immaculate Heart of Mary, to the local bishop. This meant that Lefevere and Joos both functioned as authority figures over the sisters.

Joos quickly assumed an active role as superior, and his decisions superseded any directives issued by Mother Theresa. The community received a request to minister to Irish railroad workers in Susquehanna, Pennsylvania, in 1858, and Mother Theresa Maxis accepted the challenge in the hope of keeping the community faithful to its founding premise while expanding its ministry. When they were invited to open a second mission in Reading, Pennsylvania, however, Lefevere, who had the final say in the issue, would not allow them to accept. He soon learned that Mother Theresa had not only publicly expressed disappointment over his refusal, but was appealing to him to reverse his decision. Lefevere removed her as superior and ordered her, along with two other sisters, to leave Michigan for Pennsylvania immediately. In the summer of 1859, twelve sisters left for Pennsylvania and twelve remained in Michigan. These events ultimately divided the sisters into two separate communities, each answering to the bishop of their respective diocese (Philadelphia and Detroit).[101] When the Diocese of Scranton (Pennsylvania) was created in 1868, a further division occurred because the sisters in Susquehanna were separated from their colleagues in the Philadelphia archdiocese. Despite her best efforts, Mother Theresa was unable to bring the communities together, and she spent many years residing with the Sisters of Charity of Montreal, known as the Grey Nuns, in Ottawa, Canada. In 1885, Philadelphia Archbishop Patrick Ryan (1884–1911) granted permission for Mother Theresa to spend the last seven years of her life at the IHM motherhouse near West Chester, Pennsylvania.

During the remainder of the nineteenth century the official histories of the community moved away from focusing on an African American woman who had left Baltimore to found a new religious congregation in a remote area, and began crediting Father Louis Gillet as the sole inspiration behind the Sisters, Servants of the Immaculate Heart of Mary. Reverend Edward Joos, who ultimately shaped the Monroe, Michigan, community into what it would become, emerged as the narrative's main character. Mother Theresa Maxis's successor, Mother Joseph Walker, was identified as the "true [female] foundress" of the community.[102] When all three IHM communities began to examine their collective history toward the end of the twentieth century, however, they focused on Mother Theresa Maxis rather than a French Redemptorist priest, claiming their true histories despite sensitive issues relating to race and illegitimacy and how they had been handled in the past.[103] By the end of the twentieth century, the Oblate Sisters of Providence and the Sisters, Servants of the Immaculate Heart of Mary in Monroe, Michigan, and Scranton and Immaculata, Pennsylvania, acknowledged the place of Mother Theresa Maxis Duchemin in their histories and ministries.

The Next Step

Women religious continued their roles of serving Catholics in need and aiding in the building of the American Catholic Church in the decades following the cessation of the Civil War. Sisters were often misunderstood during the first half of the nineteenth century, but as time went on, many came to know the women and their ministries through their expansive network of institutions. They responded to invitations from church leaders to establish needed ministries in urban and rural areas throughout the country, including cities and towns where Catholics were a distinct minority. As they built, maintained, and staffed schools, hospitals, and institutions dedicated to social service such as orphanages and settlement houses, Americans came to understand better the dedication of women religious to serving those in need.

3

Serving through Education

ON MONDAY, DECEMBER 1, 1958, most of the 1,668 students attending Chicago's Our Lady of the Angels School were readjusting to classroom activities after the four-day Thanksgiving holiday. Their teachers, knowing how difficult it could be to return their students' attention to school after a long weekend, had prepared a day centered on academic pursuits. Eighth-grade teachers Sisters Davidis and Mary "Hurricane" Helaine had a busy day planned for their 126 students, sixty-two and sixty-four in each class. Other sisters were thinking about Christmas, only twenty-four days away, and Sister Mary Clare Therese Champagne was getting ready to place new Christmas decorations around her fifth-grade classroom. All in all, it was a normal Monday at Our Lady of the Angels.[1]

After lunch, children returned to their classrooms for the last two hours of the school day. Around 2:30 p.m., custodian Jim Raymond saw smoke coming from the school's northeast corner. Further investigation revealed that a fire had broken out on the basement level near a stairway. Raymond, along with others who observed smoke and flames emanating from the building, began to call frantically for help. Barbara Glowacki, the owner of a nearby candy store, ran to alert the fire department. Assured that help was on the way, she returned to the school, only to discover the flames had spread. Looking up at the second floor, she realized the windows were full of children screaming, "Get me out of here! Catch me!" Their teacher, Sister Mary Seraphica, screamed for her to call the fire department. Glowacki assured her help was on the way, and then asked why the teacher had not led her class out of the building. Sister Mary Seraphica answered, "We can't. We're trapped."[2]

The Chicago newspapers reported the grim news to their readers the following day: many had escaped with no more than minor injuries, but eighty-seven children and three sisters were dead; ninety children and three sisters were injured.[3] Some had been burned so badly it was difficult to identify them. Sister Mary Seraphica was identified by her cincture, a cord tied around her waist, which was numbered 2764, her number in the community, as well as by a lock of red hair that belonged to the student who had been lying on top of her when they were found together in their classroom. The religious medal worn by Sister Mary St. Canice Lyng, who died along with twelve of her students, was used to determine her identity. Our Lady of the Angels principal, Sister St. Florence, survived, but could not stop reliving the events of the day. "I don't think I'll ever lose the picture of those children who jumped out the windows," she told another sister.[4]

Monsignor William McManus praised the sisters during their funeral liturgy, referring to them as "professional women and experienced teachers," but he did not remember them by name. They "would want to be remembered," McManus claimed, "simply as the BVM sisters who died with their pupils in the fire."[5] The deceased women were not only primarily identified by their membership in a religious community, but the survivors were not expected to speak out as individuals about their part in evacuating students from their classrooms. Sister Davidis, who survived the fire but suffered burns on her hands and face, did speak at a news conference on the day she was released from the hospital. After she discovered smoke spreading throughout the building, Sister Davidis instructed the boys to place their arithmetic books along the crack in the door to keep the smoke from seeping into the room, moved students closer to the windows, and prayed the rosary with them. As the students looked out the window, one boy decided he could jump from the window to a first-floor roof and then to the ground. Other students followed his lead until they were all out of the classroom. As Sister Davidis descended a ladder, she looked back. "With a voice broken in grief, she confessed, 'That's when I saw the little one, the one I missed.'"[6] Beverly Ann Burda had been unable to escape from the classroom. Whether they publicly spoke about their experiences or sought solace in their religious community, the BVMs at Our Lady of the Angels carried the memory of that day with them for the remainder of their lives.

A quarter of a century later, Sister Mary Adrienne Carolan—now Sister Mary Carolan—recalled her memories of the horrific fire that claimed the lives of so many. She remembered that the students pinched her legs as she led them out of the classroom to safety to make sure they were with her. "'Later,' she said, 'a doctor looked at the bruises on my legs. "What are those?" he asked. I said, "Never mind. Those are my scars of victory."'"[7] Telling her story reminded Sister Mary Carolan that the fire at Our Lady of the Angels had had an impact on her religious community, the Sisters of Charity of the Blessed Virgin Mary. "It was years before any of us who were in it could talk about it," she said.[8] John Raymond, the son of the custodian who was one of the first to discover that fire had broken out, confirmed the sisters' place in the story. "A lot of kids [they] had taught died in the fire. The nuns never forgot you. They cared about you. They went through pure hell over this."[9]

Fortunately, there are few stories of Catholic schools as tragic as the one told here. But the demographics of the school—"an ordinary parochial school virtually indistinguishable from hundreds like it in the Chicago archdiocese"[10]—are typical of a parochial school in the United States during the mid-twentieth century. Like many other parish schools, burgeoning enrollment meant space was so tight, for instance, that the two hundred children in kindergarten and first grade were housed in buildings located around the corner from the main school. What enabled Our Lady of the Angels—and thousands of other parochial schools—to enroll such a large number of students was the presence of women religious, who taught a great many students for very little pay.

The history of the educational ministry of Catholic women religious is closely connected with the creation of a massive parochial school system in the late nineteenth and twentieth centuries designed to provide generations of children with an academic and religious education. It can be difficult to tell their story, however, because sister-teachers have often been omitted from the story of parochial education in the United States. "Though historians routinely acknowledge that nuns' heavily subsidized labor underwrote the parochial school system, they give scant attention to the personalities or developments that shaped this process."[11] Women religious sometimes chose to minimize their own contributions to the story because of their desire not to call attention to themselves or their work. Sharing advice received from Reverend Philip Garrigan, vice-rector of the Catholic University of America, the Superior at Trinity College in Washington, D.C., wrote in 1901, "like the dear Blessed Mother, the Sisters were chosen to do great things and like her too, they should be satisfied that He alone be witness of their cooperation with His grace. The Blessed Virgin did not publish her history to the world; neither should we be concerned whether people know what we do or not."[12] The fact that they have been often overlooked by historians does not negate the role women religious have played in the education of generations of American Catholics.

Teaching American and Catholic Girls

The twelve Ursuline sisters who arrived in the French colonial city of New Orleans in August 1727 were operating a boarding school within three months of their arrival. By the following spring the Ursulines had become what may be the first professional elementary school teachers in the United States,[13] and the school included twenty boarders of European descent, seven enslaved boarders, and "large numbers of day students and Negresses and Indian girls."[14]

Since "social geography was suspended, if only for a time"[15] in colonial America, children of the wealthy and the working class alike received an education at Ursuline Academy. Boarders, however, were taught separately from day students. Firmly believing that women as mothers were primarily responsible for passing the Catholic faith down to their children, the Ursulines taught all future mothers regardless of their place in the social order.[16] They further manifested this belief when they began teaching catechism to African and African American slaves and Native people living in and near the Crescent City.

The young women attending Ursuline Academy were taught reading, writing, spelling, "figuring," needlework, and catechism. Following a schedule that can best be described as monastic, the school's boarders rose between 5:30 and 6:30 each morning and attended Mass with the Ursulines at 7 a.m. After breakfast, they received instruction until 10:15, paused for prayer, dinner, and recreation, and returned to class until 2:00 p.m. The students then participated in Vespers and received instruction in spelling and catechism. Supper was served at 5:00 p.m., followed by recreation and night prayers; the students retired about 8:00 p.m.[17]

One of Archbishop John Carroll's first priorities was to build an "American church," and he planned to accomplish this goal by establishing schools and colleges to educate Catholics and, as it would turn out, non-Catholics. In the United States of the late eighteenth century, public schools were few and far between, but Catholics—like all Americans—needed to know how to read and write. Because Catholics rarely encountered a priest, they did not have the opportunity to attend Mass regularly (let alone weekly), and had difficulty receiving the sacraments at the appropriate intervals and ages dictated by church law. As a result, American Catholics also needed instruction in the teachings of their church to discourage them from drifting toward one of the many Protestant denominations dotting the national landscape. To educate American Catholics, Carroll needed teachers.

The Carmelites, who had established a foundation at Port Tobacco, Maryland, in 1790, were not interested in a ministry of teaching despite Carroll's encouragement, but the bishop's luck began to change when Alice Lalor, Maria McDermott, and Maria Sharpe formed a Visitandine community and assumed responsibility for Georgetown Visitation Academy.[18] In order to support their ministry to poorer girls, the nuns began a practice that became common among women religious dedicated to teaching: the education of poor children was funded—at least in part—by tuition paid by those attending Catholic female academies administered by religious communities.

Elizabeth Seton's Sisters of Charity were the first religious community that had the potential to grow large enough to provide the number of teachers needed to begin an extensive educational ministry to Catholics in the United States. Seton recognized that education was a full-time job. "In the chapel at six until eight," she wrote of the time spent at her school in Baltimore, "school at nine, dine at one, school at three, chapel at six-thirty, examination of conscience and Rosary . . . and so it goes day after day without variation."[19] Since the students lived at the school, Seton was on duty at all times: "from half-past five in the morning until nine at night every moment is full, no space even to be troubled."[20]

Seton often acted as a kind of surrogate mother to some of the boarders and informed parents of their children's progress, offering advice on how they might help their offspring grow into responsible and productive adults. "I think you are too anxious for the fruit of your dear little tree, which is ripening very fast, and will soon be as you wish it," she advised one mother. "But we must wait for these fruits; for, if there is a true danger for one of her turn, it would be to push her too fast, and force an exterior look without the interior spirit."[21]

Before John Carroll's death in 1815, female academies had been established in Georgetown and Emmitsburg, and women religious were educating girls on the Kentucky frontier.[22] By 1830 several communities of women religious—all involved in a ministry of teaching—were attempting to meet the educational needs of Catholics throughout the United States. The Sisters of Loretto (1812), Sisters of Charity of Nazareth (1812), Dominican Sisters of St. Catherine in Kentucky (1822), Oblate Sisters of Providence (1828), and Sisters of Charity of Our Lady of Mercy (1829) were all dedicated to working with children, rich and poor. Most communities followed the pattern established at Georgetown Visitation Academy and taught girls from all socioeconomic classes. The mission of the Sisters of Charity of Nazareth, for instance, was teaching and "works of mercy"; by the late 1820s, however, the community's academy—"the only academy in the South offering 'a highly finished education'"—was also attracting daughters of the wealthy.[23]

All the schools founded by women religious in the early nineteenth century admitted non-Catholic students. In addition to the firmly held belief
that all Americans needed a basic education if they were to succeed in life,
the presence of tuition-paying non-Catholics was vital to keep Catholic
schools on a firm financial footing. Women religious did not attempt to
convert their non-Catholic students, but did try to offer all their charges
some instruction in religion. The Sisters of Loretto explained that: "[The
Sisters] deem it a duty incumbent on them to inculcate upon pupils of
the other denominations, the general principles of Christian religion and
morality. They do not, however, use any influence with the pupils of other
professions, toward inducing them to join the Catholic religion, without
the express will and consent of parents."[24] The only religious obligations
of Protestant students attending St. Benedict's Academy in Charlestown,
Massachusetts, in 1820 involved participating in generic morning and evening prayers and attending a weekly lecture by the Bishop of Boston on
"practical truths and religious duties peculiar to no sect."[25] The presence of
non-Catholic students helped ease financial burdens and allowed young
Protestant women the chance to receive a formal education.

Educating a Growing Nation

The rapid increase in schools dedicated to the education of young Catholic
women caused some consternation among Protestant proponents of female education. Catharine Beecher, daughter of the prominent Congrega-
tionalist minister Lyman Beecher, contended that these schools could not
provide a proper education for women for two reasons: first, women religious were "personally unfit for the task since they had publicly challenged
the fundamental role of women in the family by renouncing marriage and
motherhood in favor of celibacy"; second, the course of study offered at
Catholic female academies was weighted toward the ornamental and domestic arts, rather than more traditional academic subjects.[26] Beecher's
critique of the curriculum at these schools was not always justified. In the
1820s course offerings at the Ursuline Academy in Charlestown, Massachusetts, included Latin, geometry, and moral philosophy.[27]

Protestant leaders worried about the appeal these academies held for
non-Catholic parents hoping to find a school that would provide their
daughters with a quality education. "I was both surprised and pained," an
anonymous pamphleteer wrote in 1837, "by the intelligence that you had

placed your daughters in a Catholic seminary . . . and I trust I shall not be deemed impertinent or intrusive while I address you upon a subject which I feel to be of vital interest to us as American and Christian mothers."[28] The purpose of the letter, published by the evangelical American Tract Society, was to convince Protestant parents of the need to keep their daughters away from schools operated by women religious.

In order to meet the needs of a growing Catholic population on the frontier, the presence of American religious communities was essential because European congregations simply could not meet the demand for sisters. Communities sometimes struggled, however, as they tried to find the resources necessary to build and maintain ministries. Founded in 1845 in Monroe, Michigan, the Sisters, Servants of the Immaculate Heart of Mary announced that they were opening a school for boarders and day students in January 1846. However, few boarders, who paid more tuition, enrolled, and the sisters struggled to keep the school—and themselves—financially solvent. "They often have occasion to recall that they have made the vow of poverty," a priest explained, "because they have much to suffer in this connection. Their whole resources consist in the fees from the children of the school, a very moderate fee and poorly paid since most of the children are more than poor."[29] Aware that they were ministering in an area hostile to members of their faith, and anxious to prove their patriotism to non-Catholic neighbors, the school was closed on July 4, 1849.[30]

In the mid-1840s, King Louis I of Bavaria asked the School Sisters of Notre Dame (SSND) for teachers to support missions for German Catholics. Four professed sisters and one novice left Bavaria for America in June 1847, but the revolutions of 1848 forced the king to renege on his promise to pay their traveling expenses and finance a convent in the United States.[31] Several years later, Mother Caroline Friess returned to Bavaria to convince her European superiors that the sisters could not follow the strict rules of cloister when working with immigrants in the United States. In this new land, she explained, sister-teachers needed to be able to communicate with parents face-to-face.[32] After returning from Europe, Mother Caroline, along with several other sisters, opened St. Mary's School in Milwaukee on January 2, 1851. One hundred thirty students were present on the first day. In order to attract paying students, Sister Emmanuel offered music and voice lessons in the convent. "Daughters of the best families in the city flocked to 'the little sister who,' they declared, 'could sing and play like an angel and teach like a professor.'"[33]

Sister-teachers were also needed to work on missions established to evangelize and minister to Native Americans. In 1864, four Sisters of

Providence left Montreal and traveled to Vancouver, Canada; from there they traveled overland to St. Ignatius Mission in Montana, a journey of 550 miles. Jesuit priests had staffed the mission for about ten years and were developing a program of instruction for boys. They recruited the sisters to teach religion and domestic arts to Native American girls so "they would make acceptable wives and mothers for Native boys."[34] Unable to follow the pattern of founding an academy in conjunction with a school for poorer students meant that the women could not rely on wealthy students subsidizing those whose families could not afford tuition. Missionaries on reservations usually depended on aid from the United States government to support their educational endeavors, but a series of treaties ratified in 1859 made it difficult for the community to receive federal funds. The Jesuits provided food and supplies for the women and their students; the sisters reimbursed the priests by assuming responsibility for the care of several buildings, including the church, and ironed, mended, and sewed for the Jesuits.[35] They were not pleased with this arrangement, however, and decided there was only one other option open to them if they were to be self-sufficient; they reluctantly began a begging trip among men working in the region's gold mines. Although they believed begging was "repugnant to nature and humiliating," the sisters realized it was the only alternative if their mission was to succeed.[36] Their trips through the mining areas of Montana were difficult and sometimes dangerous—on one trip, when they stopped at a roadhouse to spend the night, someone slipped a pistol under their pillow so they could protect themselves—but their fund-raising campaign was a success. Annual begging tours between 1867 and 1872 yielded $9,300, enough money to pay the Jesuits and leave the sisters free to start their own teaching ministry to Native Americans.[37]

Parochial Schools and Women Religious

In the years prior to the Civil War, most church leaders endorsed the concept of free schools for Catholics, but found this idea difficult to implement. Lay teachers required a salary, and rules prohibiting most communities of women religious from teaching boys made it almost impossible to develop any sort of regional or national parochial school system. In addition, schools received very little financial support, and when they did, it was usually in the form of land. The Sisters of Loretto opened two free schools in St. Louis in 1818 and 1823 on donated property, but Bishop

Joseph Rosati was unimpressed with them, describing these facilities as "without funds, because of the poverty of our Catholics."[38] Despite the problems involved in funding such enterprises, bishops and priests viewed free schools as essential by the middle of the nineteenth century.

Parishioners were not always able or willing to support parish free schools. The members of St. Patrick's parish in Philadelphia, which was established in 1839, were poor Irish immigrants. Planning for a parish school began in 1849, eight years after the dedication of the church, but it was three more years before construction was completed. The school was originally staffed by six lay teachers, but the parish could not afford to pay their salaries and began to recruit religious communities of women and men to replace them. It took five years to contract with the Sisters of St. Joseph to teach girls, and thirteen years before the Christian Brothers agreed to teach the parish's male students.[39]

Catholics sometimes appealed to their local bishop to convince a community of women religious to undertake responsibility for a school. Dubuque's Bishop Mathias Loras reluctantly agreed to try to convince the Sisters of Charity to send teachers for a school planned for Galena, Iowa. "If I am so fortunate as to succeed in procuring some of these excellent educators of youth," Loras noted, "I shall bring them with me next summer on my return from the Council of Baltimore; but what great expense it will entail on me!"[40]

A system of Catholic education slowly took shape during the nineteenth century as the growing number of immigrants, coupled with episodes of anti-Catholicism, convinced church leaders of the necessity of establishing parochial schools. The process of formalizing Catholic education finally began in 1884 when bishops meeting at the Third Plenary Council of Baltimore voted to "command the building of a parochial school within two years 'near each church where it does not exist.'" In addition, all Catholic parents were instructed to send their children to these schools.[41] This decree had a profound impact on American sisters because it "ensured that American religious would be primarily a teaching population," and that "they would play a major role in the shaping of the American Catholic community."[42]

Staffing the schools mandated by the Third Plenary Council of Baltimore posed a perennial problem for bishops and diocesan superintendents of schools. Reverend Philip McDevitt, superintendent of schools for the Archdiocese of Philadelphia from 1899 until 1916, was constantly in need of teachers for a school system that increased in size and number during each year of his administration.[43] McDevitt, along with other Catholic leaders, lamented the shortage of vocations to religious life; there were simply not enough sisters to provide teachers to all the schools in need of their services. Writing to McDevitt, who had been consecrated Bishop of Harrisburg, Pennsylvania, in 1925, Sister Assisium McEvoy, SSJ, a Sister of St. Joseph, identified the problem: "From every school there comes a cry for help, and there are no sisters to send."[44] McDevitt and Sister Assisium both agreed that one way to increase the number of sisters teaching in parochial schools was for women religious to nurture vocations among their students.

Born Kate McEvoy, Sister Assisium attended Philadelphia public schools until she was expelled for missing school to practice for her parish's May procession. Members of her parish, St. Patrick's, were outraged and vowed to raise funds needed to build a school. Until St. Patrick's opened, Sister Assisium attended St. Joseph's school. Both were staffed by the Sisters of St. Joseph, and her experiences with these sisters convinced Sister Assisium that this was the right congregation for her.[45] Believing that her own teachers had led her to religious life, Sister Assisium hoped other sisters would do the same for their students. "Remember [that] in the classroom the children are watching you," she reminded sister-teachers in training, "and you may repel or you may attract."[46]

Encouraging vocations and appealing to members of the hierarchy were not always successful, especially if a religious community simply did not have enough sisters to fill all the requests for teachers. When Mother Aloysia Hofer was named superior of the Franciscan Sisters in Philadelphia, she determined that the community was spread too thin and refused to accept any new missions during her first term in office (1906–1912). According to her assistant, Sister Marilla Stoddard, "We may be wrong in our judgment, but it seems to us that the Community has undertaken more than it can accomplish. It is, to use a very common expression, being like a 'Jack-of-all-trades and a master of none.' We begin a little of everything and bring nothing to completion."[47] Several years later, when Mother Aloysia concluded that the community had stabilized, she began fulfilling requests for sister-teachers not only in Philadelphia, but throughout the United States.

Nativists worried about the dramatic increase in the number of parochial schools throughout the country, and claimed that public schools were the most effective vehicle for Americanizing immigrants. In 1922 Oregon voters, who had been lobbied vigorously by members of the Ku Klux Klan, approved the state's Compulsory School Law, which required all children between the ages of eight and sixteen to enroll in public schools. Aided by organizations such as the National Catholic Welfare Council and the Knights of Columbus, lawyers for the Archdiocese of Oregon City—now Portland—challenged the law on behalf of the Sisters of the Holy Names of Jesus and Mary, arguing that it violated the sisters' rights under the Fourteenth Amendment. Closing schools operated by the community would deprive the sisters of their right to property without due process. The law was overturned in June 1925 when the U.S. Supreme Court handed down *Pierce v. The Society of Sisters*; the right of parents to send their children to Catholic schools had been affirmed.[48]

The quality of education offered in parochial schools can perhaps best be described as uneven for two reasons. First, teacher preparation varied from one religious community to another. Although most congregations recognized the necessity of educating teachers, young women were often sent into the classroom with only a rudimentary knowledge of the subject they were assigned to teach. This began to change in 1911 when a teacher's college for women religious was established at the Catholic University of America.[49] Second, although they recognized the necessity of learning English as quickly as possible, members of European communities were often placed in schools before they had mastered the language. In a letter written home to Germany, Mother Anselma Felber, a member of the Adorers of the Most Precious Blood, asked for prayers that "God may loose my tongue and let me hear right . . . without a miracle I shall never know English."[50] A study conducted in Chicago during the mid-1920s found that many Polish women religious were only able to communicate in broken English. Parents were frustrated by the inability of some sister-teachers to instruct children in this subject.[51] Church leaders were especially concerned that immigrant students attending parochial schools gain fluency in English. Cleveland Bishop Ignatius F. Horstmann (1892–1908) insisted that English be taught in parochial schools; teachers were expected to be able to perform this task.[52]

Schools enrolling students for whom English was not their primary language faced special difficulties. Polish and Polish American sisters might have children who were bilingual in both languages—Polish and English—because their parents had been in the United States long enough to become fluent in English. Other students in the sisters' classes could read and write only in Polish, but spoke English; still others could speak only Polish and could not read or write at all. The Sisters of St. Francis, Sylvania, Ohio, teaching at St. Hedwig's School in Toledo, Ohio, tried to teach

English as much as possible. In 1917–1918, second graders received cate-chism instruction in Polish, but their arithmetic class was taught in English. Polish and English were spoken in spelling, reading, and writing classes. The goal was to move students toward greater fluency in English as they entered the upper grades.[53] Because many of these children were forced to leave school at an early age to help their families financially, schools were often very crowded in the lower grades but had far fewer students beyond fourth or fifth grade. Women religious teaching in these schools attempted to convince parents of the importance of allowing their children to receive an education, but they often met with resistance. Girls, for instance, did not need more than a rudimentary education because they could be taught by their mothers at home, as their mothers had been taught in Poland.[54]

Parishes composed primarily of immigrants from southern and eastern Europe recruited women religious fluent in the language of their students. These religious communities shared the problems and difficulties faced by all newcomers. All fourteen members of the Religious of Jesus-Mary min-istering in Fall River, Massachusetts, in 1880 were foreign-born; by 1920, seventy-six out of one hundred community members were from Europe. The sisters desired to learn the language and adapt to the culture of their new home, but they also recognized the importance of retaining some ele-ments of their heritage. Although they, along with many other sister-teach-ers, helped "Americanize" the children they taught, they also helped pre-serve their cultural integrity while, at the same time, encouraging students to become "economically mobile."[55]

The first Polish sisters to establish a permanent foundation in the United States, the Community of St. Felix of Cantalicio, also known as the Feli-cian Sisters, left Poland for Polonia, Wisconsin, in 1874, opening a school that same year. Between 1885 and 1900, three other communities sent sis-ters to work among Polish immigrants. As the number of parochial schools continued to increase and it became difficult for European communities to supply the number of women required to open and staff these institutions, ethnic religious communities were founded in the United States. By the end of World War I, for instance, 399 elementary and secondary schools had been established to educate the Polish American community. They were staffed by eighteen communities of women religious: four were Eu-ropean; seven had been founded in the United States; and six were able to provide some Polish-speaking sisters to schools in need of their services.[56]

The decision to develop national parishes intended to meet the needs of particular ethnic groups created a further demand for schools and sister-teachers. By 1902, 55 percent of Chicago's parochial schoolchildren attended schools connected to these parishes.[57] Since parishioners often refused to send their children to schools in other parishes, changing neighborhood patterns could lead to either dips or increases in school enrollment within a few years. "As one school stood almost empty, another [was being built] just across the street or down the block."[58] Parishioners complained when pastors could not find sister-teachers from their country of origin. "A Lithuanian parish forced to hire Polish sisters when it lacked its own teachers bitterly complained in 1899 about 'the Polish Sisters, incompetent to speak the Lithuanian language and who through ignorance convert our children into Poles.'"[59]

Italian parishes were the least active in planning and raising funds to build schools, but some pastors recruited religious communities from Italy to educate their parishioners. In 1910, when five Religious Sisters Filippini arrived in Trenton, New Jersey, at the request of the pastor of St. Joachim's Church, they were welcomed by a thousand enthusiastic Italians accompanied by a marching band. When Father Edward Griffin, a non-Italian pastor, was appointed to the parish two years after their arrival, he tried to replace the sisters with an American community and allowed the Filippini Sisters to teach only Italian and catechism. Angry parishioners confronted him, shouting, "Why did you come here? You get out of this parish. Woe to you if you dare to send our sisters away!" The new pastor was replaced by an Italian priest, but it was not until Trenton Bishop James A. McFaul (1894–1917) was replaced by Thomas Walsh (1918–1928) that the Filippini Sisters and their school received complete diocesan support. During Walsh's tenure, the enrollment of St. Joachim's School increased to one thousand students, and the sisters' work grew to include teaching catechism to public school students and ministering to the poor.[60]

Attempts to staff schools with growing enrollments sometimes led to problems when the rules and customs of women religious, especially those whose communities were closely attached to European motherhouses, conflicted with the organization and culture of the parish school. Some congregations were either unable to teach boys at all or had to cease instructing them after they reached a certain grade level because it was believed this would "endanger the virtue of the sisters."[61] The Sisters of Mercy in Rhode Island did not instruct boys in the upper grades until 1871, and the Sisters of Notre Dame de Namur were not able to teach boys above the fourth grade until 1922.[62] This complicated matters for bishops, who sometimes had to staff schools with two sets of teachers, and they often pushed women religious to modify their rule so they could teach both boys and girls. When the Holy Union Sisters, who taught primarily in Rhode Island and Massachusetts, proposed to follow the custom of their European colleagues and limit their teaching of young male students, their chaplain, James C. Cassidy, who would later be consecrated Bishop of Fall River, Massachusetts, warned community leaders that if they insisted on teaching only girls, parishes would replace them with another congregation.[63] When sisters persisted in maintaining this tradition, some parishes sought either men religious or a community whose rule was more flexible to provide instruction for boys.[64]

The issue of educating boys resulted in divisions among Elizabeth Seton's Sisters of Charity of St. Joseph. The community began its ministry in New York City in 1817, nine years after it was formally established, and by the mid-nineteenth century was staffing schools and orphanages throughout the diocese. In 1845, Rev. Louis Deluol, SS, the community's priest superior, informed Bishop John Hughes (1842–1864) that the sisters were no longer permitted to care for boys. He "was interpreting very literally a passage of the rule that specified as one of the major works of the community the teaching of girls."[65] Hughes strenuously objected to the decision, arguing that he was planning to build a boys' orphan asylum on the assumption that the sisters would administer and staff the institution. The bishop proposed that each sister be allowed to choose whether to remain in New York City or return to Emmitsburg, Maryland. Forty-seven of the sixty-nine sisters working in New York chose to remain.[66] The community divided again in 1850, when Deluol decided to affiliate it with the French Daughters of Charity. Sister Margaret George, superior of the congregation's convent in Cincinnati, objected because she believed this was against the wishes of Elizabeth Seton. In addition, the sisters in Ohio had never been pleased with the decision to remove the community from its ministry of caring for and teaching boys. On March 25, 1852, they became formally known as the Sisters of Charity of Cincinnati.[67] The Emmitsburg community changed its name to the Daughters of Charity to reflect its affiliation with the French congregation.

At times, women religious were frustrated by what they viewed as lack of parental interest in the educational process. This was especially disheartening given the large class sizes in many parochial schools. One Felician sister teaching in a Detroit school in 1896 commented, "This past year I had 130 of the younger children. Very often I just did not have the stamina or physical strength to carry on and experienced difficulty. . . . Parents don't register any concern. They want their children to study and become wise, but you can't find any such traces of parental concern or influence in the children."[68] There is no doubt that large classes of energetic students could also be a problem, especially if a sister-teacher had limited classroom management skills or had not completed enough credits to receive her bachelor's degree in education. Andrew Untener, who attended Holy Cross School (Hungarian) in Detroit from 1907 until 1910, remembered: "Our natural inclination to mischief was a source of great annoyance and vexation to the Sisters, and it was not uncommon to see Sister chasing someone around the room with a ruler, trying to catch him and administer some promised punishment."[69]

The system of segregation in the southern United States demanded separate parochial schools for white and African American children. When the Georgia state legislature considered passing a law prohibiting white teachers from educating black children, Father Ignatius Lissner, a French missionary, decided to found a community of African American women religious to assume responsibility for schools currently staffed by white sisters. On October 15, 1916 Mother Theodore Williams, who was appointed Reverend Mother Superior of the community, became the first member of the Franciscan Handmaids of Mary. Three young women entered the community as novices on the same day, and by November the congregation boasted twelve members.[70] The new congregation opened Immaculate Heart of Mary School in Savannah for grades one through three, but a combination of racism and anti-Catholicism made it difficult for the sisters to recruit students. Their financial difficulties were so severe that the women were forced to take in laundry to support themselves. The community eventually relocated to Harlem, New York, where it operated a nursery and taught at several schools, including St. Benedict the Moor. Some members of the community returned to the South during the 1950s and established several mission schools.[71]

Women religious sometimes shared the prejudices held by other Americans of their era and spoke about their students with an attitude that can best be described as paternalistic. Franciscan sisters from Germany arrived at the Lakota Rosebud Reservation in South Dakota in 1886 to teach Native American children. Although the sisters themselves had to adapt to American life and culture, they were also charged with helping their students do the same. A report written shortly after the sisters' arrival reflects the nation's prevailing attitude toward Native Americans: "The main thing in the Indian schools, you must know, is to introduce the children to work in order to get them accustomed to a productive life, given that by nature they are very idle and lie about almost all day long sunning themselves."[72]

The development of a comprehensive American parochial school system was realized in large part by the large number of women religious working for very little financial remuneration while ensuring that their schools offered a comparable education to their public counterparts. Sisters opened schools designed for specific ethnic groups, as well as the general Catholic population, and worked with African American and Native American students, even those who were non-Catholic. The great need for sister-teachers meant it was difficult for religious communities to allow their members adequate time to attain undergraduate degrees. Catholic schools could not claim to offer quality education unless they were staffed by qualified and professionally trained teachers.

From Parochial Schools to Higher Education

In 1890 about sixty Catholic colleges and universities were offering men the opportunity to receive a higher education, but there were no comparable institutions for Catholic women. This situation was rectified in 1895, when the School Sisters of Notre Dame opened the College of Notre Dame in Baltimore by expanding the academy they were already administering. Four years later, in 1899, the college's six seniors became the first women to graduate from a Catholic college in the United States.[73] The American bishops did not especially support higher education for women, but recognized that wealthy Catholics were now willing to pay to educate their daughters as well as their sons. In addition, women themselves were interested in pursuing advanced degrees, and would attend secular universities if they did not have access to Catholic higher education.

The Sisters of Notre Dame de Namur opened Trinity College in Washington, D.C.—a short distance from the Catholic University of America, an all-male institution —in 1900.[74] Because the new college did not evolve from an already existing academy, Trinity was not able to develop slowly and "unobtrusively." The college could not open without a public announcement drawing all eyes to the sisters' enterprise.[75] In a letter written to congratulate Sister Julia McGroarty on Trinity's opening, Cardinal James Gibbons (1877–1921) of Baltimore indicated his awareness of the need to offer church-sponsored higher education for Catholic women. "Such an institution . . . in the shadow of our great University," Gibbons wrote, "will, I am convinced, offer educational advantages to our young women which can not [sic] be found elsewhere in our country. It will relieve the [Catholic] University [of America] authorities from the embarrassment of refusing women admission, many of whom have already applied for the privilege of following our courses, and will be a light and a protection in faith and morals."[76]

Expanding their education apostolate to the college and university level required sister-teachers to receive post-baccalaureate degrees, a feat not easily accomplished given financial restraints, personnel shortages, and the fact that very few sisters had even completed the requirements for a bachelor's degree. When Trinity opened its doors, the faculty included three "professors" from the Catholic University of America, who held doctorates, and ten "teachers," sisters whose credentials, with one exception, were limited to teaching experience.[77] Within twenty years of the advent of Catholic women's colleges, women religious with doctorates were teaching courses in most academic disciplines with the exception of theology and philosophy; until St. Mary's Graduate School of Sacred Theology in South Bend, Indiana, opened in 1944, Catholic women were not allowed to complete higher degrees in these two areas of study.[78]

Catholic colleges founded by women religious followed one of two models. The first, exemplified by Trinity, Manhattanville College (Purchase, New York), College of St. Catherine (St. Paul, Minnesota), College of St. Elizabeth (Convent Station, New Jersey), and St. Mary's College (South Bend, Indiana), were established to emulate women's colleges such as Smith, Wellesley, and Vassar, offering a rigorous classical curriculum similar to that of their male counterparts. Sister Antonia McHugh, CSJ, of the Sisters of St. Joseph of Carondolet, assured women considering the College of St. Catherine that it would offer "all the branches that are usually taught in colleges for boys."[79] A second model, "usually urban and regional, saw their role as providing skills and training to young Catholic women of the working and lower middle classes, often the first in their families to attain a college education."[80] An example of this model was Felician College in Lodi, New Jersey, founded—like many similar institutions—as a junior college to educate members of the Felician Sisters. In 1965, one year after the college began to admit lay students, Felician began an associate's degree program in nursing; by 1967 it had been approved to offer a Bachelor of Science degree in elementary education.[81]

With one important exception, all the colleges founded by communities of women religious were exclusively female. Mother Katharine Drexel,

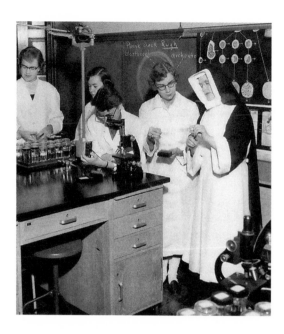

Sister Catherine Lawlor of College of St. Elizabeth Biology Department with students, ca. 1950. Courtesy of the Archives of the Sisters of Charity of St. Elizabeth.

heiress to the Philadelphia Drexel family fortune, was "probably the most powerful woman in the American Catholic Church" in the early twentieth century.[82] When her father died in 1885, he left $14,000,000 to his three daughters, making them the richest women in Philadelphia, and Mother Katharine decided to use her share of the fortune to assist African Americans and Native Americans. She founded Xavier University in New Orleans in 1925 as a coeducational institution after receiving special permission for the community to teach men as well as women.[83]

Xavier University was an important Catholic institution because many colleges, including those administered by sisters, were segregated. When Kentucky's state legislature passed an amendment in 1950 allowing "black students to attend 'white' institutions *if* courses of equal quality were not available at Kentucky State College for Negroes," the Sisters of Charity of Nazareth announced that Nazareth College, along with two other Catholic institutions, planned to desegregate its student body.[84] Within one week of the college's announcement, twenty-five African American students had been admitted for the fall; they constituted one-third of the freshmen class in 1950–1951. Integration of the student body proceeded without incident, but after 1955 the number of black students attending the college declined, as state colleges and universities began to desegregate.[85] Other southern

Catholic women's colleges followed Nazareth's example during the 1950s and 1960s. The College of the Sacred Heart in Grand Cocteau, Louisiana, integrated its student body in 1953, but St. Mary's Dominican College in the same state did not admit black students until the late 1960s.[86]

The sister-faculty and administrators at Catholic women's colleges personified the idea that a woman could assume leadership in a male-dominated society; women seldom held less than 50 percent of faculty and administrative positions at these schools.[87] In 1968, 142 Catholic women's four-year colleges boasted a total enrollment of approximately 101,000 students.[88] These numbers began to decline as student unrest and the decision of male schools to become coeducational changed the ways young women viewed the place of higher education in their lives and future work.[89] At the same time, a decrease in the number of women religious altered the financial situation of these institutions, and many communities had to either close, admit men, or look for new ways to attract students to their colleges.[90] By the end of the twentieth century, many of the 114 remaining Catholic colleges administered by women religious were primarily staffed by laypeople—men and women—including the position of president, and although members of the congregation served on the board of trustees, they were not always the primary sponsors of the institution.

Women Religious and Changes in Parochial Education

Bishops attending the Third Plenary Council of Baltimore in 1884 might have expressed surprise at the changing nature of Catholic education in the 1960s. The number of parochial schools increased significantly during the years following World War II; between 1950 and 1960 Catholic elementary schools increased 171 percent and secondary schools grew 174 percent. This growth began to slow in 1964, and by 1970 it was clear that the number of students attending Catholic schools was decreasing every year. At times, declining enrollment in a particular region was evident to all concerned. In 1968, Catholic schools in the Minneapolis-St. Paul area suffered a decrease in students that was 20 percent higher than that reported four years earlier.[91]

Part of the financial difficulties experienced by parochial schools was caused by a decreasing number of priests, sisters, and brothers; the numbers of women religious alone decreased by 48.8 percent between 1964 and 1989. During those same years, 3,929 Catholic elementary schools and

1,379 high schools closed.[92] In addition, as women religious moved away from a primary ministry of education and pastors had no choice but to hire lay teachers, the cost of staffing and administering parochial schools increased. The high cost of maintaining these schools eventually forced many to close. St. Edward's School in Philadelphia was founded in 1886 to serve the growing middle class Irish American community living within the parish's boundaries. When the Sisters of the Holy Child Jesus (SHCJ) opened the school's doors for the first time, 297 boys and 294 girls were in attendance. In the 1950s, the parish demographics changed as Puerto Rican Catholics began to move into the area. Cardinal John O'Hara (1951–1960) believed Catholic schools had the capacity to transform this latest group of immigrants into "American" Catholics, and the sister-teachers at St. Edward's—unlike their colleagues at three neighboring parishes—accepted Puerto Rican children into the school. Three sisters began to learn Spanish in order to better communicate with both the children and their parents; they also developed a plan to introduce bilingual education to the school.[93]

As the sisters assigned to the parish school adapted to their new students, their religious community was revisiting the ministries in which they were involved, including St. Edward's. The school's sister-teachers concluded that the eight decades in which the community had staffed the school "had accomplished nothing very spectacular in our corner of inner city Philadelphia," but they "took comfort in the realization that 'the very fact of our being here and the daily concern we have for the 440 Black and Puerto Rican children under our care as well as for this community . . . is reason enough for these people to realize in some way the love God has for them.'"[94] The community agreed that St. Edward's School was their primary ministry in the neighborhood; through the children, they would reach others.

In 1977, the Sisters of the Holy Child Jesus agreed that members would no longer be assigned to teach at inner-city schools like St. Edward's; they could, however, choose to teach there and sisters who did so were assured the support of their religious community. Between 1989 and 1992, under the direction of Cardinal Anthony Bevilaqua (1988–2003), the Archdiocese of Philadelphia conducted a study to determine the number of churches and schools needed in the section of the city where the parish was located. One of the report's recommendations was to close St. Edward's church and school. "In a kind of ecclesiastical triage, the decisions were based on worsening financial problems and declining Catholic population in these inner-city areas."[95] The sister-teachers were left with the job of "dismantling school and convent—pulling up roots of seeds planted so long ago by the 'Pioneer' S.H.C.J. here."[96] Although they realized the difficulties involved in financially supporting a school located in a deteriorating neighborhood, the sisters living and working at St. Edward's were reluctant to leave the place they had come to call home. On June 30, 1993 they moved out of the convent where Sisters of the Holy Child Jesus had lived for many years, but remained convinced that those women religious who had "lived or worked at St. Edward's will live on in its past students and parishioners."[97]

Just as Our Lady of the Angels School in Chicago was able to rise from the ashes and continue to educate the parish children, the closing of St. Edward's led to a new educational ministry for the Sisters of the Holy Child Jesus. Within a few months of St. Edward's closing, under the leadership of Sister Elizabeth Barber, SHCJ, Providence Center was founded. The center was designed to offer a variety of services, including an after school program, English as a second language, and health education; in short, the sisters continued to meet the needs of those they were called to serve. Providence Center remained committed to educating people living within the boundaries of what was once St. Edward's parish, albeit in non-traditional ways.

The ways in which women religious of the twenty-first century approached their educational ministry differed from previous generations of sister-teachers. Factors such as shifting immigration patterns, the growth of public colleges and universities, and demographic changes impacted parochial education on all levels. In addition, declining numbers of women religious, the expense of staffing and administering schools, and changes in the ways in which decisions were made and implemented by dioceses and religious communities altered the shape of the parochial school system. It is difficult to predict the future shape of Catholic education in the institutional church, but it will be influenced by the forces which led sister-teachers to provide a ministry of education to Catholics seeking a way to improve their own lives and those of their children from the eighteenth to the twenty-first century.

4

Serving the Sick

THE VERY MENTION of cholera was guaranteed to strike fear in the hearts of nineteenth-century Americans. The disease's symptoms are unmistakable: severe vomiting and diarrhea along with intense abdominal pain, dehydration, and shock, leading eventually to death. Many Americans believed that cholera was transmitted primarily by "bad air," a theory that gained in popularity when observers realized it often impacted poor neighborhoods—those with the most unsanitary living conditions—more severely than the rich. The disease is actually spread through "human fecal matter in drinking water," and the bacterium then "releases toxins that prevent the absorption of water." In 1826, cholera swept through Bengal, India, and spread to Russia and Western Europe, arriving in North America in the summer of 1832. From Canada cholera moved to New York, and then on to Philadelphia and points south. When the epidemic of the 1830s finally came to an end, the disease had killed as many as 10,000 Americans.[1]

When cholera broke out in Philadelphia in July 1832, the municipal government immediately instituted a program designed to prevent its spread. Attempts to purify water used for drinking, cooking, and bathing did not seem to contain the spread of the disease, however, and within a month over one hundred cases a day were being reported. The epidemic caused panic to spread throughout Philadelphia's neighborhoods and led to "an almost total breakdown of discipline within the [city's] medical profession."[2] The almshouse was particularly affected; nurses flatly refused to minister to the sick and dying even after they had demanded and received a salary increase. A report issued by the Committee of the [Alms]House explained that "In a disease which requires unremitted attention from nurses, those employed in the wards (a few excepted) were by no means suitable. . . . In one ward where the disease raged in all its horrors, where one would suppose that the heart would be humbled and the feelings softened at the sight of distress, the nurse and her attendants were in a state of intoxication [drunk], heedless of the groans of patients and fighting over the bodies of the dying and the dead."[3] The institution's director offered a solution: bring in the Sisters of Charity from Emmitsburg, Maryland, to care for those suffering from the disease.[4]

The Sisters of Charity were no strangers to Philadelphia. By the 1830s, the community was caring for the children at the city's St. Joseph's Orphanage and teaching at Sacred Heart School. Philadelphia Bishop Francis Patrick Kenrick (1842–1851) readily assented to the almshouse director's request for nursing sisters, as did Father John Hickey, the clerical superior of the community. On August 9, eight Sisters of Charity left Emmitsburg to join five members of their community already living and working in Philadelphia. Eight sisters cared for cholera patients at the almshouse, and two others tended the sick at a makeshift hospital housed in the residence of Father John Hurley, pastor of St. Augustine's Church.[5]

Following a pattern that was developing among religious communities working in health care, the sisters ministered among both Catholic and non-Catholic victims of the disease. One account claims that of the 370 patients nursed by the sisters at St. Augustine's, only 63 were Catholic. Although the Sisters of Charity nursed residents of the almshouse until the following spring, by the end of August the number of cholera patients was decreasing, and by early September few new cases were being recorded within the city. Those responsible for the administration of the institution had nothing but praise for the sisters' work, describing their services as "invaluable." "These ladies," the report observed, "left a healthy home to visit an infected city to encounter a dreadful disease, to live in an atmosphere dangerous in the extreme, to watch by the bedside of strangers, of the friendless, of the outcast, of those who generally proved themselves unworthy of kindness." The women religious declined the offer of a silver plate for each sister who had provided care to the epidemic's victims, but did ask that a comparable sum be donated to St. Joseph's Orphanage. All the sisters who ministered in Philadelphia survived the epidemic, but several members of their community performing a similar service in Baltimore died after contracting the disease.[6] Historian of medicine Charles E. Rosenberg notes that the sisters' work as nurses when others were unavailable produced "sympathy for the church to which they had dedicated their lives."[7]

The sisters' work during the cholera epidemic was not confined to victims living within Philadelphia's city limits. A group of Irish railroad laborers working in Chester County, an outlying suburb, were stricken with the disease in mid-August 1832. Far from home and family, the men had no recourse to any sort of nursing care. When four Sisters of Charity were asked to nurse the dying men, "so great was the fear of contagion that they [the four nuns] could get neither shelter nor conveyance, and tradition tells us that although jaded and worn out as they were by their vigils and duty to the dying laborers, they were forced to walk all the way back to the city, twelve miles. . . . [A]t the sight of the habits doors would be closed and all assistance refused to these persons, who had themselves risked their own lives to save that of their unknown fellowmen."[8] The traditional preference of women religious to remain anonymous means that the names of these sisters have not been preserved.[9]

The willingness of the Sisters of Charity to nurse victims of Philadelphia's cholera epidemic is a good example of one way in which a number of communities of Catholic women religious first became involved in health care: as "spontaneous responses to 'nursing opportunities' (epidemics, disasters, and wars) [rather than] as a systematic plan for sister-run hospitals."[10] Other congregations responded to a need within the Catholic community to provide care for the sick by founding and staffing hospitals throughout the United States. By the mid-twentieth century, American sister-nurses had helped to develop a comprehensive system of Catholic hospitals and nursing care facilities. Even communities that did not focus primarily on nursing often stepped in and tended to the sick when epidemics led to a shortage of trained nurses. Caring for the sick, whether in times of epidemic or war or as part of their day-to-day ministry, was an important way in which women religious served the Catholic Church in the United States.

Sisters as Nurses in the New Republic

Although the Ursuline Sisters had nursed at Charity Hospital in New Orleans since 1659, Continental soldiers fighting in the American Revolution may have been the first from the thirteen English-speaking colonies to be cared for by sister-nurses. When American troops led by Benedict Arnold attacked Quebec, outbreaks of smallpox and scarlet fever forced a number of soldiers to be admitted to a hospital. A Lieutenant Nichols, "sick of the scarlet fever," recounted his stay at the Hotel Dieu, a hospital administered by women religious in Quebec. "For several nights the nuns sat up with me, four at a time, every two hours. . . . When I think of my captivity I shall never forget the time spent among the nuns who treated me with so much humanity."[11]

During the late eighteenth and early nineteenth centuries, most American women religious were involved in teaching. Some sisters ministered to the sick and dying when no other care was available, but women religious had not been encouraged to enter the field of nursing. In a letter to Mother Elizabeth Seton, Bishop John Carroll reflected that a "century at least will pass before the exigencies and habits of this Country will require and hardly admit of the charitable exercises toward the sick, sufficient to employ any number of the sisters out of our largest cities."[12] Despite Carroll's admonition, Seton's community was the first to begin a formal ministry to the sick in the United States. Their American rule recognized the role of nursing in the congregation's work, stating: "The end which our Sisters of Charity of St. Joseph proposed to themselves was to honor our Lord Jesus Christ as the source and model of all charity, by rendering Him every temporal and spiritual service in their power, in the persons of the poor, the sick, prisoners and others."[13] In October 1823, they were able to begin an official ministry of health care when doctors at the University of Maryland opened the Baltimore Infirmary, a fifty-bed hospital managed and staffed by the Sisters of Charity.[14]

Each sister-nurse was provided with room, board, and free medical care, and received a stipend of twenty-one dollars every six months. Their official responsibilities included admitting and discharging patients, supervising visiting hours, and inventorying furniture and patient property. But the sisters were also involved in many aspects of their charges' daily care. "Instructions for the Care of the Sick," written by Mother Mary Xavier Clark, the community's superior general from 1839 until 1845, for instance, contained a section on preparing and distributing medicine, including information on the proper way to mix drugs. Mother Mary Xavier also prescribed appropriate behavior for sisters nursing in the Infirmary. They were to do no more than serve meals and distribute medicine in the men's wards; the women were not even permitted to check the pulse of a male patient. In addition, although the sisters were clearly a visible manifestation of the Catholic faith, there was to be no mention of their religion to patients identifying themselves as Protestant. "Some of these poor creatures," the superior general wrote, "are very bitter against our holy religion."[15] A crucial aspect of this ministry involved caring for those who were terminally ill, and Clark's work included three pages of prayers designed to be useful when ministering to the dying.[16]

The Sisters of Charity left the Baltimore Infirmary in September 1840 over a disagreement with the board of directors, but that was not the end of their hospital ministry. In that same year they founded the first Catholic hospital for the mentally ill in the United States, while continuing to serve those suffering from physical illnesses.[17] In 1828 the community sent four sisters to St. Louis, Missouri, where they became the first administrators of Mullanphy Hospital—also known as St. Louis Hospital—the first Roman Catholic Hospital in the United States. The hospital was originally housed in a three-room log cabin; the sisters' living quarters also served as the kitchen. In 1832 a more permanent building was built that could accommodate sixty patients.[18]

As Catholic leaders struggled to meet the needs of the large numbers of Catholic immigrants arriving in the United States, bishops recruited communities of European religious women willing to provide necessary services to poor and needy Catholics, including health care. The Irish Sisters of Mercy who arrived in Pittsburgh in 1843 opened that city's first hospital—and the first Mercy hospital in the world—when they established Mercy Hospital on January 1, 1847 in hopes of alleviating "the daily misery they witnessed."[19] They supported their ministry by charging those able to pay three dollars for a bed on a ward or five dollars for a private room, and asking local pastors to provide financial assistance for indigent parishioners.[20] Six Franciscan Sisters of the Poor from Germany were able to establish St. Mary's Hospital in Cincinnati within a year of their 1858 arrival in the United States. They opened St. Elizabeth's Hospital in Covington, Kentucky, one year later, and founded hospitals in Hoboken and Newark, New Jersey; Brooklyn, New York; and Quincy, Illinois.[21] Some religious congregations believed hospital ministry was the most effective way to reach those they had come to serve because this work contributed to the healing of both the physical and spiritual ills of the area's Catholic poor.[22] The hospitals they founded quickly became known for the quality of their care, however, and the sisters "were disciplined and careful nurses decades before nursing developed into a trained occupation."[23]

Women religious, even those whose primary ministry did not involve nursing, often volunteered their services when epidemics threatened to bring American cities to a standstill, and were welcomed by physicians and city officials alike. When cholera swept through Baltimore in 1832—the same year the Sisters of Charity were asked to work with the disease's victims in Philadelphia—four Oblate Sisters of Providence volunteered to nurse the sick in the city's almshouse.[24] The trustees had asked for eight Sisters of Charity to help them through the crisis, but when only four sisters were assigned to the task Sulpician Father James Joubert was asked if the Oblates could help. Joubert replied that the sisters' rule did not require them to care for the sick—their mission was the education of young African American girls—but he would inform them of the request. All eleven of the community's sisters volunteered, and four spent a month nursing at the almshouse.[25]

The work of the Oblate Sisters in Baltimore serves as a reminder that racial discrimination was found in all aspects of American society, including health care. The 1832 cholera epidemic was especially hard on the city's free black population. During one week, 254 Baltimore residents died from the disease; 104 of the victims were black. Although African Americans comprised only 14 percent of Baltimore's population, during that week they accounted for one-third of the deaths caused by the disease. Many public and private institutions did not accept blacks, and those that did were strictly segregated. Despite their readiness to minister to both blacks and whites, the Oblate Sisters may have themselves been victims of discrimination. Writing to city officials to assure them that the sisters were anxious to help during this time of emergency, Joubert "also told these gentlemen that I [Joubert] should wish these colored Sisters in a department of the hospital entirely separate from those of the Sisters of Charity, so that they would not come in contact with them. The gentlemen understood perfectly, and promised that this should be done."[26] When the disease no longer threatened Baltimore residents, both communities returned to their respective ministries and the Sisters of Charity "received significant public acknowledgment of their efforts." The Oblate Sisters, on the other hand, received only one letter from Archibald Stirling, secretary of the trustees of the Bureau of the Poor.[27]

By 1849, five of the sixteen communities of women religious living and working in the United States were involved in hospital care. The size of the hospitals ranged from New Orleans' five-hundred-bed Charity Hospital, for which the Sisters of Charity had assumed responsibility in 1834, to the much smaller Mercy Hospital in Pittsburgh, which could hold sixty patients. Beginning in the late 1840s, the Sisters of Charity staffed and administered St. John's Infirmary in Milwaukee. This hospital, like many others founded by religious communities, included wards and private rooms and was open to patients who could afford to pay for medical care as well as the indigent. The sisters deferred to physicians in matters of patient care, but often distributed meals and medicines to the sick.[28]

Angels of the Battlefield

When the Civil War broke out in 1861, women religious were staffing or administering about thirty hospitals in the United States.[29] As a result, they were already trained to provide much needed nursing care to soldiers from both the Union and Confederate camps. Prominent reformer Dorothea Dix (1802–1877) was placed in charge of those willing to nurse the wounded on northern battlefields. Dix, a Protestant, required her nurses to be at least thirty years of age, "plain looking," and to wear black or brown dresses. In addition, Surgeon General Robert C. Wood insisted that they be certified as able nurses by two physicians and found morally upright by two members of the clergy.[30] Despite Dix's anti-Catholic views—she seldom hired a Catholic if a Protestant nurse was available—she found herself supervising sisters willing to nurse wounded and dying northern soldiers because they were among the very few women with any real nursing experience during this era.[31]

Medical and army officers specifically requested sisters to tend to the wounded. Some doctors had worked with nursing sisters before enlisting in the war effort and admired their ability and work ethic, and those who had not came to respect the knowledge and skills of those women with whom they came in contact. As they cared for the wounded and dying, women religious usually agreed to work wherever and whenever necessary, even if it meant laboring in dangerous and sometimes hostile territory. Their duties included housekeeping, cooking, personal care, distributing food and medicine, assisting in surgery, supervising hospital wards, and ministering on the battlefield. In short, they were willing to perform any task necessary to ease the suffering of the wounded and the work of military physicians.[32]

Shortly after the war began, the Daughters of Charity (Emmitsburg) began nursing soldiers in their Norfolk, Virginia, hospital. On May 15, 1861, Confederate medical personnel asked the sisters to admit wounded and sick soldiers to their infirmary in Richmond. These two events began a pattern that continued throughout the war years: hospitals operated by religious communities were requested to take in wounded and sick soldiers, but sisters were also asked to provide nursing care in hospitals administered by the government. If necessary, sisters whose ministry did not include nursing joined those trained as nurses to care for those wounded in battle.[33]

American women religious from the North and the South responded to the many requests they received to provide nursing care to the wounded. While a few demanded formal contractual agreements setting out the terms and conditions under which they would work, all the sisters expected at least to be able to attend Mass on Sunday. It was not always easy, however, for women religious to fulfill this obligation; chaplains—of any denomination—were few and far between. Baltimore Archbishop Francis Patrick Kenrick reflected on this problem in a letter to Arcbhishop John Hughes of New York: "The Sisters may experience difficulty in regard to their spiritual duties unless some arrangement be made for chaplains. . . . It is hard for the Sisters to hear Mass even on Sundays." Even when Kenrick was able to find a priest to serve as a chaplain for women religious, the appointment was not always accepted. "The Surgeon General asked me some months ago to designate a priest for them," the archbishop continued, "and took no notice of my request to have him appointed and provided for."[34]

Sisters struggled with their inability to attend Mass and spend time in prayer and meditation. A Daughter of Charity nursing in Marietta, Georgia, wrote: "Five weeks without Mass. At last, two sisters went to Atlanta, where there were two priests—did not get one to come for Mass on Easter."[35] Those finding themselves in this situation were often reassured by a superior reminding them of the extenuating circumstances under which they ministered. Sisters of St. Joseph of Philadelphia were told: "Go to Holy Communion when you have that favor. . . . Make your meditation in the morning after your prayers and be not troubled if you can say no other prayers of the community, not even if you are deprived of Mass on Sundays."[36] In another missive, members of the same community were instructed: "Offer up all the actions of the day, attend to those poor people and I think Our Lord will be satisfied."[37] If circumstances permitted, sisters participated in community devotions. A Sister of Mercy, who journeyed to Oxford, Mississippi, to care for the wounded, remembered, "Here, as we ate our corn bread without salt and drank our sage tea, or sweet potato coffee . . . Reverend Mother read us our morning lecture, as the distance to the various wards was so great that we could only return at meal time."[38]

Sister-nurses unable or unwilling to work in areas where Mass was unavailable had to make difficult decisions about caring for wounded soldiers and sailors. The Daughters of Charity were forbidden from nursing on hospital transport boats because no chaplain was available to celebrate Mass for the sisters. Writing to his superiors in France, Father Francis Burlando, the priest-director of the community, explained the situation. Even though these floating hospitals were in desperate need of nurses and the sisters were happy to provide assistance, they were "deprived of all spiritual assistance; no mass or communion even when they entered the port, it was hard for them to go to church, either because they did not know where there was one, or because the distance would not allow them. We were therefore obliged to remove and place them in the organized hospitals on land, where they can at least rely on the assistance of a priest."[39] On occasion, the reluctance of priest-superiors and local bishops made it difficult for sisters to become involved in the war effort. In a letter to Francis Kenrick, New York's Archbishop John Hughes, complained, "I am now informed indirectly that the Sisters of Charity in the diocese would be willing to volunteer a force of from fifty to one hundred nurses. To this latest proposition I have very strong objections."[40]

The inability to attend Mass was—in some respects—the least of the women's worries. Sister-nurses often labored under conditions that can best be described as horrendous. When a battle took place close to the Dominican sisters' convent in Perryville, Kentucky, in 1862, the building was quickly turned into a hospital receiving wounded soldiers. According to the community's annalist, "Long after midnight of that memorable October 8 and 9, 1862, wagon loads of bruised and shattered heroes were still being brought to St. Catharine. There some Sisters were on duty receiving the soldiers, while others remained for additional service on the battlefield, helping to lift the sick and wounded onto the wagons."[41] Other communities, such as the Sisters of the Holy Cross, often performed the very difficult task of ministering to the wounded and dying on the battlefield. In one instance, a physician's wife working with the sisters, noting the "sight of a macerated face and stench of [a soldier's] wounds," suggested they leave the wounded man and help others. One sister, "conscious of the religious motivation that enabled her to endure the situation, gently reminded the woman of the Scriptural passage, 'Whatsoever you do to the least of mine, you do to Me.'" The community's annals noted that all remained on the battlefield that day.[42]

Sister Mary Serena Klimkiewicz, a Daughter of Charity from Emmitsburg, experienced perhaps the most difficult situation possible for a battlefield nurse. Because of their proximity to Gettysburg, members of the Emmitsburg community reached the battlefield on July 5, 1863, nursing first on the field itself and later in makeshift hospitals that had been set up in the town. As Sister Serena moved among the wounded and dying, she stopped to wash blood from the face of a soldier who turned out to be her brother

Thaddeus. He was later sent to a hospital where Sister Serena nursed him until he recovered. She later remembered, "He was then but eighteen I, a few years older. I was a young Sister and I was sent by my Superiors with several other Sisters to nurse the poor wounded soldiers at Gettysburg and I found my dear Thaddeus among the number."[43] Her brother died about a year after the battle.

Father Edward Sorin of Notre Dame, Indiana, viewed the sisters' nursing service as an opportunity not only to help the wounded, but to lessen the public's prejudice against Catholics and their church. In 1861, at his request, the Sisters of the Holy Cross from Saint Mary's Academy in Indiana, led by Mother Angela Gillespie, volunteered their services as nurses in Cairo, Illinois, and other areas on the Western front. The following year, Dr. John Brinton, a Union physician, replaced secular nurses at the military hospital in Mound City, Illinois, with the Holy Cross Sisters. He reported great improvement in the patients as a result of the sisters' care, and claimed that the women were respected by all.[44] Not only did sister-nurses work in military hospitals, they also served on the first naval hospital ship, the *Red Rover*.[45]

Religious communities recognized that many of the men among whom they ministered were not Catholic; some could even be described as anti-Catholic. Soldiers unfamiliar with women religious were sometimes hostile and did not allow the sisters to touch them; some "even spit, cursed, or struck the sisters."[46] At times, the women were falsely accused of espionage, and some leaders on both sides worried that spies disguised as women religious would attempt to infiltrate enemy camps. On other occasions, such as when the Union navy asked the Sisters of St. Joseph of Carondelet to stand on the deck of a naval vessel bound for Richmond from Philadelphia so Confederate soldiers would recognize that they were on a peaceful mission, they were viewed as an asset.[47] Unfamiliarity with women religious sometimes led to humorous situations. A Mississippi soldier, seeing the Sisters of Mercy, asked the priest with whom they were traveling if the sisters were his daughters. "Poor things!" he commented, "I suppose their Mother is dead."[48] Most of those fighting in the war, however, did not question the women's dedication to the sick and dying. Although the sister-nurses did not try to convert the soldiers and only spoke about religion to non-Catholics if a patient raised the issue, they took comfort in the spiritual benefits resulting from their work.[49] Sister Ambrosia, a Sister of Charity of Cincinnati remembered, "Our duties [were] fatiguing and often disgusting to flesh and blood, but we were amply repaid by conversions, repentances, and the removal to a great extent of certain prejudices to our holy Faith."[50]

When the war ended, sister-nurses tried to return to their former ministries, but that was sometimes easier said than done. The Sisters of Mercy in Mississippi refused the Union army's offer to evacuate them during the Battle of Vicksburg in 1863 because they preferred to remain with their patients. In 1865, when the war was drawing to a close, the sisters, who had continued to tend the wounded, were captured by northern forces. Sister Stephana Warde, who was originally from Pittsburgh and had arrived in Mississippi via Baltimore, was detained as a prisoner of war and held until the winter. When she was finally released, Sister Stephana decided to return to the congregation's motherhouse in Pittsburgh. Wearing an army coat, she knocked on the convent door after being away from Pittsburgh for twelve years, and discovered that no one recognized her. Sister Stephana proved her identity by taking a locket from around her neck that contained the vows she made when she entered the community. After spending some time regaining her strength, the thirty-four-year-old woman left Pittsburgh to care for wounded veterans at Stanton Hospital in Washington, D.C.[51]

The sister-nurses' dedicated care of the wounded and dying on both sides of the conflict, Catholic and non-Catholic, earned them a good deal of praise when the war ended. Women religious returned to their ministries and many seldom spoke about their work on the battlefield. "[They] resumed their former duties as if they had never left them," wrote an admiring sister in Philadelphia [about the Sisters of St. Joseph]. "Seldom did they allude to their war experiences . . . nor did they ever record their story."[52]

According to Sanitary Commission leader, Mary Livermore, "The world has known no nobler and no more heroic women than those found in the ranks of the Catholic sisterhoods."[53] In recognition of the nursing care provided by women religious during the Civil War, a monument was erected in Washington, D.C. The inscription at the monument's base states: "To the memory and in honor of the various Orders of Sisters who gave their services as nurses on battlefields in hospitals and on floating hospitals in the wars in which the United States has engaged."[54] Indeed, not only did the sisters improve their public images, but through their work as Civil War nurses they contributed to the development of modern nursing in the United States. The work performed both by women religious and laywomen of all denominations during this period, including the adoption of sanitary techniques endorsed by Florence Nightingale, advances in medicine, and the heroic stories of nursing under less than ideal conditions, led to the founding of the first nurses' training academies in the 1870s.

Nursing a Growing Church

After the war ended, much of the work of sister-nurses involved founding new hospitals to meet the needs of an expanding church. In 1866, Bishop of Galveston Claude Marie Dubuis (1862–1892) requested the Order of the Incarnate Word and Blessed Sacrament, a French community, to send sisters able to nurse victims of epidemics in Galveston and San Antonio, Texas. Sisters Blandine, Joseph, and Ange arrived the same year, and became the original members of the American branch of this community, known as the Sisters of Charity of the Incarnate Word. The congregation opened Santa Rosa, San Antonio's first hospital, in 1869.[55] The sisters' daily schedule kept them busy: they rose at 4:30 a.m. for prayer and devotions; accompanied doctors on rounds at 8 a.m.; served breakfast to patients at 9, followed by religious exercises; ate lunch at 11; participated in prayers and recreation until 1 p.m.; visited the wards in the afternoon; brought supper to the hospital's patients at 5; and ate their own dinner at 6. During the evening, they visited patients again at 6:45, and retired after evening prayer at 8:25.[56] The hospital's Remark Book illustrated the sisters' policy of treating both black and white patients: "Thursday 20 January 1898. Operation on Mrs. Sophie Butler the colored lady, by Dr. A. Herff assisted by Dr. Oldham and the sisters. They removed a large tumor from her bowels."[57]

Some communities established hospitals dedicated to meeting the needs of a particular ethnic group. Although Philadelphia's first Catholic hospital, St. Joseph's, was founded in 1849, a second, St. Mary's Hospital, opened in 1866 to serve the needs of the city's German immigrants. Rev. John B. Hespelein, pastor of St. Peter's parish, began laying the groundwork for the hospital in 1855 when he organized the Sisters of the Third Order of St. Francis.[58] Within three years the community consisted of twelve sisters involved in teaching, caring for the sick and elderly, and providing for the needs of the poor.[59] By 1860, the new community had opened the twenty-bed St. Francis Hospital, which was replaced by St. Mary's in 1866; the new hospital contained eighty beds, a dispensary, and operating rooms.[60] Located in the Kensington section of the city, where many of the 120,000 residents were employed in factories, the hospital often treated workers who had

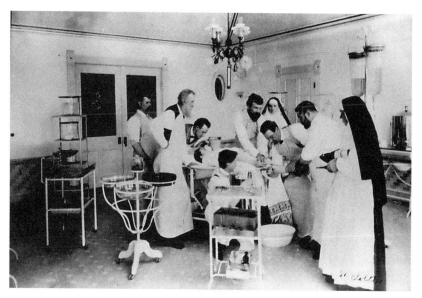

Two Sisters of Charity of the Incarnate Word oversee physicians, including Drs. Ferdinand and Adolf Herff at Santa Rosa Infirmary, San Antonio, Texas, early 1900s. Courtesy of University of Texas, San Antonio Library, Special Collections

been injured on the job.[61] The Sisters of the Holy Family of Nazareth came to Chicago from Poland in 1885. They orginally planned to focus primarily on a ministry of education, but when they realized that the city's Polish community desired a hospital staffed by medical personnel who spoke their language, the sisters opened Holy Family Hospital in 1894.[62]

Toward the end of the nineteenth century, Pope Leo XIII (1878–1903) expressed concern about the conditions in which Italian immigrants were living, and encouraged priests and sisters to consider a ministry to those leaving Italy to make a new life in the United States. In 1887, Frances Cabrini, a young Italian woman who believed she was called to be a missionary, met with the pontiff to seek approval for a community of women religious she was in the process of founding. Her original plan was to establish a group—they would become known as the Missionary Sisters of the Sacred Heart of Jesus (MSC)—whose ministry involved missionary work in Asia, but when Cabrini arrived in Rome she met Bishop Giovanni Scalabrini, who informed her of the many difficulties facing Italian immigrants in the United States. Leo XIII concurred with the bishop and told the young foundress, "Not to the east, but to the west. . . . The institute is still young. It needs resources. Go to the United States. There you will find the means which will enable you to undertake a great field of work."[63] Cabrini followed the pope's advice, and in March 1889 she and her sisters boarded a vessel bound for the United States. Although they purchased second-class tickets, Cabrini was deeply moved by the inadequate quarters assigned to those traveling third-class, "whose accommodations resembled a stable." During the trip across the Atlantic, the woman who would one day be named the patron saint of immigrants regularly visited those in steerage, beginning a tradition that continued on her many trans-Atlantic voyages. Sister Gabriella Linati, who accompanied Cabrini on several ocean crossings, later remembered that "she always made certain she was near the poor emigrants to lend words of comfort, to inspire confidence in God. She was always ready to give them whatever [goods] she had available."[64]

Under Cabrini's leadership, New York's Columbus Hospital was founded in 1892, and in 1905 the community established Columbus Hospital in Chicago. Six years later, Columbus Extension Hospital—later Saint Cabrini Hospital—was opened in Chicago. The hospitals were the property of the community, but Cabrini always informed the local bishop of the sisters' work and asked permission to raise money to support these institutions.[65]

Like other communities of women religious involved in nursing, the MSCs, led by Cabrini, viewed health care from a holistic perspective. Their hospitals had two purposes: to heal the bodies *and* the spirits of their patients. In addition, the sisters recognized the importance of interacting with their patients' families. Two years after it was founded, Columbus Hospital (New York) opened a children's pharmacy, which allowed the sisters to offer advice to mothers trying to create a healthy environment for their families at a time, Cabrini said, "when almost no one knows what family means."[66]

The sisters did not limit their health care outreach to hospitals founded by Mother Cabrini; they also visited Italian immigrants admitted to public hospitals, where they served as interpreters between doctors, nurses, and patients, contacted family members when necessary, and offered solace to those who did not speak English. If circumstances permitted, the sisters also provided spiritual comfort. English-speaking hospital chaplains were not always willing to minister to the immigrants, and immigrants were not always enthusiastic about speaking with an American priest. As they prayed with and comforted the sick, the sisters tried to convince worried patients and their families to meet with the hospital chaplain.[67]

Although women's religious communities involved in nursing established many hospitals—between 1866 and 1926 nearly five hundred hospitals began operating under the auspices of Catholic sisters—these institutions could not always meet the health care needs of communities suffering from epidemics.[68] As they had during the cholera outbreaks of the early decades of the nineteenth century, religious communities continued to stretch beyond traditional hospital care when the spread of contagious diseases threatened the resources of both public and religious hospitals. In 1878, the Sisters of Mercy in Mississippi were asked to nurse yellow fever victims at Vicksburg's Charity Hospital because "not only the wards but even the corridors were full; men were lying on the floor, and the nurses had fled in terror."[69] The sisters complied with the request, despite the fact that five would eventually die from the disease, and were pleased when some of their patients converted to Catholicism.[70] Sister Ignatius Sumner remembered, "The Sisters who were able visited the sick from morning to night; many received the Sacraments and were baptized. . . . [Tea], chicken soup and jelly were constantly dispensed to the sick irrespective of creed while the Sisters almost forgot the requirements of nature themselves."[71] A few months later, two sisters left Vicksburg to care for residents of Yazoo City. Remembering the sisters' willingness to nurse under dificult conditions, a resident of the city wrote: "Day and night they were by our bedsides, trying to comfort us, to gratify our wishes, so far as possible. A mother could not have done more or been more self-sacrificing than were these good Sisters."[72]

The Sisters of Our Lady of Christian Doctrine, a community founded to work in social settlements and teach religious education, assumed the role of practical nurses on New York City's Lower East Side during the 1918 influenza epidemic. Sister Rosaria Perri remembered that the sisters nursed the sick and buried the dead: "The homes we went into were scenes of horror and sadness. The members who were already dead (and at times there would be two, three and more) could not be taken out for burial because of the great number dying in the district and undertakers were inadequate."[73]

During the late nineteenth and early twentieth centuries, some religious communities were founded with the specific mission of ministering to the sick and dying. Convert Rose Hawthorne Lathrop (1851–1926), daughter of the famous New England writer and thinker, Nathaniel Hawthorne, trained at the New York Cancer Hospital after studying nursing with the Grey Nuns of Montreal. She nursed the sick poor in her home–a rented two-room apartment–in order "to be of the poor as well as among them," and in 1899 joined with two other women to form a community now known as the Dominican Sisters of Hawthorne. Hawthorne, whose religious name was Mother Alphonsa, and her community only worked with those poor suffering from incurable diseases.[74]

Sisters were sometimes the only nurses willing to provide care in remote, rural locations. A physician in Missoula, Montana, asked Father Laurence Palladino, the Jesuit superior at St. Ignatius Mission, if the Sisters of Providence—who were already staffing an Indian school in the area— would be willing to bid on a contract to care for the county's poor. Palladino was not interested, but the sisters were and they asked Mother Caron, superior general of the Sisters of Providence in Montreal, to consider establishing a hospital in Missoula. The sisters' facility opened in 1873 and consisted of "two private rooms and a small ward ready and comfortably furnished for the accomodation of patients."[75] Between 1873 and 1890, only three to six members of the community and several paid workers staffed the hospital at any one time. In addition to administrative work, the sisters "attended to orphans, the elderly, and the insane on the premises; visited the sick and elderly in their homes; served meals to the needy; and, starting in 1874, ran the Academy of the Sacred Heart, a boarding school that also taught day students."[76] When scarlet fever struck Missoula, the sisters found themselves nursing sick children in their homes as well as taking care of two children admitted to their hospital, one of whom needed to be watched throughout the night. The community's annals explained that "[w]hen there were only two or three sisters who could sit up on nights [on vigils], their turns came around frequently."[77] In 1878, the Sisters of Charity of Leavenworth, who had begun a health care ministry to miners in Montana, opened a hospital in Deer Lodge, having traveled by rail and stagecoach from Leavenworth, Kansas.[78]

The Sisters of St. Joseph of Carondelet were invited to open a parish school and hospital in Georgetown, Colorado, a mining town with a significant Catholic population, in 1880. The presence of a hospital in the town meant that women involved in other occupations, such as managing a boardinghouse, were no longer expected to care for men to whom they were not related; they could leave that task to the Catholic sisters and their hospital. Three years after opening Georgetown's first hospital, the sisters moved to a larger building, which included a ward and eight private rooms. More than 90 percent of the patients consisted of men between the ages of twenty-one and sixty-five.[79] The sisters left Georgetown in 1917, when the end of the mining boom meant that they were no longer able to support and maintain the hospital.[80]

Several communities were involved in building hospitals for lumberjacks, which were financed by insurance the sisters sold to the men working in logging camps. The money collected provided for the building and maintenance of hospitals, and the lumberjacks were assured of care if and when they required it. Sister Amata, a Benedictine who traveled from camp to camp in the 1880s selling insurance, was fondly known as the "lumberjack sister."[81] Money she raised was used to build and equip hospitals in northern Minnesota.

As they had during the Civil War, American sisters, including four Sioux women religious from South Dakota, tended to those wounded during the Spanish-American War (1898), receiving accolades from physicians with whom they worked. One doctor commented, "The only fault I had to find with the Sisters was that they would not rest, would not take care of their own health. After the long hours which their hospital service demanded, they devoted a portion of the time needed for rest to religious exercises. They arose so early in the morning for this purpose that they deprived themselves of necessary sleep, and by thus lowering their vitality, exposed themselves to disease."[82] Although a few sister-nurses were recruited to nurse the wounded during World War I, the "Spanish-American conflict represents the last general recruitment of sisters as wartime nurses."[83]

By the end of the nineteenth century, women religious had established themselves as important figures in the development of the nation's Catholic health care system. The twentieth century brought new stories of success and challenge as sisters continued to provide quality nursing and medical care to those who depended upon them, Catholic and non-Catholic.

Healing in the Twentieth Century

As the nineteenth-century charity hospital was transformed into the comprehensive health-care facility of the twentieth century, Catholic institutions began to be judged on the "professional standing of their medical staff and the technological sophistication of their diagnostic equipment."[84] As a result, religious communities devoted to nursing became increasingly concerned about the education of their members. About twenty Catholic training schools for nurses were operating by the end of the nineteenth century, but the number of sisters caring for those wounded in the

Spanish-American War meant that some hospitals were faced with a per-sonnel shortage. The ten Sisters of St. Joseph of Carondolet sent to work with wounded troops, for instance, meant that there were not enough trained nurses to staff Kansas City's St. Joseph's Hospital, and hospital ad-ministrators began the process of establishing a nursing school.[85] Other Catholic hospitals followed suit because as the number of patients con-tinued to increase, both women religious and laywomen needed sufficient training to ensure that hospitals were adequately staffed.[86] By 1915 com-munities of women religious were sponsoring approximately 220 nursing schools, many of which were open to laywomen as well as sisters.[87]

The founding of the Catholic Hospital Association (CHA) helped re-ligious communities utilize advances in health care during the twentieth century. Jesuit Charles Moulinier, the Association's first president, believed the CHA would discourage competition among religious congregations administering hospitals and solve the problem of "professional isolation" experienced by nurses and administrators whose rule prohibited them from traveling or associating with non-Catholics. Such limitations often "restricted their access to the information they needed to modernize their hospitals."[88] Two hundred sisters, lay nurses, and doctors from forty-three hospitals attended the first CHA convention, held in Milwaukee in 1915.[89] Although the first president of the organization was a priest, the group was viewed as a "sister's organization"; community regulations may have prevented women religious from assuming leadership positions until the 1960s, but sisters "have been well represented among the officers, the ex-ecutive board, and the leadership of the various committees that planned the [annual] convention" since 1915.[90]

Ministries of healing in the twentieth century encompassed more than nursing and hospital administration. In 1925, Austrian-born physician Anna Dengel (1892–1980), along with one other doctor and two sisters, formed the nucleus of a new religious community, the Society of Catho-lic Medical Missionaries, now called the Medical Mission Sisters. Dengel spent four years among Muslim women in India, and after discovering that their religious leaders did not permit them to be examined by a male physician, concluded that the ministry of women doctors was an essential component of work in the mission field.[91] Michael Curley, Archbishop of Baltimore (1921–1947), formally permitted the establishment of the new community, but Dengel received her most enthusiastic support—moral and monetary—from Philadelphia's Cardinal Dennis Dougherty (1918–1951).[92]

At the time the Medical Mission Sisters were established, the Vatican prohibited women religious from practicing obstetrics or surgery. This restriction, Dengel claimed, hindered the formation of her new community because the sisters planned to work with women who had no other access to medical care. Dougherty was convinced by her argument and lobbied Pope Pius XI (1922–1939) for the ban to be lifted. On February 11, 1936, Propaganda Fide, which is responsible for issues relating to the church in non-Catholic countries, issued *Constans et Sedula*, permitting sisters to perform surgery and obstetrics.[93] This decree not only allowed Dengel and the Medical Mission Sisters to carry out their mission in a more effective manner, it permitted other nursing religious communities to meet state standards in nursing education by providing training for their members in surgical and obstetric nursing.

As nurses and doctors, the Medical Mission Sisters served those in need of health care throughout the world, including the United States. Dengel was especially aware that African Americans often did not receive quality health care, and in *Missions for Samaritans*, published in 1945, she noted the paucity of medical services available to the black community. Only nine Catholic hospitals—the Sisters of Charity of Nazareth were planning to build a tenth in Ensley, Alabama—and fourteen clinics, Dengel explained, currently served African Americans.[94]

Prior to the civil rights movement of the 1960s, southern hospitals and some northern health care facilities, including those administered by women religious, were segregated. The Sisters of the Holy Cross, for instance, nursed black patients admitted to St. Mary's Hospital in Cairo, Illinois, in a separate annex.[95] In 1946 the Dominican Sisters of Springfield, Illinois, purchased an infirmary owned by a group of doctors in Jackson, Mississippi. The sisters reopened Jackson Infirmary as St. Dominic's Hospital, determined to provide quality health care to the area's African American residents. One of the community's first acts upon taking possession of the hospital was moving the beds that had been reserved for blacks from the basement to the first floor. The women also promised to treat members of both races in as equal a manner as possible, and to pay African American employees the same wage as their white coworkers.[96] Not everyone was happy with the sisters' decisions. When St. Dominic's administrator, Sister Rita Rose Monaghan, invited an African American porter to have a seat in the lobby while waiting for her to finish a task, she was informed that people would not respect a woman who "allowed a black man to be seated in her presence."[97] Sister Rita Rose was also discouraged from allowing the sisters to perform any sort of manual labor, including carrying typewriters. "Let the colored do it," she was told.[98]

Although the Dominican Sisters of Springfield tried not to differentiate between their black and white patients and employees, St. Dominic's was in fact a segregated hospital in compliance with the laws of Mississipi. In 1964, several months before the passage of the Civil Rights Act, a group of Jackson's black Catholics petitioned Richard Gerow, Bishop of the Diocese of Natchez-Jackson (1924–1967), concerning the hospital's policy of racial separation. Citing segregated lobbies, eating facilities, rooms, and the nurses' training program "(WHITE ONLY)," the petitioners asked, "Why does the Church permit Catholic Charities (St. Dominic Hospital) to be operated on a strict segregation basis, when it knows it is against the teachings of the Catholic Church?" Sister Rita Rose explained that the lobby was beginning to be desegregated, and a later memo revealed her desire to integrate the professional staff.[99]

Three articles published in the Catholic weekly magazine *Ave Maria* criticized St. Dominic's policy of segregation in 1965, reporting that there were even separate doors for whites and African Americans. Although the hospital's public entrance consisted of a "triple set of double doors," a letter responding to the accusation stated, there were no longer separate entrances; the black door was being used as a service entrance, and all patients were using the same main approach to the lobby. Although it is not clear how patients and visitors acutally used the entrance, all public areas of the hospital were integrated by the end of 1965.[100] The advent of Medicare in that same year required patients to be assigned rooms without regard to "race, color, creed, or national origin. . . . The federal Department of Health, Education, and Welfare recognized St. Dominic's compliance [with federal civil rights laws] on August 9, 1966."[101]

Other communities involved in health care responded to the civil rights movement in ways that reflected both their own convictions and the culture in which they lived and worked. The Sisters of St. Joseph (SSJ), Rochester, New York, first began hospital work in 1908 in Elmira, New York. In 1940, after Edmundite Father Francis Casey asked for sisters willing to work with him in the segregated South, several sisters left New York for Selma, Alabama. The first members of the congregation assigned to the city were designated "missionaries," and even wore a white habit like their sisters stationed in Brazil. They were originally charged with teaching African Americans the importance of conforming to the "norms of Catholicism," and in 1941 founded a school for black children. Three years later, they prepared to begin a nursing ministry when Casey negotiated the purchase of the city's Good Samaritan Hospital, an all-black facility, which had been founded by Baptists in 1922 and administered by a group of local doctors since 1937.[102]

When the Rochester-based community assumed supervisory responsibility for the hospital, they discovered that blacks were treated very differently from patients in white hospitals. There were no laundry facilities, for instance, and the designated number of toilets and bathing areas was insufficient for the number of sick. The only source of heat was open fireplaces—dangerous and inadequate—and a shortage of utensils meant patients often had to eat with their fingers.[103] The sisters immediately began to improve the conditions under which their black patients received care.

In 1950 the Good Samaritan School of Nursing was established under the direction of Sister Louis Bertrand Dixon, SSJ. Alabama's first school for the training of practical nurses, Good Samaritan accepted members of all races, but its student body was primarily non-Catholic and African American. By 1966, 300 students were enrolled in the school, 8 of them men.[104] In that same year, the hospital had 109 beds, 40 of which were designated for the elderly, and 150 employees, "90 percent of whom were black"[105]

Sisters working at the hospital were impacted by the civil rights movement as early as 1960, when a group of employees met with Sister Louis Bertrand over issues related to salaries and working conditions. In addition to requesting a raise in pay and reimbursement for cab fare if assigned an evening shift, the workers asked to be addressed as either Mr., Mrs., or Miss.[106] During this time, the sisters had been trying to demonstrate their support for both civil and voting rights by refusing to shop at grocery stores that did not serve African Americans. They found themselves in the middle of one of the movement's major events when civil rights' marchers were beaten by police as they tried to cross the Edmund Pettis Bridge in Selma on March 7, 1965, a day now known as "Bloody Sunday." Long before the events of that day, Mobile Archbishop Thomas J. Toolen (1927–1969) had announced that any Catholic sister involved in civil rights "would be on the first bus out of Alabama."[107] The sisters, however, were able to participate in the protests in a variety of subtle ways.

Prior to the march, Sister Barbara Lum, SSJ, distributed first aid suplies to some of the demonstrators. She then left the hospital, prayed in the community's chapel, and joined the other sisters at Sunday dinner. As the radio broadcast news of the violence taking place on the Pettus Bridge, the sisters left the convent to tend the wounded arriving at the hospital. Lum recalled, "We hardly even said anything as I remember, we simply went back to the hospital."[108] The community in Selma also participated in the movement by continuing to teach and nurse, while helping northern sympathizers get to and from the airport, and offering hospitality and nursing care to those who stayed with them. "I remember one sister who came from California, maybe, whose feet were blistered at the end of the day," an SSJ nurse recalled. "And she came back and I put medicine on her feet and bandaged her in the emergency room the next day before she went back out on those same poor feet."[109]

The passage of legislation creating Medicare and Medicaid in 1965 stipulated that hospitals requesting payment through these programs had to prove compliance with the 1964 Civil Rights Act, which outlawed racial discrimination. The integration of hospitals in Selma and its surrounding area meant that both doctors and patients now had other options when choosing a health care facility. In 1970, the School of Practical Nursing closed when the state opened a similar school in the city that was integrated. The Sisters of St. Joseph, Rochester, discontinued their work at Good Samaritan in 1971, but several continued to work in clinics dedicated to the black and white rural poor.[110]

The Story Continues

By the mid-twentieth century, Catholic hospitals were "an economically viable, politically powerful player in the American health care system."[111] The women religious who staffed and administered these institutions, however, were not always appreciated by church leaders, and sisters were not always consulted when decisions were made affecting their health care facilities. In 1955, for instance, the Diocese of Brooklyn merged two local hospitals and placed the new institution under the administration of the Sisters of Charity. Before informing the congregation of the proposed changes, diocesan officials received permission from the Hospital Council of Greater New York to implement their plan. The consolidation of hospitals meant that the Sisters of Charity could not provide the number of sisters needed unless they withdrew from Holy Family Hospital, an institution with which they had been connected for forty-six years. The decision prompted one sister to write, "The thought of leaving a work [Holy Family Hospital] into which our Sisters for a long period of years have put so much hard work and self-sacrifice was a cause of painful regret." The community was simply unable to staff both hospitals. "We could continue what we were doing," she explained, "but we could not take on additional obligations."[112]

The passage of Medicare and Medicaid and the development of new technologies, combined with significant changes in communities of women religious, led to transformations in the administration of Catholic hospitals during the 1960s.[113] "Nuns . . . [had been] trying to do modern jobs under medieval systems," and as a result, "Women religious in responsible positions of authority in hospitals and schools lived according to traditions that stipulated such anachronisms as kneeling to ask for permission from a superior." One sister described her situation by noting, "I am responsible for a $3 million budget but I can't drive to a meeting at night without special permission."[114] By the 1970s this situation had changed, and sisters working as health care professionals were involved in continuing education, attending evening and weekend meetings, and participating in national organizations. As women left religious life in increasing numbers, however, their role in health care diminished. Between 1965 and 1975, "the number of sisters involved in health care fell from 13,618 to 8,980."[115] In addition, Catholic hospitals, including those administered by women religious, were often forced to either merge or close as rising health care costs and changes in government policies made it difficult to remain financially viable.

In some instances, women religious found themselves in public disagreement with the nation's bishops over the contentious issue of health care reform. In 2010, Network, an organization of women religious dedicated to lobbying the federal government for "federal policies and legislation that promote economic and social justice,"[116] joined the Catholic Health Association, representing "1,200 Catholic sponsors, systems, facilities, and related organizations," in endorsing a health care bill that was eventually passed by the United States Senate despite opposition by Catholic clerical leaders.[117] In a letter sent to members of Congress, the sisters reminded legislators of their experience as health care professionals, writing: "We have witnessed firsthand the impact of our national health care crisis, particularly its impact on women, children and people who are poor. We see the toll on families who have delayed seeking care due to a lack of health insurance coverage or lack of funds with which to pay high deductibles and co-pays. We have counseled and prayed with men, women and children who have been denied health care coverage by insurance companies." Religious communities involved in ministry to the sick and dying believed supporting health care reform was central to their mission. "In this Lenten time," the letter continued, "we have launched nationwide prayer vigils for health care reform. We are praying for those who curently lack health care. We are praying for the nearly 45,000 who will lose their lives this year if Congress fails to act. . . . For us, this health care reform is a faith mandate for life and dignity of all of our people."[118] Network's Executive Director, Sister Simone Campbell, SSS, a Sister of Social Service, defended the groups's endorsement, stating: "When I read the Gospel, where is Jesus? He's healing the lepers. . . . It's because of his Gospel mandate to do likewise that we stand up for health care reform."[119] Although she did not criticize the American bishops' position on the bill, Campbell speculated that "some people could be motivated by a political loyalty that's outside of caring for the people who live at the margins of health care in society."[120]

The health care ministries of women religious have changed a good deal between 1823, when the Sisters of Charity assumed responsibility for the Baltimore Infirmary, and the twenty-first century. Sisters continued to nurse the sick in a variety of settings, including visiting those confined to their homes, but seldom served as the face of Catholicism for the sick and dying. In 1960, for instance, "virtually every department of every Catholic hospital was run by a nun, from pediatrics to dietary to billing." Only eleven women religious were employed by the nation's largest network of Catholic hospitals in 2011; none worked as administrators.[121] In addition, other ways in which nursing sisters functioned as a manifestation of Catholicism for many people no longer required their services by 2000. Epidemics—fortunately—are no longer common in the United States. The armed services do not require the work of sister-nurses; sick and wounded military men and women receive medical care through a system of government health care installations. In addition, the rise of hospitals, rehabilitation centers, and skilled nursing facilities throughout the United States meant that sisters were no longer called upon to staff hospitals in remote outposts for miners and lumberjacks.

Neither advances in medicine nor complicated regulations regarding insurance and treatment plans deterred women religious from maintaining their committment to providing health care for those in need, including charging patients based on a sliding scale, treating those without health insurance, or refusing to work with physicians who did not accept Medicaid.[122] Their commitment to nursing and health care ministry was one way sisters heeded their call to serve those in need and work with groups that were invisible to many, such as orphans, immigrants, and the poor. In doing so, they provided the church with additional forms of ministry and served as representatives of Catholicism to those who had limited contact with the institutional church.

5

Serving Those in Need

MARION GURNEY, a recent convert to Catholicism, was convinced there was only one way to bring salvation to New York City residents in the early twentieth century. "[T]he city of New York will be saved if it is," Gurney claimed, "not by the distribution of clothing and groceries, nor yet by the study of Browning and the cultivation of fine arts, but by regeneration of individual human lives as one by one they are brought back to the Sacraments of the Catholic Church."[1] Gurney, a graduate of Wellesley College, was an enthusiastic advocate of social settlements, which gave middle- and upper-class Americans the opportunity to live among the poor and working classes while offering them a variety of educational and social services. When Clement Thuente, OP, a Dominican priest who was pastor of St. Catherine of Siena parish on New York's East Side, decided to open a settlement house within the parish boundaries, he turned to Gurney for assistance because she "knew the needs of the neighborhood as well as the priests who had thoroughly surveyed it, understood settlements thoroughly, and generously offered her services to organize a Catholic settlement, no matter how humble and poor."[2]

In the late nineteenth and early twentieth centuries, immigrants from southern and eastern Europe found themselves dealing with a host of practical problems, including finding a place to live, securing employment, and keeping their children safe. In addition to recognizing the many difficulties faced by these newcomers to the United States, Gurney was concerned about their spiritual lives, and contended that Catholic settlement houses could effectively provide religious education and sacramental preparation classes for children and adults. Called to religious life, she had difficulty finding a congregation that combined the active and contemplative ministries in exactly the way she envisioned. After a period of time spent in prayer, meditation, and consultation with her spiritual director, Gurney decided to found a religious community dedicated to the work she believed God was asking her to do.

In 1908, a notice in *Church Progress* announced the formation of the "Institute of Our Lady of Christian Doctrine," which would train women to minister in rural parishes without a resident pastor. The Institute was not designed as either a teaching or nursing community of women religious, and could not "undertake any form of institutional work."[3] Gurney hoped this new community would serve the church by preparing children for First Communion and Confirmation, developing a parish library for volunteer catechists, and publishing material related to the field of religious education. Their ministry, she informed New York Cardinal John Farley (1902–1918), served as an additional way of counteracting Protestant missionaries seeking to draw Catholic immigrants away from their faith.

Gurney and four other women begin living as a religious community on September 8, 1908. Unlike most other young women entering religious life in the early twentieth century, they were not cloistered while they were being formed, or educated, for religious life. Instead, the sisters organized and staffed a Sunday school at Our Lady Help of Christians parish on the Lower East Side. During the three years the women worked at the parish, enrollment in religious education classes increased from 20 to 700 students. When the new community was asked to work at St. Joachim's—also on the Lower East Side—the sisters discovered that it was very difficult to interest the parish's children and their parents in either religious education or sacramental preparation. Gurney's work in settlements enabled her to diagnose the problem: "They [the sisters] were not a part of the neighborhood life, in touch with all its humble joys and sorrows."[4] If they were to succeed in bringing the Word of God to the people of St. Joachim's, they would have to meet the physical and spiritual needs of those they were called to serve. As important as it was to save the souls of those living on New York's Lower East Side, it was also vital to ensure that the poor received food, clothing, job training, and an opportunity to experience social, cultural, and educational activities.

In response to a memorandum detailing the conditions among which the residents of the Lower East Side were living, Farley permitted the women to open the Madonna House Day Nursery on Cherry Street in September 1910. Within six months, the day nursery had grown into Madonna House, a Catholic social settlement dedicated to serving the people of the neighborhood. The sisters and their settlement would provide educational, social, and religious programs for their neighbors until changes in the field of social work combined with a deteriorating physical plant led to the closing of Madonna House in 1960.

The Sisters of Christian Doctrine were founded as a religious community dedicated to a ministry that extended beyond the boundaries of education and health care. Communities of women religious staffed and administered orphanages—some of which remain in existence as residential facilities for troubled children and adolescents to this day—opened social settlements, answered the call to work among African Americans, Native Americans, and Latino/as, and journeyed to other parts of the world to offer material and spiritual sustenance to people who had never seen a Catholic sister. The work accomplished by these women contributed to the development of an extensive network of institutions designed to "take care of the church's own," but it also led them to participate in public debates over the role of charity in uplifting the poor and to enter into discussions that led to the passage of social welfare legislation at the national, state, and local level.[5] Sisters were encouraged in this work, most of which focused on women and children, by clerical leaders worried about Protestant attempts "to rescue poor children from what they considered the baneful and antidemocratic control of the Catholic church and from the poverty and degeneracy of their parents."[6] Women religious whose ministries encompassed these areas often worked outside traditional Catholic schools and hospitals—on Native American reservations and in African American communities, for instance—and as a result, served non-Catholics as well as their coreligionists.

Although their contribution to the development of the Catholic Church in the United States often received less recognition than those of their sisters involved in teaching or nursing, women religious working in these areas visibly manifested the church's concern for the poor and struggling. At times, of course, communities involved in these ministries also administered schools and hospitals, but their call to work outside the traditional areas associated with Catholic sisters meant that they provided another avenue for women called to serve their church and its people.

Sisters and Children

As early as 1729, the Ursulines ministering in New Orleans established an orphanage to care for children left without parents or guardians. During the early nineteenth century, religious communities were often asked to administer orphanages that were originally founded as a response to epidemics. Philadelphia Catholics, for instance, established St. Joseph's

Orphan Asylum to care for children orphaned by an outbreak of yellow fever in 1797. Nine years later they organized the Roman Catholic Society of St. Joseph for the Maintenance and Education of Orphans. In 1814, three Sisters of Charity arrived from Emmitsburg, Maryland, to administer and staff St. Joseph's Orphan Asylum.[7]

When they arrived in Philadelphia, the sisters discovered that conditions at the orphanage were less than ideal. The thirteen residents were essentially unsupervised, boys and girls were sharing the same facilities, and the institution was mired in debt. Local Catholic women organized a Society of Lady Managers charged with raising money to pay the sisters' annual salaries—thirty-six dollars—transportation costs, and shoes. The society also provided $600 a year to support the work of the orphanage, and other local Catholics offered help when they were able. One sister remembered that "Sometimes when we would return from early Mass on a week day we would find a barrel [sic] of flour at our kitchen door; sometimes find the table strewn with produce of the market, and our kind friends would leave us to guess the name of the donor."[8] Within three years of the sisters' arrival at St. Joseph Orphanage, the debt had been paid and the number of resident children had doubled.[9]

Other cities followed Philadelphia's lead and requested sisters from Emmitsburg to care for Catholic orphans. After New York Bishop John Connolly (1814–1825) informed Mother Elizabeth Seton that "many pious and zealous Catholics of this City are most anxious that we should have here for the relief and education of destitute Catholic children, such an Orphan Asylum as exists at Philadelphia," three sisters began working in that city's Catholic orphanage.[10] In 1829, Edward Fenwick, OP, the first bishop of Cincinnati, asked the Mother Superior at Emmitsburg for sisters to settle in the Queen City and establish an orphanage. "Confident that great good may be done in this city by the establishment of a female orphan asylum under your zealous and charitable care," Fenwick wrote, "I have written to . . . your Superior, to beg of him 3 or 4 of your pious Sisters who are well calculated to conduct such an establishment in this place." In October that year, four sisters arrived to establish the eighth mission of the new community. They began caring for five orphans and opened a school for six other children; by 1834, thirty-two children were housed in the orphanage.[11]

At times, women religious began caring for orphans in conjunction with other ministries. When Sisters of Charity in St. Louis received money from John Mullanphy, a wealthy Catholic resident of the city, they designed one building that was able to accommodate both the foundlings—abandoned children—for whom they cared and destitute elderly women in need of a place to live. Housing both groups in one location allowed the sisters to make more efficient use of space, financial resources, and personnel.[12]

Many communities began caring for orphans as a result of administering and staffing Catholic hospitals. Amadeus Rappe, Cleveland's first bishop (1847–1870), personally asked the French Sisters of Charity of St. Augustine (Augustinians) to send sisters to Ohio to open hospitals and orphanages. After leaving France in 1851, the sisters began caring for the sick shortly after arriving in Cleveland and, since many of their patients had no one to care for their children while they were in the hospital, the sisters often assumed responsibility for them. If one or both parents died, they usually became the children's caretakers. Another community working in Cleveland, the Daughters of the Immaculate Heart of Mary, was caring for girls, but an additional facility was needed to accommodate orphaned boys. The Augustinians received permission to build an orphanage specifically for boys, and on May 20, 1853 the first resident, a ten-year-old boy, was admitted to St. Vincent's Orphan Asylum. Fourteen boys resided in the orphanage by the end of the year, and by 1886, two hundred boys and thirty sisters called St. Vincent's home.[13]

The Sisters of Charity of the Incarnate Word began caring for orphaned children shortly after opening Charity Hospital—later St. Mary's Infirmary—in Galveston in 1867. The orphans lived in a part of the hospital, but when smallpox spread throughout the city in 1872, it became clear that they needed a separate building, and St. Mary's Orphanage was built along the coast in 1874. The new orphanage allowed the sisters to expand their work with children because the hospital could only accommodate girls and infant boys.[14]

St. Mary's Orphanage was destroyed in the great storm that struck Galveston in the late summer of 1900. Storm warnings were posted along the Texas coast on September 7, and by noon on the following day, heavy rain and winds reaching thirty miles per hour were impacting the area. By three o'clock that afternoon, the long-distance wire connecting Houston to Galveston snapped, and the city was cut off from the outside world. The sisters and their charges watched the storm worsen while trying to remain sheltered from the high winds and torrential rain. The children were moved into the girls' building, and the sisters led them in prayers and hymns, including "Queen of the Waves," which the first members of the community had brought with them from France. Hoping to protect them from the storm, the children were tied together in groups and attached to a sister, but the plan was not successful. Ten sisters and ninety children died in the storm; three boys managed to survive. Undeterred by the tragedy, the sisters rebuilt St. Mary's within the Galveston city limits, and the orphanage remained in operation until 1965.[15]

When the Sisters of St. Joseph of Carondolet, who had already established a number of Catholic schools and hospitals, assumed responsibility for St. Joseph's Home for Boys in St. Louis, Missouri, it marked the beginning of their ministry to orphans. One year later, they began administering a boys' orphanage in Philadelphia. Because some European communities were prohibited from working with male children, bishops were especially enthusiastic about this congregation's willingness to care for orphan boys.[16] In 1851, four members of the Carondolet community left St. Louis to open a school in St. Paul, Minnesota. They began nursing the sick and caring for orphans during a cholera epidemic that swept through St. Paul, and by 1854 were operating both a hospital and an orphanage.[17] Other communities found themselves caring for orphans almost before they had time to consider whether they had the financial resources or personnel to become involved in such work. The Sisters of Mercy were about to open a mission in Bangor, Maine, in 1865, when a priest accompanied by a young girl knocked on their door, asking "Have you any room in your house for this little girl?" At that moment, the small community began caring for children in need.[18]

Many of the children residing in Catholic child care institutions were not technically orphans, but their parents were unable to care for them. Those admitted to St. Joseph's Orphanage in Cleveland during one month in 1895, for example, included one case where the father had died and the mother had "left." Other situations involved one or both parents abandoning the family, or problems resulting from unemployment or alcoholism.[19] Women religious did not usually attempt to solve the problems that led to parents leaving their children with them, but sisters often tried to teach the children entrusted to their care skills that would enable them to find employment as adults. Girls at Cleveland's St. Mary's Orphanage received sewing lessons, and their handiwork was sold at events designed to raise money to support the children and sisters.[20]

The Sisters of Charity opened the New York Foundling Asylum in New York City in 1869 to care for babies whose mothers were unable to provide for them. The new institution offered one response to the growing concern about the 100 to 150 infants abandoned in the city each month. In addition to the asylum's policy of accepting infants without determining the marital status of the mother, the sisters placed a crib outside the convent, which allowed women to leave their babies without revealing their identity.[21] When the bell near the crib was rung, the sisters knew a child had been brought to them.[22] The large number of babies and young children left at the Foundling Asylum forced the sisters to place them in foster homes, some of which were located in other parts of the country. Believing that the rights of natural parents—especially mothers—were of utmost importance, they did not develop a policy of allowing children to be legally adopted until 1900. By 1919, 23,301 children had been reunited with their parents, and 3,200 had been legally adopted.[23]

In 1897, the Sisters of Charity administering the Foundling Asylum hired George Whitney Swayne as their agent, and charged him with placing orphaned and abandoned children with families living in the western United States. Fifty-seven children between the ages of two and five left New York for the territory of Arizona in the fall and winter of 1904–1905, accompanied by Sisters Anna Michaella Bowen, Ann Corsini Cross, and Francis Liguori Keller, and four lay nurses. Seventeen children were placed with families in either Missouri or Arkansas, and the remaining forty-seven were supposed to be adopted in Arizona. When the train reached its destination in Clifton, Arizona, nineteen children were placed with some of the town's poorest families, many of whom were Mexican. The following morning the rest of the children were taken to live with families in a nearby town.

Issues of race and class complicated the situation almost immediately. The sisters apparently did not consider race when placing children with adoptive families. "The only identification that mattered to them was, were they Catholics?"[24] The Anglo women who stood at the train station to view the new arrivals, however, became upset when they learned that Mexicans were the "prospective parents for the lovely white orphans."[25] Later that evening, "men on horseback" forcibly removed the children in Clifton from their new homes. After spending the night in a hotel lobby, the orphans were placed with some of the town's more prominent white families, many of whom were either non-Catholics or Catholics no longer practicing. Most of the other children returned to New York with the sisters and nurses.[26]

The sisters petitioned for the children removed from their original foster homes to be returned to their custody. In *New York Foundling Hospital v. Gatti*, the Arizona Supreme Court ruled against the Sisters of Charity, and prohibited the children still living with foster parents from being placed under their care. The Court's decision claimed that the foster parents had demonstrated "that more than ordinary ties of affection bind them to these children, and that in no other homes that can be found for them are they so likely to fare as well."[27] When the U.S. Supreme Court refused to reverse the lower court's decision, the hospital discontinued its policy of placing children in the Far West and fired George Whitney Swayne, replacing him with Sister Anna Michaella Bowen, who served as the child placing agent between 1905 and 1917.[28]

Orphanages were a significant part of the network of social services sponsored by the Catholic Church in the United States until the second half of the twentieth century, when social workers, psychologists, and child advocates began to revise their views on the institutionalization of minor children. New theories of child development contended that only children with psychological or emotional problems should live apart from families and guardians. Religious communities that staffed and administered orphanages had to transition to this new model even though many of their staff members were neither trained social workers nor psychologists.[29] By 1962, Cleveland's Catholic child care institutions, including St. Vincent's Orphanage, were a part of the Parmadale System of Family Services. Although a sister headed the facility's Social Service Department, Parmadale employed a number of full-time and part-time social workers to provide services for children classified as emotionally disturbed. As the numbers of women religious began to decrease in the mid-1960s, Parmadale hired laypeople for jobs originally held by the Sisters of Charity of St. Augustine.[30] By 1996, only a few children resided on the site, all with "serious emotional or behavioral problems"; most of those receiving psychiatric and social services offered by Parmadale lived throughout the greater Cleveland area.[31]

Ministering to Women in Need

Women religious caring for children sometimes expanded their work to include the mothers of their young charges. Almost as soon as the Sisters of Charity opened the New York Foundling Hospital, they were confronted by a young woman threatening to commit suicide if she could not remain with her child. Their decision to allow her to stay marked the beginning of a ministry to "poor and unwed mothers."[32] Women opting to remain with their infants were expected to nurse them and one other baby in order to help those who might otherwise "fail to thrive."[33] The women's residence eventually expanded to include a maternity hospital that did not require a woman to be married, "day care for working mothers, and training and placement for unwed mothers in domestic service positions in which they could keep their children."[34]

Other congregations worked with recently arrived female immigrants in America's cities. At the urging of New York Archbishop John Hughes, seven Sisters of Mercy from Dublin arrived in New York City in 1846 to offer "shelter, training in domestic service and sewing, and job placement for women of 'good character only.'"[35] Hughes encouraged and supported the sisters' work because he believed that they could prevent young female immigrants from becoming involved in crime or prostitution. In 1848, for instance, he mandated that a collection be taken in every parish in New York, Brooklyn, and Jersey City to help build the community's proposed House of Mercy.[36]

Unlike communities whose work with women in need constituted only one part of their larger mission, the Sisters of the Good Shepherd, who first arrived in the United States in 1842, "dedicated themselves specifically to the care of wayward, abandoned, and unfortunate women and girls."[37] They were not as well-known as other communities of women religious because they were primarily a cloistered community. Only a few members of the community, known as tourières, or outside sisters, were allowed to leave the convent without permission from either the local bishop or the motherhouse. Outside sisters were responsible for interacting with the community beyond the cloister; their tasks included: shopping, handling mail, and sometimes begging or "collecting."[38] The Good Shepherd Sisters divided the women they worked with into two groups. The first, known as penitents, consisted of delinquent women and girls; the second was composed of the orphans and children cared for by the community. "Delinquents" sent to the House of the Good Shepherd from the courts were free to leave when their time had been served. Some, however, chose to stay, and they were also divided into two groups based on their commitment to the community and its work. Consecrates, who dedicated themselves to Our Lady of Sorrows, did not take vows and lived in a "semireligious" state that permitted them to leave if and when they chose to do so. Magdalenes took solemn vows and "formed a separate contemplative order of nuns" apart from the Sisters of the Good Shepherd; six Magdalenes began living in community in Chicago in 1869.[39]

The mission of Chicago's House of the Good Shepherd, which opened in 1859, did not involve changing a society that drove women to prostitution; rather, the sisters' aims included bandaging "the wounds of the erring sheep," providing women with skills that would allow them to support themselves, and teaching them "with a view to their eternal salvation."[40] During the community's early days in Chicago, most of the women either arrived at the house voluntarily or were brought to the sisters by a local family member or priest. Later, they were sent by either their relatives or the courts. Some were prostitutes; others had been arrested for vagrancy or drunkenness. Still others, however, were there simply because those close to them were concerned that the women were exhibiting signs of "immorality," such as staying out late and associating with people disapproved of by their family.[41]

By 1880, 336 women, including 43 women religious, 22 Magdalenes, and 271 "inmates," were listed as residing at Chicago's House of the Good Shepherd. Parents able to contribute to their daughters' support were asked to do so, but the sisters did not turn away those unable to pay. Women who were eighteen years of age or older when they came to the house usually stayed about two years; most of the younger women remained until they turned eighteen. When they left the home, the women were given all they had brought with them. Those who had been living and working with the sisters for a while were provided with clothes and money. Most returned to family and friends, and the sisters helped former residents enter the workforce. All were welcome to return to the House of the Good Shepherd at any time.[42]

Because they worked with "troubled" women—including those convicted of prostitution—some clerical leaders did not support the work of the Sisters of the Good Shepherd. Although a group of Catholic laywomen, along with the Protestant matron of New York City's workhouse on Blackwell's Island, were willing to raise the funds necessary to bring the Good Shepherd Sisters to New York, they had difficulty convincing Archbishop John Hughes that the community would be a great help to struggling young women. Hughes finally allowed the sisters to open a Magdalene Asylum in 1854, writing in a pastoral letter that, "after years of hesitation on our part, we have at last been almost compelled to give our consent to the founding of a Magdalene Asylum." The Archbishop did not finally approve the project until three years later, however, and only on the condition that laywomen raise the funds needed to establish the convent.[43]

Although the sisters received donations from individuals, their main source of income came from taking in sewing and laundry. Hughes's lack of support meant that this community was less well known among Catholic New Yorkers than other religious congregations approved to receive archdiocesan funds and benefit from special collections. Despite Hughes's unwillingness to fund the sisters' work, the number of facilities to help women in difficulty remained few and far between, and the community was often forced to turn away potential residents for lack of room.[44]

Meeting the Need of Immigrants

The American Catholic Church experienced significant growth in the late nineteenth and early twentieth centuries. In 1880, 6,259,000 Catholics lived in the United States; by 1910 that figure had increased to 16,363,000. This growth resulted in a change in the ethnic composition of American Catholicism. In 1882, for instance, 87 percent of Catholic immigrants came from northern and western Europe; by 1907 80.7 percent were southern and eastern Europeans. Catholics of Irish descent were not always hospitable toward the newcomers, and resented their presence in a church they believed belonged to the Irish. In addition, most of these new arrivals, many of whom settled in the cities of the East or the Midwest, were desperately poor and strained the resources of the institutional church.[45]

As they had during the first half of the nineteenth century, church leaders depended upon women religious to provide necessary services for the recent immigrants. Many religious communities served those living in the slums of congested urban areas, and their work was supplemented by southern and eastern European sisters willing to send members to the United States to work with their own ethnic group.

As we have seen, one way in which women religious attempted to meet the needs of Catholic immigrants was through social settlements. Stanton Coit established New York City's Neighborhood Guild, the first settlement house in the United States, in 1886. Chicago's famous Hull House, founded by Jane Addams, opened in 1889, and within a few years secular and Protestant social settlements were operating in most major cities.[46] Bishops distrusted settlements initially, considering them little more than breeding grounds for socialists. They were slowly persuaded, however, that Catholic settlement houses offered one way to reach the urban poor. Social settlements, "with a prudent administration under Catholic auspices and control," claimed James B. Curry [a New York City priest], "would mean much for the Catholics of the crowded districts of our great cities."[47]

In 1897, Cincinnati Archbishop William Elder (1883–1904) asked the Sisters of Charity of Cincinnati to begin a ministry to the city's Italian immigrants. In response to Elder's request, Sisters Blandina and Justina Segale—who were also biological sisters—opened the Santa Maria Institute, the first Catholic social settlement in the United States. Immigrants themselves, Sisters Blandina and Justina believed the settlement house would help prevent Cincinnati's Italian immigrants from leaving the Catholic Church. "Our work among the Italians," Sister Justina wrote, "has disclosed to us countless ways by which our Catholics lose the faith, Young Men's Christian Unions, Young Women's Christian Associations, 'Settlements,' 'Missions,' Kindergartens, Sewing Classes etc."[48]

The sisters began their ministry by visiting Cincinnati's Italian residents. Going block by block, they encouraged Italian Catholics to attend Mass and receive the sacraments, recited the rosary, and explained Catholic doctrine.[49] They believed personal contact was essential to their mission, and in the early days of their work spent their entire budget on streetcar fare as they traveled to Italian neighborhoods throughout the city.[50] Sisters Blandina and Justina originally intended to establish a school for Italian children, but as they determined the community's needs, they concluded that adults needed a settlement house, "a place to which they [immigrants] could turn in their perplexity, certain of receiving advice, and, if necessary, material aid; where the young people might find recreation, free from dangerous influences; where the children could be instructed in the ways of better living."[51]

With the help of lay Catholics, the Santa Maria Institute offered a variety of services and activities. The first annual report, issued in 1898, informed readers that, in addition to conducting a Sunday school, the settlement provided shelter to women and girls and offered classes in domestic science. By the following year, Santa Maria had established a night school for boys and offered both sewing classes and a Christian Mothers Class, where women were taught how to make clothes for their children. By 1906, the sisters were operating a Fresh Air Farm and had established English and Italian circulating libraries.[52]

Although Elder asked the Sisters of Charity to develop a ministry to Italian immigrants, Sisters Blandina and Justina did not limit their work to any one ethnic group. One day in 1914, for example, a Ruthenian, a Greek, and a Hungarian immigrant came to the settlement seeking assistance, and Sister Justina was called to the community's hospital to translate for an Italian mother who neither spoke nor understood English. Sister Justina reflected on the day's events, writing, "I wonder what nationality will apply before the day is over? But we are all children of the good God who understands all languages, and more so the unspoken language of the heart."[53] A year later, Poles, Mexicans, Germans, Irish, Syrians, Hungarians, Italians, and "Negroes" had received assistance from the Santa Maria Institute.[54]

Sisters who ministered in social settlements hoped to provide for the spiritual needs of those they served while helping them procure material assistance. Many, such as the Segale sisters and Mother Marianne Gurney, offered classes in religious education and sacramental preparation along with programs traditionally found at social settlements, including citizenship classes, instructions in practical skills such as sewing and woodworking, and social activities, such as dances and scout troops. Catholic settlement workers believed that their institutions played a vital role in preventing Catholic immigrants, especially Italians, from deserting their church for one of the many Protestant churches found in American cities.

When the seven Missionary Sisters of the Sacred Heart of Jesus (Cabrini sisters) arrived in New York City in 1887, they immediately began ministering to the Italian immigrants attending St. Joachim's Church on the Lower East Side. The community's annals record that after only three days in the city, the sisters had already "heard of the hatred that there is for the Italians." Cabrini wrote home and requested material to make habits and veils so that the sisters would make a good impression on the Americans they encountered. "Otherwise," she wrote, "they will call us 'guinea-pigs' the way they do the Italians here."[55] The sisters experienced the same difficulties encountered by other Italians as they tried to learn the language and customs of their adopted country. Cabrini reported that although she was slowly beginning to understand English, "at first [she] really believed it was the language of the geese."[56]

Although New York Archbishop Michael Corrigan (1885–1902) assisted the community in several ways, he insisted that their fund-raising efforts be limited to Italian residents of the archdiocese. Most Italian immigrants, however, lived in poverty, and the sisters found it difficult to raise the money needed to support their ministries. Although interaction among communities of women religious varied depending on the situation, congregations often offered assistance and hospitality to sisters new to an area. During this difficult time, Mother Cabrini and her sisters were grateful for those women religious who came to their rescue, allowing them to at least support themselves. The New York Sisters of Charity, for instance, invited the Italian sisters to stay in two of their convents and assisted them during their first weeks in a strange country. Sister Irene Fitzgibbon, who opened the New York Foundling Hospital in 1869, offered monetary donations as well as vases, candelabra, vestments, and altar cloths for their chapel, and twenty-two bedsteads for their new orphanage.[57] This generosity helped the Cabrini sisters to open their first school and orphanage. Their work rapidly expanded beyond New York City to encompass a network of charitable, educational, and medical institutions throughout the United States.

Much of the Felician sisters' work involved teaching, but they also cared for orphans, and established St. Casimir Orphanage, the first Polish institution of its kind in the United States, in LaSalle, Illinois, in 1878. Three years after the orphanage's opening, however, a mother accused the sisters of mistreating the children she had entrusted to the community's care. In response to her charge, the sisters claimed that the five children had been neglected by their mother, and that their "bodies were covered with festering sores" when they arrived at the orphanage. Four of them were nursed back to health during their time at St. Casimir's. The community was eventually acquitted, but withdrew from the orphanage in 1881.[58]

Despite the difficulties they encountered at St. Casimir's, the Felician sisters continued to work with orphans in other parts of the Midwest. In Jackson, Michigan, they began caring for girls at the Guardian Angel Home in 1882; beginning in 1912, orphaned boys were housed at St. Joseph's. Children not adopted by the age of fourteen were placed in private homes as domestic servants, and the sisters visited them once a month until they reached the age of twenty-one. In 1946, the congregation accepted twenty-five Polish children orphaned as a result of World War II. Like other communities whose original purpose involved ministry to a particular ethnic group, the Felician Sisters expanded their outreach as the number of Polish immigrants in need of social services decreased. About thirty girls from Cuba, for instance, were being cared for at the Michigan orphanage in 1962.[59]

The needs of Latino and Latina immigrants, who struggled with both poverty and racism, were often ignored by national and church leaders. Even Mexican American sisters suffered "pain . . . humiliations and difficulties" in their religious communities, were usually assigned menial jobs such as cooking, cleaning, and laundry, and seldom received additional education.[60] In addition, congregations that ministered to the Mexican community in Texas in the early twentieth century expressed prejudicial opinions about those with whom they worked. One newsletter reported that two sisters assigned to the Guadalupe parish school in Houston, Texas, "[went] every morning . . . to *civilize*, catechize and Christianize these Mexicans."[61]

Missionary Sisters of the Sacred Heart of Jesus (Cabrini Sisters) with orphans of the Yellow Fever epidemic, New Orleans, 1905. Courtesy of Cabriniana Room, Holy Spirit Library, Cabrini College, Radnor, Pennsylvania.

Some sisters worked to ease the poverty of Mexican Americans and bring them into the mainstream Catholic Church. In 1915, Sister Mary Benitia Vermeersch, a member of the Congregation of Divine Providence (CDP), was the principal at Houston's Our Lady of Guadalupe School. She routinely provided hot meals for the students and often sent food home to their families.[62] Sister Benitia also organized the parish's young women into the Missionary Catechists of Divine Providence. The catechists, who ranged from sixteen to twenty-two years of age, were trained to teach religion to public school children, but also served as Sister Benitia's "eyes and ears," informing her of the community's needs and concerns.[63]

In the mid-1930s, the congregation's superior general, Mother Philothea Thiry, began to train sisters as professional social workers for San Antonio's Mexican residents. Several years later, in 1939, the community bought two houses in San Antonio; one was used as a convent for the society of catechists and the other became a center offering social services for those in need. One way the sisters attempted to enhance a family's socioeconomic status was to train young women as domestic workers. Mexican Americans were so poor, they believed, that any job was preferable to none. Sister Mary Immaculata Gentemann explained that this program was one way for the sisters "to meet the needs of the time." By the 1950s, however, the community decided that the women they were placing as servants in affluent households were both exploited and underpaid. "[W]hile the value of earning some badly-needed money by the girls had great value," they noted, "the amount was in direct contradiction to a living wage in the light of Christian principles relating to social justice."[64] The Missionary Catechists of Divine Providence also underwent a transformation as the sisters looked for new ways to meet the needs of the Mexican American community. By 1945, the catechists were being formally trained as social workers.[65]

Ministries to African Americans and Native Americans

In the second half of the nineteenth century, some women religious began to reach out to marginalized non-Catholics, including blacks and Native Americans. A lack of available priests made it difficult to provide a visible Catholic presence on Native American reservations, and as a result, women religious were asked by bishops and clergy to help "sustain Indian missions."[66] The need for sisters to work in this area increased during the 1870s, when President Ulysses S. Grant (1869–1877) initiated a program known as the Peace Policy to encourage cooperation between the private Board of Indian Commissioners and the federal government's Office of Indian Affairs as they attempted to assimilate Native Americans into white society. Even though the opinions of Native people were excluded from the process leading up to the implementation of Grant's policy, both agencies expressed their belief that reservation schools combining "religious, linguistic, and vocational training" were the first step in the process of assimilation, and supported the founding of mission schools. Religious denominations were assigned to reservations to prevent competition among Christian churches. Only two reservations, Standing Rock and Devils Lake, were given to the Catholic Church, and agents began to seek out missionaries willing to work with Native Americans.[67]

Several Grey Nuns left Canada in 1874 to live and work among Native Americans living on the Fort Totten Indian reservation in northeastern North Dakota. Major William Forbes, the Indian Agent at the fort, invited the Canadian sisters to work with the Devils Lake Sioux after he failed to persuade women religious in the United States to undertake this work.[68] The school opened by the Grey Nuns in February 1875 taught reading, writing, and arithmetic to both boys and girls. Boys received additional instruction in "manual or industrial vocations," including gardening and caring for stock; girls were trained in domestic arts such as cooking, housekeeping, and sewing. All students lived at the school because it was assumed that assimilation could not take place unless children were separated from their families.[69] By 1880, one hundred students were enrolled at St. Michael's Mission, and the number of sister-teachers had increased from five to eight.

Although the Grey Nuns staffed what was by all accounts a well-run school, they encountered problems during the course of their work on the reservation. First, it was difficult for the sisters to communicate with their students during the first year of the school's existence because they did not speak or understand the Sioux language. Since the community's headquarters were in Montreal, Canada, some of the sisters were not even particularly fluent in English. They solved this problem by hiring a woman to assist with classes and to provide instruction in the Sioux language for the sisters. Second, the community's rule prohibited them from teaching boys over the age of twelve. This meant that a significant portion of young people did not have access to the education offered by the sisters. Agent James McLaughlin, who replaced Forbes at Fort Totten, eventually convinced a group of Benedictine monks to begin a ministry of education to boys on the reservation, allowing the sisters to continue their work with girls and young women. A third problem developed when the sisters learned that they would no longer be able to receive rations distributed by the agency. The community's precarious financial situation simply did not allow them to pay for rations, but McLaughlin helped negotiate a compromise between the Grey Nuns and government officials. The cost was deducted from their pay, but the sisters received a salary increase large enough to cover the amount.[70]

During the 1880s, Grant's Peace Policy and the practice of assigning a particular denomination to a reservation was criticized by several Protestant groups. As a result, the system of schools operated by groups such as the Grey Nuns was replaced by boarding schools administered and operated by the federal government. The community's school was turned over to the Indian Service in 1890, and the sisters functioned as civil service employees while continuing to teach girls and young boys. Although their transition to government workers had very little effect on their day-to-day lives, the sisters' inability to speak English and their Canadian citizenship were both called into question. Those members not fluent in English had to be assigned tasks that did not involve interaction with the school's students. When advised that they should apply for naturalization to avoid being dismissed from their positions, the Canadian sisters immediately sought American citizenship.[71]

Sisters often responded in the affirmative when asked to work in Catholic Indian missions. Sarah Theresa Dunne, who received the religious name of Sister Amadeus after taking vows as an Ursuline in 1864, answered Cleveland's bishop Richard Gilmour's (1872–1891) request for volunteers to travel with Jesuit missionaries to the western United States. Along with four other Ursulines, Sister Amadeus established missions among the Cheyenne in Montana between 1884 and 1889, before beginning work with the Inuit and Aleuts in Alaska in 1908. Given the title "Chief Lady Black Robe," she tried "to be present among the native women and prepare them in a holistic manner, with attention to their education and physical and spiritual development."[72]

Religious congregations sometimes experienced difficulty when attempting to educate Native Americans. In 1880, several Irish Sisters of the Presentation of the Blessed Virgin Mary arrived in the Dakota Territory after a trip that included twelve days spent crossing the ocean, trains to Chicago, Omaha, Sioux City, and Yankton, South Dakota, and a steamboat ride that carried them to their final destination of Wheeler, located between Fort Randall and the Yankton Indian Reservation, ninety miles northwest of the nearest railroad station. The women opened St. Ann's Mission School, and taught their Indian female boarders, who were between the ages of seven and seventeen, reading, writing, and arithmetic, while trying to instill "basic Christian values." Students "earned their keep" by helping with the cooking and laundry. The Vicar Apostolic of the Dakota Territory, Martin Marty, OSB (1879–1889), a Benedictine, originally envisioned a mission school with an enrollment of two hundred children, but since many families had moved further west or to Canada, the school enrolled fewer than twenty children.[73]

The sisters had difficulty communicating with their students, many of whom did not speak English, but at the same time were discouraged from teaching in the Indians' native language. In addition, textbooks and supplies were scarce. Although they managed to survive their first year at St. Ann's, the women's clothing did not protect them from a series of blizzards that swept through the region during the winter of 1880–1881. Winter storms were followed by spring floods, and Marty decided that the sisters should abandon their effort. In the fall of 1882, the community began teaching non-Indian children in Fargo, North Dakota.[74]

In addition to the Grey Nuns and the Sisters of the Presentation, Benedictines from Switzerland and Sisters of St. Francis from Germany journeyed to what was then known as the Dakotas to serve as teachers, working with both white and Native children.[75] Although several Indian women had entered the Benedictines, Father Francis Craft, a diocesan priest from Nebraska assigned to the Standing Rock Reservation, was concerned that communities ministering to Native Americans were not doing enough to foster vocations. Envisioning a religious order made up entirely of Native Americans, in 1891 he brought Sister Mary Catherine, OSB—the former Josephine Crowfeather—and five postulants from the Benedictine convent at Yankton, South Dakota, to St. Edward's School, located on the Fort Berthold Indian Reservation in North Dakota. Two years later, he formally named the group the Congregation of American Sisters.[76]

Craft's plan to establish a school never materialized because he was unable to secure government funding, but he simply changed the work of the new congregation from teaching to nursing. By 1896, eleven sisters were living together in community and working at the hospital Craft founded on the reservation. Unable to convince both government and church leaders of the importance of such a community, the women received little financial support. When detractors leveled charges of sexual impropriety against the sisters and government employees, most of the women returned to their camps. The congregation served as sister-nurses during the Spanish-American War, and in 1899 Craft and four sisters opened an orphanage in Cuba. By the end of that year, one sister had died and two had left Cuba for the United States. Craft and the remaining sister also returned home, and nothing more was done to build a religious community comprised entirely of Native American women.[77]

Katharine Drexel (1858–1955) and the Sisters of the Blessed Sacrament (formerly known as the Sisters of the Blessed Sacrament for Indians and Colored People) are perhaps the best-known women religious involved in a ministry to African Americans and Native Americans. In 1889, Omaha Bishop James O'Connor (1885–1891) encouraged Drexel to found a community dedicated to the work she believed God was calling her to undertake. "I was never so sure of any vocation," he wrote the young heiress, "not even my own as I am of yours. If you do not establish the order in question, you will allow to pass an opportunity of doing immense service to the Church which may not occur again."[78] O'Connor's letter helped convince

Drexel to form a congregation dedicated to ministering among blacks and Native Americans, and in that same year she entered the novitiate of the Sisters of Mercy in Pittsburgh to begin training for the life of a woman religious. Two years later, in 1891, Katharine Drexel became the first member of the Sisters of the Blessed Sacrament for Indians and Colored People. Along with eleven women who hoped to join the community, she moved into a temporary convent in eastern Pennsylvania while building a more permanent institution. The grounds of the new motherhouse included a school for African Americans, but some of the sisters' neighbors objected to black children living and attending school in the area. When a formal ceremony to lay the cornerstone of the building was planned on July 16, 1891, rumors circulated that critics intended to disrupt the scheduled events, and perhaps even blow up the grandstand, but the day passed without incident.[79]

Drexel used her money to fund schools and missions staffed by her new community, but she also assisted other religious women and men working with Indians and blacks. In 1890, for instance, she came to the aid of two Benedictine sisters working on the White Earth Reservation in Minnesota by helping to build a new three-story school with a capacity for a hundred and fifty children. In addition, she paid tuition and board for needy students, monthly salaries for priests and women religious, and covered the costs of insurance and groceries.[80]

Some Catholics were unhappy with Drexel's decision to use her family's wealth to fund missions to African Americans and Native Americans. Paulist priest Walter Elliott wrote to a friend in 1894, expressing his anger over Drexel's refusal to grant him $500 for a special project. "[S]he said in effect," Elliott wrote, "no poor white trash need apply. Only black and red are the team they [Drexel and her sisters] will back."[81] In general, however, most members of the hierarchy supported her decisions, relieved "that the missions of the 'Indian and the Colored' could be left to Katharine Drexel."[82]

In 1894, Patrick Ryan, Archbishop of Philadelphia, allowed the new community to send sisters to work on missions throughout the United States. Several sisters were immediately assigned to St. Catherine's in Santa Fe, New Mexico, a school that had been built by Mother Katharine. Eight years later, in 1902, sisters began working at St. Michael's School on the Navajo Reservation in Arizona. Mindful that African Americans in northern cities were also in need of women religious willing to educate their children, Drexel sent six members of the community to open a school in

Chicago's St. Monica's parish in 1912. Until the Sisters of the Blessed Sacrament arrived in that city, there had been "no concerted effort to educate black children, the majority of whom were not Catholic." When the women moved into the parish neighborhood on Chicago's South Side, whites still lived there. Within ten years, however, the Sisters of the Blessed Sacrament were among the few white women residing in that section of the city.[83] Schools administered by the congregation, including St. Monica's, were never segregated, but very few white children ever enrolled. Since the sisters' living expenses were paid from Mother Katharine's inheritance, tuition was minimal. By 1925, a thousand students were attending the school, which was staffed by sixteen sisters.[84]

When Katharine Drexel founded the Sisters of the Blessed Sacrament, a few predominantly white communities of women religious were already involved in a ministry to African Americans. The Mill Hill Missioners arrived in the United States from England in 1881. Known as the Franciscan Sisters of Baltimore, they worked closely with the Josephite Fathers, a community of priests and brothers dedicated to serving the African American community, and was the only white community ministering "exclusively in behalf of blacks."[85] Previous attempts to engage white women religious in this work had often ended in failure. Augustin Verot (1858–1876), whose jurisdiction as Bishop of Savannah, Georgia, included Florida, requested French Sisters of St. Joseph to work with former slaves in that state. Within five years of the bishop's death in 1876, the Sisters of St. Joseph of St. Augustine, Florida, were teaching twice as many white as black children.[86]

Because there were already communities such as the Oblate Sisters of Providence and the Sisters of the Holy Family designated for African American women, Mother Katharine decided not to admit black candidates to the Sisters of the Blessed Sacrament. This rule was relaxed in the 1960s, at the same time other religious and societal institutions began ending policies that discriminated against African Americans. At the end of the twentieth century, there were more African American members of the Sisters of the Blessed Sacrament than any other predominantly white religious congregation.[87]

Serving Those in Other Lands

In addition to extending their ministries to include African Americans and Native Americans, women religious began ministering in other countries

during the late nineteenth century, hoping to meet the physical and spiritual needs of those with whom they interacted. In 1879, the Franciscan
Sisters, Allegany, New York, became the first congregation founded in
the United States to send sisters overseas when three of their members
joined a Scottish community of Franciscans working in Jamaica.[88] Ten
years later, at the request of Archbishop Michael Corrigan, five Sisters of
Charity, Mount St. Vincent-on-Hudson, agreed to staff a mission in Nas-
sau, the Bahamas. By the end of their first week, the sisters had opened
two schools—St. Francis Xavier Academy for students able to afford the
tuition and St. Francis School for Colored Children, which was free. Like
many sisters working in the United States, the women often struggled to
make ends meet and to furnish their facilities. Sister Veronica Mary described their working conditions by explaining, "We have nothing to work
with, no place to store any equipment, no plans, but we are happy in the
realization that under such conditions the work will really and truly be
God's and not ours."[89]

Marianne Cope (1838–1918) was serving as major superior of the Franciscan Sisters of Syracuse, New York, when she received a letter from Father Leonard Fouesnel, a missionary priest in Hawaii, explaining that he
was looking for sister-nurses willing to work in Honolulu. The community voted eight to one to send sisters to Fouesnel's mission, and Mother
Marianne herself, along with six others, left for Hawaii in October 1883.[90]
Shortly after their arrival, the sisters began working at Kakaako Hospital,
where those suspected of Hansen's disease, or leprosy, were quarantined.
In April 1884, they were placed in charge of the hospital and asked to set
up a second health care institution on Maui. Their first act after assuming
control of the hospital was a thorough cleaning of the facility, followed by
a beautification program, which included painting patients' residences and
planting trees and flowers. Several years later, they took an additional step
and removed the wall separating the patients' quarters from those of the
sisters. "Redrawing the lines of the leper hospital to include the convent
building signified the Sisters' willingness to identify with the lepers, and
particularly with the least of the lepers, the women."[91]

By the end of the nineteenth century, the United States had become an
international power, and in 1908 the Vatican announced that the country
was no longer considered missionary territory. In 1911, Fathers James A.
Walsh and Thomas Price, hoping to create an American Catholic missionary presence in Asia, established an order of priests and brothers known as
the Catholic Foreign Mission Society of America, or Maryknoll.[92] A year

later, they were joined by several women, including Mary Josephine Rogers (1882–1955), who also expressed an interest in missionary work in that part of the world. Although Walsh's original plan called for the women to cook and clean for the Maryknoll seminarians, Rogers and her colleagues were determined to serve in the mission field. Rome recognized the women as the Foreign Mission Sisters of St. Dominic, or Maryknoll Sisters, in 1920, and they began working among Japanese immigrants in Seattle and Los Angeles. In 1921, several moved to Hong Kong to open a mission.[93]

When the Maryknoll Sisters began working in mainland China in 1922, they cared for orphan girls, who were not valued as much as boys for reasons related to both economic and social status. Sons not only worked for the family and brought in more money than daughters, but they were viewed as a status symbol in Chinese culture.[94] These orphanages saved the lives of countless females whose families might otherwise have left them to die.

Maryknoll missionaries shared with other American sisters a desire to spread the Christian message to China's "teeming millions . . . living in darkness."[95] A mission magazine published in the United States offered a blunt explanation of the message to be conveyed to the Chinese and implicitly noted the link between Catholicism and American civilization. "We [American Catholics] owe it to ourselves as Americans; we owe it to the heathen; we owe it to the Giver of all things. . . . We must become in deed what we are in name, 'the connecting link of the ancient and modern civilization.'"[96] As the sisters cared for abandoned girls and established schools for Chinese children, they supported the philosophy that espoused the importance of converting the Chinese to both the Catholic Church and the western way of life and thought.

The community remained in China after the Japanese invaded the country in 1937. Those working in both Hong Kong and on the mainland found themselves threatened by the Japanese and confined to house arrest. Their sisters stationed in the Philippines, Maryknoll's largest mission after China, managed to survive the Japanese invasion, but by 1944 forty-six were imprisoned in Los Baños internment camp. The sisters shared their section of the camp with Catholic priests and brothers and Protestant missionaries. Conditions at the camp were poor, to say the least, but the sisters did their best to make life bearable for themselves and those around them. They participated in a Christmas celebration, for instance, that included midnight Mass, caroling, and a small tree trimmed with ornaments made from tin cans. Gifts were exchanged: lumps of sugar, mustard greens, and a

coconut shell. "It was the most peaceful, happy Christmas," remembered a
Maryknoll Sister, "and we didn't have one material thing."[97]

When the war ended, and the sisters confined to Los Baños were liber-
ated, they learned that most of their schools and convents in the Philippines and China had been destroyed. The sisters returning to China faced
an especially difficult situation due to the battles between Communists
and Nationalists taking place throughout the country. Because they had
not fled their adopted countries when war broke out, however, Maryknoll
Sisters no longer "carried the stigma of the foreign missionary, who . . .
could always return home to a less austere life. By staying at their posts,
even when the Japanese were at the gates . . . the Maryknollers changed
that perception. A deeper bond was forged between the missioners and
their adopted peoples—the bond of those who together have endured a
calamity and survived."[98] When the Communist forces took control of the
country in 1948, they attempted to force the sisters to ask for permission
to leave the country. The Maryknoll missionaries resisted the government,
but during the early 1950s most of them were expelled from mainland
China.

Changes and Adaptations

As sisters expanded their ministries beyond nursing and teaching, they often became involved in issues not usually associated with Catholic nuns.
Administering orphanages, for instance, meant that they placed children
in foster care, advocated and arranged for adoptions, and negotiated with
state and municipal leaders concerning the care of abandoned and neglected children. Founding settlement houses led sisters to interact with
political leaders, help immigrants work their way through the process leading to citizenship, and develop recreational and social programs that kept
children and young adults safe during long, hot summers. Sisters immigrating to the United States to minister to a particular ethnic group found that
they too had to become Americanized if they were to be a viable part of the
American Catholic Church. Religious communities dedicated to working
with Native Americans and African Americans, along with those called to
spread the Gospel overseas, often initiated ministries that included teaching and nursing, but in a very different environment from those staffing
parish schools and complex health care institutions.

The years following World War II brought significant changes to both the Catholic Church and American society and greatly affected the lives and work of women religious. The ways in which they responded to these changes, in turn, impacted the way in which the vast network of Catholic social service institutions operated. As new government programs, such as Head Start, altered the way services were provided to the needy, social settlements slowly disappeared from the urban landscape, leading the Sisters of Christian Doctrine to close Madonna House in 1960 rather than renovate the deteriorating building.[99] St. Aemilian's Orphanage, established in 1849 by the Sisters of St. Francis of Assisi, Milwaukee, as a response to a cholera epidemic, was transformed into a residential facility dedicated to working with emotionally disturbed and delinquent youth.[100] As fewer immigrants from southern and eastern Europe settled in the United States, communities such as the Felician sisters no longer found it necessary to confine their work to a specific ethnic group. The congregation continued to minister to those living in the former Polish neighborhoods on Milwaukee's South Side, sponsoring the Child Development Center of St. Joseph, a nonprofit, community-based school for preschool and kindergarten age children.

The Sisters of the Blessed Sacrament, along with other communities whose apostolate included ministry to African Americans and Native Americans, adapted their work to meet the needs of the poor and dispossessed in the twenty-first century. Although few sisters remained on the faculty of St. Michael's School, located on Arizona's Navajo Reservation, by the end of the twentieth century, the community was committed to subsidizing the school. The concept of missionary work also changed in the 1960s, and the Maryknoll Sisters' work in Asia and Latin America began to reflect the new dynamics of mission as they developed a deeper awareness of the systemic causes of poverty and oppression.

Other sisters, after reading the "signs of the times," began to advocate for changes in American society. Women religious became involved in campaigns to abolish the death penalty, marched arm in arm with civil rights demonstrators, lobbied for immigration reform, committed civil disobedience at factories where nuclear weapons were built, and supported many other campaigns related to peace and justice.[101]

The changes experienced by women religious in the second half of the twentieth century did not mean that they abandoned their call to serve those in need, but they did so in ways that met the needs of Americans living in the late twentieth and early twenty-first centuries. Before examining these changes and the response of women religious, it is important to give some attention to those nuns who did not enter into ministries of teaching, nursing, or social service. The ministry of contemplative nuns is one of prayer for the world and its people, and although they are less well known than other women religious and are rarely seen in public, their ministry is equally important to the work of the Catholic Church.

6

Praying for the World

"MOST PEOPLE ARE thrilled to have someone write about them," claims freelance journalist and writer Kristen Ohlson in her 2003 book *Stalking the Divine*. "A few refuse," she acknowledges, "knowing how often journalists botch their characterizations of people either through spite or just because it's so hard to get the details right. In either case, people tend to think it's a big deal."[1] Ohlson's experiences did not prepare her for what happened when she developed a plan to write about the Poor Clares and St. Paul's Shrine in Cleveland, Ohio. After attending Christmas Mass at St. Paul's, she found herself wondering about these cloistered contemplative nuns, and hoped her proposed project would "construct a framework for trying to make sense of [the nuns'] faith and, perhaps, learn to build some kind of faith of my own."[2]

Ohlson wrote to the Poor Clares informing them of her intention, and asked to interview members of the community. She was surprised when six weeks passed without a response, and decided to approach them as they greeted people from behind their grate after a Sunday Mass. Standing in front of Mother Mary James, the superior, Ohlson introduced herself as the "one who wrote the letter."[3] The superior politely nodded, "but seemed unconcerned about [Ohlson's] request." "We've had so many things to do," she explained. "We haven't had time to think much about it yet."[4] Surprised by Mother Mary James's response, Ohlson concluded that her "proposal was so far on the periphery of their world that they could hardly see it."[5]

The experience of convincing the Poor Clares to talk with her helped Ohlson understand a good deal about the community that had come to fascinate her. Mother Mary James and the Cleveland Poor Clares, she learned, were committed to a ministry of prayer. "They pray *all* the time," she was told. "They pray all day and all night. They pray for the city and its people. They take requests from people. They take requests from people who call in or write to them—they'll pray for this one's sick child or that one's aging parent."[6] The nuns did not bemoan living in the heart of Cleveland, but embraced the city. A visiting sister, worried that the community lived in a struggling neighborhood, once suggested to the superior that the Poor Clares consider moving to more comfortable quarters in a safer area. The nuns refused, informing the sister that they often took the time to pray for the city from the monastery roof, "noting the twinkle of each distant light and the wavering lines of streets that radiated from downtown into the darkness beyond." They did not want to leave the city because "[t]hey were afraid they wouldn't be able to watch over it in the same way if they moved."[7]

Ohlson's experiences help confirm two common views held by many Americans related to the lives and ministries of contemplative women religious in the United States. First, Catholics as well as non-Catholics are intrigued by women who leave the world for a cloistered religious community in the twenty-first century, and wonder if "ordinary moments have greater meaning because of their [the nuns'] faith? Was their faith more powerful because it was compressed between the walls of their monastery? How had they converted from ordinary women to these hidden brides of Christ?"[8]

Second, people tend to be curious about what exactly takes place inside a cloistered monastery, and share Ohlson's surprise when they learn that the nuns lead busy and productive lives that, although revolving around a schedule of prayer and meditation, include both work and shared responsibilities for maintaining community life. Their ultimate vocation, however, is prayer, which, Mother Mary James explained to Ohlson, is "a calling to live our lives for prayer. It's God's grace."[9] When Ohlson asked the superior why she had chosen the Poor Clares, the response was clear. "It was the perpetual adoration. It's Jesus, really Jesus right there. We're going to be doing that for all eternity, adoring God. When you do this, it's like your heaven begins on earth."[10]

According to a 2007 ABC News report, only about 1,400 women religious in the United States are members of a contemplative community.[11] Since those who are familiar with sisters and nuns have usually become acquainted with them through an experience in either educational or health care institutions, nuns—the technical term for those who remain cloistered—remain a mystery to many, including Catholics. What leads a young woman, many ask, to leave the world they have known and enter a monastery where they will separate themselves from society? Why does someone choose a ministry of prayer, rather than an active apostolate of teaching, nursing, or social work? Women called to this life believe the cloister—with its silence—offers an atmosphere conducive to contemplation and prayer. A life of prayer not only allows nuns to give their undivided attention to God, but to ask for God's intercession in the struggles of the world's people. Although virtually invisible, these nuns are not unaware of the world around them. "Cloister enables a particular form of Christian witness"; members of these communities get their information from the world, and then contemplate the "deeper mystery embedded in it."[12] Contemplative congregations have full access to all that the modern world has to offer; many monasteries even developed websites so that those interested in the contemplative life can gather information to help them decide if they indeed have a vocation that is centered on prayer.

Contemplatives Come to the United States

The four Carmelite nuns who arrived in Port Tobacco, Maryland, in 1790 were members of a community whose roots go back to a group of pious men and their decision to live as solitary contemplatives in the Latin Kingdom of Jerusalem in the early thirteenth century. Moving to Europe in 1238, these Carmelites eventually developed a rule that was approved by Pope Innocent IV (1195–1254) allowing them to live together in urban areas, and to enjoy the privileges granted to other members of the clergy.[13] During the thirteenth and fourteenth centuries, individual women attempted to emulate the lifestyle developed by their male counterparts. Some lived alone near a church or monastery; others lived in community, wearing a habit and following some sort of rule. The women had no apostolate, but simply "led quiet Christian lives."[14]

Carmelite convents were established in Florence, Italy, and Gueldre, Holland, in 1452. In that same year, Pope Nicholas V (1447–1455) issued the papal bull, *Cum nulla*, permitting a second order of Carmelites; priests constituted the first order, nuns the second. Although each convent was autonomous, the local provincial of the first order—a priest—served as the women's superior.[15] By the fourteenth century, all European nuns were expected to be cloistered, "to live in houses where no one came in and no one went out."[16] Not all nuns, however, lived the cloistered lifestyle dictated by their church. *La Encarnación*, the monastery which St. Teresa of Avila (1515–1582), the Spanish mystic, entered in 1535, was "as large and busy as a modern hotel."[17] The women living in *La Encarnación* did not observe enclosure and were free to leave the grounds. In addition, the monastery was structured according to class; poorer women lived in dormitories, while women from wealthy families enjoyed private apartments where they lived with servants and other relatives.

Teresa was uncomfortable with the way her monastery had evolved, and in the 1560s began a reform of the Carmelites. Believing monasteries should be small and simple, she mandated that they should not be dependent upon wealthy supporters, should contain a maximum of thirteen members, and should maintain strict enclosure. Visitors were to be few and far between, and the nuns were expected to spend their days in silence so that they could concentrate on prayer and meditation.[18]

The Carmelites in Port Tobacco lived according to the reforms promulgated by Teresa of Avila, but adapted their rule to the situation they found in the United States. Although it was expected that the high walls surrounding the monastery would effectively prevent cloistered nuns from interacting with the world, for instance, it was difficult to build such a structure in late-eighteenth-century America. The Maryland monastery originally consisted of eight one-story buildings, including a kitchen, priest's house, infirmary, and chapel. Either logs or weatherboards were used to construct the buildings, and all the rooms, with the exception of those in the infirmary, were unplastered. In keeping with their vow of poverty, the only fire was in the kitchen, and the nuns filled a small iron pot with coals to keep their cells warm in cold weather.[19] Despite Teresa's concern that the Carmelites not receive monetary support from wealthy patrons, the Port Tobacco community had no choice but to rely on financial assistance from several wealthy Europeans anxious to develop communities of women religious in the United States.

Mother Clare Joseph Dickenson (1755–1830), who arrived in Maryland with the first group of Carmelites, became the second prioress, or superior, of the small community, serving in that position until her death in 1830. In addition to administering the business and financial affairs of the monastery, Mother Clare Joseph watched over the sisters' spiritual lives. In 1814, for example, she reminded them "to watch more & more narrowly every motion of your heart in order to banish from it, everything that is not pleasing to your Spouse [Jesus], & and to make it a pleasing residence for the Sacred Heart."[20] She went on to list ways in which members of the community could maintain "the first fervor of spirit," including "poverty perfectly observed," respect for each other, "humility and mortifications," observing the rule and constitution of the community, as little conversation as possible with outsiders, and a desire to save souls and reach perfection.[21] The lifestyle and spirituality of the Carmelites as expressed by

Mother Clare Joseph Dickenson attracted young women who believed they were called to a contemplative religious community. The congregation's numbers increased to the point where it was able to send five sisters to St. Louis to open a second foundation in 1863.[22]

Establishing Contemplative Life in the United States: Poor Clares and Benedictines

It was difficult for contemplative nuns to establish monasteries in the United States. Women religious committed to this type of lifestyle did not want to support themselves by teaching or nursing, and as a result, as we have seen, were not always welcomed by bishops in need of sisters willing to build and maintain the American Catholic Church. Communities such as the Visitandines operated educational institutions, but did not leave their enclosure, which consisted of the convent and school. In 1826 Edward Fenwick, OP, Bishop of Cincinnati, invited two Poor Clares, Sisters Frances Vindevoghel and Victoria de Scille, both from Bruges, Belgium, to open a boarding school in the Queen City. Although the nuns were members of a cloistered congregation, Fenwick dispensed them from parts of their rule so that the nuns were able to teach.[23] The nuns complied with Fenwick's request, but later moved the school to Pittsburgh, where they began to attract young women interested in joining their community. Following disputes over property and the place of enclosure within community life, Sister Frances and those who agreed with her moved to Detroit and opened a school; she later opened a second school in Green Bay, Wisconsin. Sister Victoria, along with five nuns and three externs—sisters who serve as liaisons with the outside community—returned to Bruges in 1839.[24]

Almost fifty years later, in 1875, Italian Poor Clare Sisters Maddelena (1834–1905) and Constance (1836–1902) Bentivoglio—who were also biological sisters—found themselves stranded in New York City when a plan to establish a foundation in Belle Prairie, Minnesota, failed to materialize. Believing they had no other options, the nuns asked New York Archbishop John McCloskey (1864–1885) for permission to remain in the city. The answer was "no," Sister Maddelena reported. "The Cardinal told us, kindly yet firmly, that he could not admit us into his diocese, as he did not consider our Institute to be in keeping with the spirit of the age, and still less in accordance with the trend of the mind of the American people."[25]

McCloskey, according to Sister Maddelena, was not interested in "mendicant orders 'that do not assist the neighbor.'" "If we should open a school," she explained, "oh, then, yes to be sure we might remain, but the time has not yet come for God to give to the Heads of the Church, the light to be able to understand the great value of the Contemplative Orders."[26]

The nuns were taken aback by McCloskey's refusal, because they believed Pope Pius IX (1846–1878) had specifically directed them to bring the Poor Clares to the United States. The Italian Poor Clares community with which the women were affiliated was forced to vacate its San Lorenzo Monastery in Rome when it was taken over by the Italian government in 1870, and the pope hoped that religious missionaries would help develop enthusiasm for Catholicism in the United States. "You, my dear daughters," the pontiff told them, "must be to the people of your new home an example by your detachment from all earthly things. This will be to them a silent preaching, which together with your prayers and your communion with God, will obtain for many souls the grace to understand that true happiness is not found in material temporal things."[27]

At the suggestion of New York priest Edward McGlynn, who believed the nuns would serve as a positive role model for adult Catholics, the Poor Clares then asked Archbishop John Purcell of Cincinnati (1833–1883) to allow them to establish a monastery within his diocese. Because he was facing severe financial difficulties, Purcell was unable to accept them. Philadelphia Archbishop James Wood (1860–1883) initially granted permission for a monastery in Philadelphia, but later changed his mind, claiming they were unsuited to the Catholic Church in that city.[28] The Poor Clares were finally invited to New Orleans by Archbishop Napoléon-Joseph Perché (1870–1883), who wrote Sister Maddalena that "The good Archbishop of Philadelphia was, no doubt, obliged to take into consideration public opinion which, in this country, does not appreciate contemplative life or understand the efficacy of prayer."[29] The nuns were placed under the jurisdiction of German Franciscan Father Gregory Janknecht, OFM, who visited the nuns in New Orleans in 1877 as part of an American tour of Franciscan communities. According to Janknecht, the house in which the Poor Clares were living was too small and expensive to maintain, and the lack of a regular chaplain meant that the nuns had to leave the enclosure to attend Mass and receive Communion at a nearby parish. When Perché refused to provide a chaplain for the community, Janknecht would not allow them to stay in New Orleans, and asked Bishop Richard Gilmour of Cleveland to accept them into his diocese.[30]

Sisters Maddalena and Constance, along with two postulants, arrived in Cleveland on August 9, 1877. By the end of the year they were joined by a group of German Poor Clares, who had moved to Holland in the 1870s when a series of policies aimed at reducing the church's influence, known as the *Kulturkampf*, were enacted, After a nineteen-day ocean voyage, the nuns arrived in Hoboken, New Jersey, where they were met by two Franciscan Sisters of the Poor. The Poor Clares stayed overnight with the Franciscans and left for Cleveland by train the following day. Sister Maddalena, who had been appointed abbess, or superior, by Janknecht, along with Sister Constance and the community's postulants, met them at the train station.[31]

Sister Margaret Mary Wickern, an extern sister, was thirty-four years old when she arrived in the United States. Since her role as an extern was to serve as the liaison between the nuns and the world outside the enclosure, Sister Margaret Mary was responsible for procuring food for the community. Her job was complicated by the fact that she did not speak English and often had to beg for food. Since she was unfamiliar with the city, she was sometimes lost and was forced to stand in the street calling, "Bread, Bread," hoping someone would step forward and help with both directions and material assistance. Her efforts were supplemented by Cleveland's community of the Sisters of the Good Shepherd, who were willing to share what they had with the Poor Clares.[32]

Mother Maddelena left Cleveland in 1878, taking Sister Constance and a group of novices with her. The group eventually established a monastery in Omaha, Nebraska. Gilmour, who believed the superior should have consulted him before leaving the city, expressed concern that the community was proving unable to adapt to the American way of life. "There is no place in the American Church," he stated, "for drones and non-workers as are the Poor Clares. They get and give not—consumers and un-producers. They have no place in the American Church in Civil life."[33] The Poor Clares remaining in Cleveland moved to a larger convent in 1881. Six years later, they began Perpetual Adoration in the monastery; each nun was assigned to spend a portion of her day or night praying before the Eucharist. In 1933, the community's chaplain, Father Louis Johantges, organized a Perpetual Adoration Guild whose members shared in adoration of the Eucharist with the Poor Clares. By 1941, 390 men and boys and 1,153 girls and women were enrolled in the guild. Members spent from one hour a month to one hour a day before the Eucharistic presence.[34]

Like other contemplative communities, the Cleveland Poor Clares were interested in and aware of significant world and national events. During

World War II, for instance, they prepared packages containing flour, dried beans, rice, sugar, powdered milk, raisins, and rolled oats for those suffering from hunger in Europe. They also collected clothing that was sent to orphanages and European relatives, and twenty-seven nuns and nine externs were certified as air raid wardens.[35] Neighbors from the area surrounding the monastery, as well as those from farther away, began to turn to the Poor Clares for help with prayer intentions, and the nuns were asked to pray for everything from "the needs of the Holy Father and the Universal Church to good weather for the St. Patrick's Day parade."[36]

In 1950, the nuns were invited to establish a new foundation, known as a daughter-house, in Campina Grande, Brazil. The story of their journey to Latin America is reminiscent of women religious traveling to the western United States during the nineteenth century. Arriving in Brazil at eleven o'clock in the evening, Sisters Mary Patricia Hernon and Mary Gabriel Schraff soon realized that the priests they were supposed to meet had been delayed. After explaining their dilemma to airport personnel, a young American man offered to take them to the mission where they were to spend the night. They drove down a dark road, and the nuns waited in the car while their guide went to tell the priests they had arrived. Mother Patricia remembered that they "thought of our lovely, peaceful chapel back in Cleveland where at the moment two sisters were now keeping vigil before the Blessed Sacrament exposed on the throne, and where we ourselves could have been safe and secure! . . . Then the thought came, 'why did we ever leave Cleveland?'" Answering her own question, Mother Patricia continued, "Well, just because we wanted to do our little part toward providing one more wonderful, beautiful peaceful convent of Poor Clares like the one we had in Cleveland, where our dear Eucharistic Lord would be enthroned day and night and where other souls would lovingly keep vigil."[37]

The next leg of their journey required them to travel to Recife. When their plane landed in that city around 8 p.m., a fellow passenger offered the nuns a ride to their destination. They finally arrived at the convent, only to discover that no one there spoke English, and the Americans did not speak Portuguese. Mother Patricia solved the problem by taking out a dictionary, "not a pocket edition but a real large one!" After speaking with several people, they finally determined that the local bishop had arranged a car to transport them to Campina Grande the following morning. As the two nuns neared their destination, they asked to be let off at the bishop's house, but were told that he did not have a permanent residence in the town. "In reply to our question as to where the Bishop was (all this in our American

Portuguese, of course!), we were quietly told that he was traveling in the 'interior' (which means out in the country someplace), and [it was not known] when he would return, perhaps after a few weeks!"[38]

When the nuns finally arrived in Campina Grande, they were left at the wrong convent. The sisters living there promptly hailed a taxi and sent the Poor Clares to the Colegio de Immaculda Conceicao, where they received "a hearty and sincere welcome." It had been arranged for the Americans to stay at the Colegio until they were able to move into the monastery being built for them. When the local bishop visited, he expressed his concern over the difficulty of building a community with only two nuns, and asked that five other Poor Clares from Cleveland join their sisters in Campina Grande. Sisters Mary Louise Gauchat, Mary Cecilia Knoblauch, Mary Agnella Klausman, along with extern Sisters Mary Clara Frost and Mary Helen Girten, arrived on September 30, 1950, and the seven nuns began to function as a community.[39]

The nuns moved into their monastery on December 31, 1950. After preaching a sermon in which he explained the Poor Clares' vow of enclosure, life of contemplation, and practice of Perpetual Adoration, the bishop "placed the monstrance on the altar throne and gave us the wonderful privilege of having the Blessed Sacrament exposed all day long—every day—just for the seven of us as the people were not permitted to enter the enclosure. The tabernacle had a glass door, and I had permission to draw the curtain aside for exposition during the midnight Office. . . . [W]e had Mass every morning and Benediction every evening."[40]

Although the apostolate of the Cleveland Poor Clares is very different from that of sisters involved in ministries of education, health care, and social services, their experiences as they opened new foundations both in the United States and beyond its borders resonate with those of active women religious. Accounts of the nuns' adventures as they traveled to their monastery in Campina Grande echo stories detailing journeys to rural areas that often involved travel by boat, stagecoach, horseback, train, and wagon. Like their twentieth-century counterparts in Brazil, nineteenth-century women religious often arrived at their assigned locale only to discover that accommodations were primitive, to say the least. These commonalities related to the establishment of new foundations—schools, hospitals, or enclosed monasteries—serve as reminders that the histories of active and contemplative women religious are not as different as they might appear at first glance.

Other communities developed temporary ministries in education when they arrived in the United States, but returned to the contemplative lifestyle as soon as it was feasible. Benedictine nuns trace their origins to some of the first recorded organized women religious in history. Tradition claims that Benedict's sister, Scholastica (480–547), who was later, like him, canonized as a saint, served as the head of a monastery. Very little is known about these early women religious, but by the end of the fifteenth century almost every European community of women religious followed one of three rules: Benedictine, Augustinian (used by Dominicans), or Franciscan. The first Benedictines, a group of active—not contemplative—sisters arrived in the United States in 1852 in St. Mary's, Pennsylvania, to teach the children of German immigrants.[41]

In 1874, the Benedictine Sisters of Perpetual Adoration arrived in the United States to open a monastery in Missouri. The community was founded in 1857, when Sisters Vincentia Gretener and Gertrude Leupi began to fulfill their dream of living a religious life that was focused around the adoration of the Blessed Sacrament. They were invited to the United States by Benedictine monk Frowin Conrad, who warned the nuns that life in the United States was very different from that in Europe.[42] "The clothing they bring," he wrote, "must be light for summer, but very warm for winter. They should also bring forks and knives, as well as sewing and embroidery needles. Here everything costs so much and often the simplest things cannot be procured."[43]

Like the Poor Clares, contemplative Benedictines experienced tension between the priorities of their lifestyle and the need for women religious dedicated to teaching and nursing. Despite their commitment to Perpetual Adoration of the Eucharist, the nuns were expected to teach and administer a school, cook and keep house for the local Catholic priest, serve as a choir, take up the collection at Mass, and care for the pastor's horse and chickens.[44] When the nuns arrived in Missouri, they took stock of the people they met and discovered that they liked their neighbors very much, writing that "If you were to meet them you would admire their friendliness, kindness and courtesy."[45]

The Benedictines supported themselves by teaching school and administering an orphanage, but by the 1920s their lives were primarily governed by a ministry of prayer and Perpetual Adoration. According to their first constitution, the sisters were to "consider as their first and primary occupation the perpetual adoration which has been established for the purpose of rendering constant worship and adoration to the eucharistic God." At this time, the community began adhering to a strict rule of enclosure. The nuns no longer left the monastery to visit family members, even for reasons related to death or serious illness. In addition, members of the congregation did not work outside the monastery's grounds. "Consequently, they are not to teach in parochial or public schools; they shall not engage in hospital work or any other occupation which necessitates their absence from the monastery of perpetual adoration."[46]

Living as cloistered nuns did not prevent the Missouri Benedictines from taking an active interest in national events. When women received the right to vote in 1920, for instance, an informed friend of the community was brought in to make sure the sisters understood the issues being decided. About seventy left the cloister to participate in the electoral process; the nuns were quite aware that the Ku Klux Klan was gaining in popularity in the 1920s, and they wanted to be sure that no member of that organization was elected to office. In 1928, the nuns voted in the first national election that included a Catholic candidate for the presidency, New York Governor Alfred E. Smith.[47]

Shoots and Branches

As their numbers increased, contemplative communities began to establish new monasteries to accommodate their members. In 1911, three nuns left the Carmelite community in Baltimore to open a convent in Davenport, Iowa; it was later moved to Bettendorf, and then to Eldridge. Shortly after its opening, Emma Seelbach (1881–1936), a native of Kentucky, entered the community and was given the name Sister Theresa of the Trinity. When the Carmelites in Iowa decided to open a daughter-house at an undetermined location, the prioress chose Sister Theresa to play a key role in the process, hoping she would assist in establishing a monastery in Louisville, Kentucky. The new foundation finally opened in New Albany, Indiana, in 1922, and as the community outgrew its original quarters, Sister Theresa planned a move to Indianapolis. In October 1932, Bishop Joseph Chartrand (1870–1933) celebrated the first Mass at the newly completed Indianapolis monastery. "Intoning the solemn rites of the church, he consecrated the 'Carmel of the Resurrection' and then locked the small community in behind a polished enclosure door." The five nuns, three of whom entered the new community in Indiana, were now "dead" to the world, dedicating their lives to solitary prayer and community life.[48]

Before Chartrand consecrated the Carmel of the Resurrection, the monastery was open to the public. Since no visitors were allowed to enter once the nuns were enclosed, many people took advantage of the opportunity to see the inside of a cloister. Indiana Governor Harry G. Leslie, William Lowe Bryan, president of Indiana University, and the president of the Indiana Board of Agriculture, O. L. Reddish, received a private tour, and the next day priests and women religious were invited to visit the monastery. The approximately 50,000 people who toured the monastery and grounds during the two days it was open to the general public were obviously curious about what might be found behind convent walls.[49] Although some of the visitors undoubtedly expected to find that the inside of a convent was somehow "different" from other institutional residences, they were not especially concerned about any negative impact the nuns might have on the surrounding neighborhood. Unlike the mob that burned the Charlestown convent to the ground in 1834, the residents of Indianapolis and its environs showed no hostility toward the congregation.

The new community suffered two difficult setbacks during the first few years that the nuns lived in the monastery. Mother Theresa Seelbach died in 1936, and a year later Sister Hilda Ammann, who had come with her from Iowa, suffered a nervous breakdown. By January 1938, the community consisted solely of three young Carmelites: Sisters Miriam, age 31; Anne, who was 32 years old; and Agnes, age 29. At the time of Mother Theresa's death, a new wing was being added to the monastery; it was completed under the direction of the three young nuns.[50] In addition to their administrative responsibilities, the women followed the rule developed by Teresa of Avila, abstaining from meat, sleeping little, working hard, and fasting—eating only one meal a day—for several months during the course of a year.[51]

The death of Mother Theresa meant that the three remaining nuns, as the next generation of congregational leaders, needed more education in the ways of the community. Since the Carmel of the Resurrection was a daughter-house of the Iowa monastery, Mother Aloysius and Sister Emmanuel came from Bettenforf to assist the nuns as they learned the intricacies of Carmelite life. Under the tutelage of the more experienced women, they learned the "complicated ceremonials necessary for the proper recitation of the Divine Office."[52] In addition, they spent two hours each day in private prayer, read material designed to enhance their spiritual lives, recited the Divine Office according to schedule, and participated in community life. When Mother Aloysius returned to Iowa, she left behind dedicated women willing and able to live as cloistered women religious according to Carmelite principles.[53] The knowledge gained from the Bettendorf nuns allowed the Indianapolis Carmelites to teach others the rule of Teresa of Avila as they began new foundations in Terre Haute, Indiana (1947), and Reno, Nevada (1953).[54]

Tuscon Bishop Daniel Gercke (1923–1960) invited the Benedictine Sisters of Perpetual Adoration to establish a foundation in his diocese in 1936. The nuns founded the Benedictine Sanctuary of Perpetual Adoration of Christ the King in temporary quarters, and five years later moved to a permanent location. During the move, the community demonstrated its devotion to the Eucharist as "the most Blessed Sacrament was brought processionally from the little temporary chapel, by auto, over a five mile route."[55]

The Poor Clares also established daughter-houses as their numbers increased during the first half of the twentieth century. By 1920, they had opened communities in Bordentown and Trenton, New Jersey, and Philadelphia. Monasteries in other areas, including Chicago (1893), Rockford, Illinois (1916), Aptos, California (1921), and Newport News, Virginia (1971), offered contemplative women a chance to expand their communities throughout the United States. The Chicago, Aptos, and Newport News monasteries later established daughter-houses of their own.[56] Bishops, however, remained reluctant to allow contemplative convents within their dioceses if they did not think the community had the ability to support itself. In 1956, Mother Mary Stella, abbess of the Poor Clare monastery in Evansville, Indiana, asked Cincinnati Bishop Karl Alter (1950–1969) for permission to send sisters to live and pray in that city. Alter refused, informing Mother Mary Stella that there was already a contemplative community residing in Cincinnati, and it was "hard pressed for the help needed." A Poor Clare convent was finally opened in the diocese in 1992.[57]

Establishing Contemplative Communities in the Twentieth Century: "The Pink Sisters"

Contemplative orders of women religious continued to spread throughout the United States during the twentieth century. In 1915, nine Holy Spirit Adoration Sisters, commonly known as the Pink Sisters because of the color of their habit, left Steyl, Holland, for Philadelphia. On their first morning in the city, they attended Mass and visited various churches and religious institutions before Archbishop Edmund Prendergast (1911–1918) closed the cloister. Sister Baptista, one of the nine, was impressed with the way the nuns were welcomed, writing home to Steyl that "[t]he Americans are very obliging and kind towards us. Several convents have offered us their services. The way they recognize and esteem our vocation is really touching."[58]

Like other contemplative congregations, the Pink Sisters were eager to establish daughter-houses throughout the United States. In 1921, Mrs. Theresa Kulage, a wealthy widow residing in St. Louis, asked Archbishop John J. Glennon (1903–1946) to allow the community to send nuns to that city; she herself pledged to support the venture. Glennon hesitated because three other contemplative communities had already asked to open monasteries in St. Louis, but Kulage persisted, and in 1927 the cornerstone for Mt. Grace was laid. In a letter to the superior of the Philadelphia convent, Glennon explained the reason for reversing his decision. "I doubted whether a congregation with strict enclosure and without a significant source of income could maintain a house in this city. . . . Now I have recently met Mrs. Kulage again and she repeated her generous offer. Then again the many recommendations I have received from Philadelphia have persuaded me to set aside any misgivings I had about the matter."[59] Writing to Mother M. Michael, the superior at Steyl, Kulage claimed that her "only desire [in financing the convent in St. Louis] was to establish a home for God, a place where he is undisturbed and where he is constantly being adored."[60]

The close ties between convents led the Pink Sisters in the United States to assist their sisters living in Europe and Asia during World War II. European nuns received coffee, tea, rice, custard powder, jelly, noodles, soap, toothbrushes, and stockings from the Pink Sisters in the United States. Those living in the Philippines also benefitted from the nuns' generosity, writing that "[t]he good Sisters in America sent us useful things and so from 15 August we could wear our pink habit again."[61]

Bishop Louis Reicher (1947–1971) of Austin, Texas, invited the congregation to his diocese in 1953. After Sisters Salvatora and Fidelis traveled to Texas to meet with the bishop, they decided the area was a suitable spot for a third foundation. Austin, according to Sister Salvatora, was a city "where all the people live in detached houses. There are no trams because all the people have their own private cars. The population is financially well off but spiritually poor and the bishop earnestly hopes that he will be able to enrich these people through our prayers and sacrifices."[62] Financial constraints, however, prevented the Pink Sisters from opening their Austin convent until 1958. The nuns remained in that city until trouble with the building's foundation forced them to look for alternate quarters; in 1971, the community relocated to Corpus Christi.[63]

Contemplative Life in the Modern World

Religious life underwent a major transformation during the second half of the twentieth century, and although contemplative communities did not change as dramatically as those involved in teaching, nursing, or social work, they also responded to events taking place in both the Catholic Church and the larger society. Responding to the 1950 apostolic constitution *Sponsa Christi*, in which Pius XII (1939–1958) recommended forming federations of monasteries in order to consolidate personnel and resources, nuns who had previously interacted only with members of their own community began to explore cooperating with other groups. The Cleveland Poor Clares, for instance, initiated discussions concerning a federation of those Poor Clare communities that associated themselves with the fifteenth-century French reformer St. Colette of Corbie (Colettines). Benefits offered to monastery-members of the federation included assistance to those in need of money or personnel, promotion of vocations, and arranging for the transfer of a nun to another community.[64] In 1969, the Association of Contemplative Sisters (ACS) was founded to enable members of these communities to work together to promote a better understanding of this form of religious life.

A number of communities adapted their lifestyle and prayer schedule to respond to changes they were experiencing in the second half of the twentieth century. As early as 1959, the Pink Sisters in Philadelphia reported that they were feeling the impact of events taking place outside their walls. The deterioration of the neighborhood was keeping visitors away, and as a result the nuns curtailed some of their devotional activities traditionally open to the public. Friends and benefactors had died or moved away, and the congregation sought new sources of support.[65] Although the Pink Sisters remained cloistered, courses in biblical exegesis, moral theology, and liturgy were offered at the monastery, and two nuns attended a course on group dynamics and shared their knowledge with the community. In addition, they received permission to play volleyball, badminton, and basketball. Nine members of the community were allowed to leave the convent to see Pope John Paul II (1978–2004) when he visited Philadelphia in 1979.

The Carmelites in Indianapolis also experimented with change in the 1960s. Grilles and grates that separated the nuns from their visitors were removed during this decade, and nuns began to leave the monastery for doctor and dentist appointments, meetings, and to vote for candidates for public office.[66] In 1964, the community began to recite the Divine Office

A Poor Clare in prayer before the Eucharist. Courtesy of the Poor Clare Monastery, Langhorne, Penn.

in English, rather than Latin, and that same year they gathered around the television to watch Pope Paul VI (1963–1978)—the first pontiff to visit the United States—address the United Nations. Other changes allowed those desiring to live within the cloister as hermits to do so, at least on a limited basis. A "hermit day" in July 1965 permitted those interested to spend the day in solitude after attending Mass as a community.[67]

Contemplative nuns serve the world and its people through prayer and meditation, but admit it has not always been easy. When Kristen Ohlson told Poor Clare Sister Thomas that she did not understand prayer, she received an unexpected response. "'Well, who does?' she [Sister Thomas] answered quickly. 'Prayer is a mystery. . . . God leads us. . . . Sometimes God draws you deeper, and sometimes he just wants you to remain in his presence and not reflect on anything.'" Ohlsen asked if Sister Thomas always felt God's presence during prayer. "Sometimes there is the dark night of the spirit when it seems that prayer is impossible. . . . We contemplatives have to live by faith,' she continued, 'and it's sometimes very hard." When questioned as to how one persevered during those times when it seemed as if God was not present, Sister Thomas reminded Ohlsen that "he does not leave us without the strength to carry on in our religious life and in our prayers. We go on but it's difficult, and God permits this."[68]

Congregations of contemplative nuns may capture the imagination of some Americans, but it is difficult to document the ways in which they have either contributed to the growth of the Catholic Church in the United States or impacted the larger society. Catholicism recognizes the importance of both individual and group prayer as important ways of communicating with God, and although everyone is encouraged to make time for spiritual activity during the course of a day, very few make it the focus of their life and work. The Cleveland Poor Clares and other contemplative congregations have maintained a strenuous work schedule that is tailored to accommodate their main focus on prayer and adoration because that is the way they have chosen to serve the church and the world. Although it is not a life dedicated to teaching, education, or social service, the nuns praying for the church and its people are nonetheless following a call to serve.

7

Redefining Sisterhood

ETHEL MARIAN DANFORTH earned a graduate degree in journalism and worked as a reporter for the *Pittsburgh Press* before entering the Maryknoll Sisters in 1933, receiving the name Sister Maria del Rey. Mother Mary Columba Tarpey, Maryknoll's Mother General from 1947 until 1958, appreciated Sister Maria del Rey's talents, and assigned her to tasks that resulted in the engineering of "a series of stunning publicity coups, including a flattering story [about Maryknoll] in *Time* magazine."[1] Thanks to Sister Maria del Rey's efforts, Mother Columba was chosen to represent women religious on the cover of *Time*. Additional feature stories in *Look* and *Cosmopolitan* led to *Bernie Becomes a Nun*, a book authored by Sister Maria del Rey. Published in 1956, the book is essentially the story of a young woman's entry into a religious community devoted to work in the foreign mission field. The main character, Bernadette Lynch, entered Maryknoll in 1949, when she was nineteen years old.[2]

The opening chapter of *Bernie Becomes a Nun*, "You Make Up Your Mind," suggested that young women pray and seek advice before deciding to enter religious life. "Go to someone," Sister Maria del Rey advised. "[A] priest, preferably. Speak to him in Confession; say exactly what is on your mind and how you feel about it. He knows many religious orders and can help you choose the one best suited to you. Or, talk to a Sister. Ask what she thinks of your chances to fit into the life."[3] Potential candidates should tell their parents, but not their friends—at least not right away—because it was "a solemn question between [a woman] and God." Once the decision was made, young women were sometimes given a shower, which followed the same format used for brides and expectant mothers. At this event, a candidate's family and friends had a chance to say good-bye while presenting her with practical gifts that could be used in her new life. The book offered suggestions for useful gifts, including black gloves, a small penknife, and a pen and pencil set (black).[4]

Interested readers learned what is was like to live as a postulant or novice in the 1950s. Postulants usually received their habits when they became novices, and in some communities a woman wore a wedding gown on reception day "to offer herself as a symbolic Spouse of Christ, reemerging... in the habit of the order."[5] During this ceremony, the presider conferred a name on the sister to symbolize her new identity as a woman religious. Although the two-year novitiate was sometimes compared to college, formation for religious life in the mid-twentieth century was much more regimented than the undergraduate experience.[6] The purpose of the novitiate was to teach candidates how to pray and live as women religious; future sisters took classes that explained the vows of poverty, chastity, and obedience, studied the community's constitutions, and received instruction in Christian Doctrine and Scripture. Perhaps the hardest lessons learned by novices in all congregations involved living in community and dealing with homesickness. When Mother Mary Joseph Rogers, Maryknoll's founder and first Mother General, spoke with young sisters, she encouraged them to cry, explaining that they would experience times of loneliness throughout their lives.[7]

In addition to learning how to live as women religious, postulants and novices were expected to immerse themselves in the history and mission of their community. "Above all," Sister Maria del Rey explained, "during the novitiate you take on, so to speak, the spirit of your congregation." Like families, she continued, religious communities are known for certain characteristics. The Franciscans, for instance, "love poverty," and the Dominicans have a reputation for being learned. "Maryknollers are a cheerful tribe, willing to take on any job in the blithe expectation that they can do it with the help of God; they believe in the motto—both of themselves and their benefactors—'The Lord loveth a cheerful giver.'"[8]

Bernadette "Bernie" Lynch—who received the name Sister Alma Bernadette—entered a religious congregation deeply involved in foreign missionary work, but her first assignment was teaching school in New York City's Chinatown. "It was so different now," Sister Bernadette explained, "I had a purpose in life; I was to love God and to bring others to love Him."[9] After a year in lower Manhattan, she was transferred to a Maryknoll mission in Bolivia. *Bernie Becomes a Nun* concluded with the young sister planning to spend at least ten years in Latin America.[10]

The thousands of young women entering religious life during the post–World War II years often hailed from strong, stable Catholic families, and parents usually supported their daughter's vocation. Families felt honored to have a daughter or son choose religious life, believing that God was bestowing a special blessing on them. The great majority of candidates were high school graduates, and some had either finished a year or two of college or spent some time in the workforce before committing themselves to a religious community. In addition, they had often developed connections with professed women religious who encouraged their vocations, answered all their questions, and responded to their concerns.[11] "For Catholic girls taught by nuns in the twenties, thirties, and forties, going to convent school and then entering the novitiate as a teenager was a plan as reasonable and almost as common as a young woman's pursuit of a business degree is today."[12]

Women entering a religious community in the 1950s were introduced to a lifestyle that had changed very little over the past several centuries. Sisters usually publicly confessed their failings, for instance, at a community meeting known as the Chapter of Faults that was held every week. Even though their offenses were often minor, such as opening a window without permission, the chapter was taken seriously by most congregations.[13] At the same time that sisters were living in convents with rules that were centuries old, however, the world around them was rapidly changing. The postwar baby boom, coupled with the beginning of a Catholic exodus to the suburbs, was placing increasing pressure on religious congregations to "meet the ever increasing demands of pastors for teachers while being sure beginning teachers were qualified."[14] During the 1950s, communities of women religious began to examine ways both to meet the growing need for sisters and to adapt their lifestyles to the rapidly changing world of the mid-twentieth century. By the 1970s, religious life had changed dramatically, and the convent that Sisters Maria del Rey and Bernadette Lynch entered in the early 1950s was almost unrecognizable to a young woman looking for a suitable religious congregation in the 1980s.

The Sister Formation Movement

Less than three months after he was elected pope in 1958, John XXIII (1958–1963) announced his intention to call a council that would engage the church with the modern world. The Second Vatican Council helped facilitate the response of communities of women religious to the twentieth century, but it was really one in a series of events leading to changes that transformed the lives and work of American sisters. In 1929, Pius XI, in *The Christian Education of Youth*, encouraged women religious to receive the education necessary for staffing the growing parochial school system. Pius

XII echoed his predecessor's concerns and informed those gathered at an international meeting of women and men religious that sisters needed to be educated appropriately for any ministry in which they were involved. The pontiff later went a step further, and called for the "spiritual renewal [of religious communities] in light of the foundress, and adaptation [of the community] to contemporary needs."[15]

About twenty years after Pius XI called for women religious to receive a proper education, the National Catholic Education Association (NCEA) began to examine the need for professional education and training of Catholic teachers. Because the NCEA was the only organization "open to American women religious and their needs," sisters recognized that they had to cooperate with this organization if they wanted to receive the education endorsed by both Pius XI and Pius XII.[16] At the NCEA convention held in 1949, Sister Madeleva Wolff, CSC, president of St. Mary's College in South Bend, Indiana, and founder of the college's graduate school of sacred theology, presented a paper that proved to be a "turning point" in the movement to promote the educational and spiritual formation of American women religious. "The Education of Sister Lucy" focused on a young woman who, because she had chosen to enter religious life, "faced the difficulty of having to teach without a degree, with only partial preparation."[17] Sister Madeleva asked her audience, "[D]oes that mean she does not need to get her degree?" A religious community, she explained, answering her own question, was responsible for ensuring that its members were able to perform their jobs to the best of their ability. In conclusion, she offered an ideal solution: "If all our religious communities begin this year to complete the education of our young sisters before sending them out to teach, practically all of the immediate generation will have their degrees and licenses in two or three years. After that, our teaching communities will have established this pattern of time and study training. They will have the same number of sisters to send out each year, with this incalculable difference, that they will all be adequately prepared."[18]

Sister Madeleva's concern that women religious were entering the classroom without appropriate training was justified. The results of a study conducted by the NCEA in the early 1950s disturbed many American sisters. Between 1940 and 1953, the cost of living had risen 93 percent; sister-teacher salaries increased only 25 percent during the same time period. Women religious teaching in parochial schools received an annual salary of $511.25, but living expenses consumed $489.50 of that amount, leaving a paltry $21.75 contribution to the support of their congregations. Sisters received only one-half of the salary of men religious—Brothers—who were paid about 50 percent less than public school teachers.[19] The low wages offered women religious meant that sisters constituted the vast majority of teachers in parochial schools, and pastors and their parishioners were unwilling to replace them with lay men and women requiring a higher salary. As a result, women religious often found themselves standing in front of a classroom with very little formal training in educational methodology or practice.

Ensuring that sister-teachers did not enter a classroom without the necessary credentials had been a problem faced by religious congregations since the nineteenth century. Young women often came to religious life shortly after completing high school. The first members of the Sinsinawa Dominicans, founded by Samuel Mazzuchelli, OP, in 1847, did not even have high school diplomas. Mazzuchelli held classes for them three evenings a week, teaching history, Christian doctrine, mathematics, natural sciences, Latin, French, Italian, and philosophy. Although the congregation quickly became known for its schools and academies, the Sinsinawa Dominicans struggled to meet the demand for teachers *and* allow their members to complete their undergraduate education.[20]

How, Sister Mary Emil Penet, IHM, asked during a presentation at the 1952 NCEA annual convention, could this situation be allowed to continue? Religious communities were unable to prepare young women for teaching during a six-month postulancy and two-year novitiate. Once they began teaching, most sisters were only able to attend college classes on Saturdays and during the summer, and it was not unusual for a sister to spend between fifteen and twenty years completing her bachelor's degree. Teaching under these circumstances, Sister Mary Emil argued, was unrealistic, and she offered several suggestions to rectify the situation and respond to the concerns voiced by Pius XI and Pius XII. First, communities were to set a ratio of women religious to lay teachers so that more sisters could be sent for full-time undergraduate study. Second, church and educational leaders needed to determine what resources were needed to implement her proposal. Third, Sister Mary Emil advocated the establishment of an organization that would allow religious communities to share information about the role their colleges played in the formation of sisters.[21]

By 1954, the organization proposed by Sister Mary Emil had evolved into the Sister Formation Conference (SFC). Given five years to accomplish its goals, the Conference was placed under the College and University Department of the NCEA. The SFC "inaugurated the beginning of a carefully planned education and formation of women religious for their ministries."[22] Sisters Mary Emil and Ritamary Bradley, CHM (Congregation of the Humility of Mary) met with major superiors and other congregational leaders to prepare them for a series of scheduled conferences on the subject of sister formation.[23] In 1956, fifteen women religious journeyed to Everett, Washington, to help design a curriculum for educating sister-teachers. Known as the Everett curriculum, it reflected the 1950s emphasis on the liberal arts, as well as Catholic social teaching, an awareness of a world that was increasingly shrinking, and an "effective approach towards effecting structural change in society."[24] The planners believed theology and philosophy ought to hold a primary place in the new curriculum, but recognized the difficulty of implementing this goal because women were excluded from Catholic seminaries and graduate schools of theology. Committee member Sister Jean Marie Neuman, SSND (School Sisters of Notre Dame), one of the few Catholic women holding a Ph.D. in theology at the time, suggested following the curriculum of the School of Sacred Theology at St. Mary's, Indiana, "affording the sister-student a genuine experience of theological reasoning, a solid foundation for her spiritual life, and an indispensable preparation for her apostolate."[25]

In a 1964 article in *TIME*, Sister Annette Walters, CSJ, who was appointed executive director of the SFC in 1960, reiterated that the main interest of the Conference was the integration of sisters' spiritual and educational training. The question was: what sort of spiritual training should a twentieth-century woman religious receive? The SFC believed "that nuns should take a wider and more active mission role in the world," so sisters studying sociology at Marillac College in St. Louis, Missouri, for example, spent time observing the court system, "learning how laws operate."[26]

The Conference suggested that religious communities either establish their own colleges or cooperate with congregations already involved in higher education so that sisters could complete their undergraduate degrees in a timely manner. Often referred to as juniorates, these institutions allowed sisters to receive an education appropriate for future teachers, nurses, or social workers while adhering to their community's schedule for spiritual activities. Marillac College, which one commentator referred to as "West Point for Nuns," became a center for sister-education in the United States. Founded by the Daughters of Charity in 1955 to educate members of their own community, sisters from other congregations also enrolled at Marillac without charge. About two-thirds of the students were Daughters of Charity enrolled in a five-year program; their novitiate took place between the second and third years of college. Most other sisters entered during their sophomore year and lived off campus with members of their community and a mistress of novices, enabling them to "maintain the distinctive spirit of their orders."[27] Young sisters attending Marillac were involved in activities that would have been prohibited to them at other colleges and universities, including the newspaper, student government, and theater. An article in the college newspaper described the sister-students as having "the energy of IBM, the perseverance of a mosquito, the curiosity of a psychiatrist, the neatness of a pin, and the speed of a jet as [they go] from one class to another in a single minute."[28]

Sister Annette firmly believed that the education of women religious was of utmost importance to the work of the American Catholic Church in the latter half of the twentieth century. Describing sisters as "first line fighters in the political, social, and cultural struggles of our time," she suggested that they could meet the needs of the twentieth century by becoming involved in new ministries of social justice on both national and international levels.[29] Her philosophy echoed the view of women religious promoted by Belgian Cardinal Leo Suenens (1904–1996) in his widely acclaimed book, *The Nun in the Modern World*. Many sisters read Suenens's book, and resonated with his response to the question, what is a religious? A member of a religious congregation, Suenens claimed, should be "[a] modern woman—not one of the eighteenth or nineteenth century—who has dedicated her life to God for the salvation of the world through the congregation to which she belongs."[30]

The SFC successfully encouraged communities of women religious to educate sisters before sending them to teach in parochial schools. In 1955, for instance, only 16 percent of sister-teachers had completed three years of college before receiving their first assignment; by 1964, 80 percent did not begin teaching until they had finished at least three years of undergraduate education.[31] Despite the positive statistics, a number of church leaders, including some major superiors, questioned the SFC's work. When the Conference of Major Superiors of Women (CMSW) was established in 1956 by Pope Pius XII "as a permanent national conference to facilitate dialogue and cooperation between the superiors of women's congregations in the United States," questions arose almost immediately about the relationship between the two organizations.[32] Tensions developed as the two groups of women religious debated how to share responsibility for the educational and spiritual formation of women religious.[33]

In 1963, the Vatican sent Archbishop Paul Philippe and Reverend Bernard Ransing to investigate the conflict between the SFC and CMSW.

After speaking with Sisters Annette Walters and Ritamary Bradley, the men ruled in favor of the CMSW. The SFC became the Sister Formation *Committee* and was subordinated to the major superiors.[34] By 1964, a new set of by-laws suppressed the original organizational format of the Sister Formation Conference, and the views on training for religious life endorsed by the CMSW began to be implemented. Formation, according to the superiors, was a "spiritual enterprise in which women were to seek perfection through withdrawal from the profane and polluting elements of the world into spheres of religious enclosure in which they devoted themselves to contemplation, prayer, and service to the Church."[35] The Sister Formation Conference, on the other hand, had moved beyond this traditional interpretation and viewed religious life as a "prophetic, public expression of God's transformative love in the world"; it also endorsed the "active character of the religious apostolate."[36]

The CMSW was reconstituted as the Leadership Conference of Women Religious in 1976 and in its new guise endorsed the original initiatives of the Sister Formation Conference.[37] The SFC was renamed the Religious Formation Conference (RFC) in the same year to indicate that it was now involved in the formation of both men and women religious. Despite its struggles with both the institutional church and major superiors of religious congregations, the influence of the SFC on untold numbers of women religious, many of whom were anxious to work in apostolates dedicated to the promotion of social justice, profoundly impacted the role of sisters in church and society throughout the second half of the twentieth century.

Apostolates of Social Justice

The planners of the Second Vatican Council did not offer Catholic women, lay or religious, a role in what quickly became a momentous event in the history of the Catholic Church. Women were neither asked for their opinions nor invited to attend Council sessions until Cardinal Suenens noted that "half of humanity" was unrepresented at Vatican II. As a result, twenty-three women were invited to attend the third and fourth sessions as auditors; they could observe, but not speak.[38] Ten of the invitees were women religious, and one, Sister Mary Luke Tobin, SL (1908–2006), a Sister of Loretto, was an American. Although some bishops welcomed a female presence at the Council sessions, others did not. Archbishop Pericle

Felici, who served as secretary of the Council, sat near the women but did not acknowledge them. When the men socialized and lobbied during breaks, the women were expected to mingle with each other in a coffee station that had been set aside for them.[39]

Vatican II resulted in a number of important church documents, but sisters were especially interested in a proposed statement on religious life. Their supporters asked Italian Cardinal Ildebrando Antoniutti, head of the commission drafting the document, if they could attend the group's meetings. Antoniutti denied their request, suggesting they might "try again at the Fourth Vatican Council."[40] Two Council documents, *Lumen Gentium* (1964) and *Gaudium et Spes* (1965) especially resonated with women religious because they called sisters to work with the poor in cooperation with clergy and laity; no longer placed clergy above the laity; and defined the church as the "people of God."[41] When read in combination with *Perfectae Caritatis* (Perfect Love, 1965), the Decree on the Renewal of Religious Life, women religious believed they were being asked to "return to the original inspiration behind the founding of their communities and infuse that spirit into their contemporary lives and ministries."[42] Most congregations readily endorsed the Council decrees and began to search for ways to better serve the modern world.

The combined forces of the Sister Formation Conference and the Second Vatican Council led some women religious to support the civil rights movement and inspired other sisters to enter into what has been called the "racial apostolate." They had been prepared for this work by SFC workshops that "supported ecumenism and interreligious cooperation," and allowed sisters to interact with non-Catholics, racial and ethnic minorities, and women religious in other countries.[43] The National Catholic Conference for Interracial Justice (NCCIJ), recognizing that sisters could play a valuable role in the struggle for civil rights, created a department designed to channel women religious into this apostolate. School Sister of Notre Dame Margaret Traxler became head of the education department of the NCCIJ in 1964, and helped to implement programs to train women religious for work in urban areas. In 1967, the Educational Services Department of the NCCIJ developed CHOICE (Cooperative Help of Integrated College Education), which placed northern sister-professors in historically southern black colleges, allowing faculty at those schools to spend the summer finishing advanced degrees.[44]

Other women religious advocated for civil rights in their own neighborhoods and institutions. The first Catholic sisters to march in support of racial justice included seven Franciscans, six School Sisters of St. Francis, and one Sister of St. Francis of Mary Immaculate, who protested discrimination as practiced by the Illinois Club for Catholic Women in 1963.[45] Two years later, in June 1965, the Daughters of Charity of St. Vincent de Paul participated in a march protesting policies of segregation in Chicago's school system; they were among the 150 demonstrators arrested. Not all the city's Catholics agreed with the sisters' actions. One detractor referred to them as "[t]hese peacemakers stirring up trouble because they have to follow their conscience—God forbid." Another wrote to the diocesan newspaper expressing frustration with women religious participating in demonstrations and protests: "How dare these so-called religious go back to the class rooms and hypocritically instruct their students in love of God, respect for country! . . . I hesitate to use the word 'sister'—it somehow doesn't appear appropriate for them."[46] Remarks offered by Sister Mary William Sullivan, DC, director of Marillac House, a social settlement, confirmed that the sisters had listened to Popes Pius XI and XII, as well as the decrees of Vatican II. Sister Mary William claimed that she and her sisters had acted as "representatives of the Church and the Daughters of Charity." The community's founder, St. Vincent de Paul, she explained, had told the first members of their congregation to have "no cloister but the streets of the town."[47] She did seem to understand why the sisters' actions might be viewed in a negative light, commenting ruefully, "On every street corner along the line of march is a nice, big policeman who has either a daughter or aunt or cousin who is a nun."[48] Women religious marching for civil rights clearly did not fit the traditional image held by many Catholics.

When Martin Luther King, Jr., asked religious leaders to support civil rights marchers in Selma, Alabama, in March 1965, sisters joined priests, ministers, and rabbis traveling south to express their support of the movement. African American Sister Antona Ebo, a Franciscan Sister of Mary working in St. Louis, Missouri, heard that 600 civil rights marchers had been attacked by police as they marched for voting rights in Selma—a day that became known as "Bloody Sunday"—when she arrived at work the following morning. As a semicloistered woman religious, she had no access to television, radio, or newspapers.[49] During a conversation with coworkers, Sister Antona remarked, "You know, I think if I didn't have this habit on, I would probably be down there with those people." The following evening she received a phone call from Sister Eugene Marie, the local superior, informing Sister Antona that the two had received permission to join a group of St. Louis religious leaders, including two Sisters of Loretto, two Sisters of St. Joseph, and several Adorers of the Blood of Christ, traveling to Selma.[50]

The St. Louis contingent arrived at Selma's Brown's Chapel, a Methodist church, and Sister Antona, dressed in her religious habit, stood out from the crowd. When the women entered the chapel, she remembered, "[I]t was like the parting of the Red Sea. . . . The congregation began to whisper, 'They brought the nuns. They brought the nuns.'" The church's pastor offered Sister Antona a seat in the place of honor, the pastor's chair inside the sanctuary, where "she joyously joined in singing the powerful Negro spirituals."[51] Although she was not prepared to speak, Sister Antona stepped to the podium when introduced by the pastor. "My name is Sister Mary Antona," she began. "I am a Negro, a Catholic nun and I am here to witness to your rights to register to vote. Just yesterday in the City of St. Louis I voted without having to go through what you are going through and on Monday morning, . . . I made a statement that if I had not had this habit on, I would be in your midst. I believe this is God's way of calling my bluff."[52] She received a standing ovation.

At the conclusion of the service in Brown's Chapel, the crowd began marching to the Dallas County courthouse, a few blocks away. The St. Louis sisters took their place at the head of the march, but after walking only about one hundred yards, Wilson Baker, Selma's Director of Public Safety, stopped them and said, "[T]here will be no march today." A minister introduced Mayor Joseph Smitherman to Sister Antona, saying, "[W]e have in our midst one of our only sisters, Sister Mary Antona." When she visited Selma years later, Smitherman, who was still mayor, told her that he had not believed she was a woman religious, but had dressed that way for publicity purposes.[53]

When the sisters returned to St. Louis, they learned that not all the city's residents supported their trip to Selma. When two Sisters of St. Joseph, Sisters Ernest Marie and Thomas Marguerite, appeared on a local radio phone-in show, the number of callers trying to reach the station was so great that they were asked to return. About twenty thusand calls were received at the station that day, and opinion was almost evenly divided on the sisters' participation in a civil rights demonstration. One positive response claimed that "If both the state and the federal government refused to act against an overt moral wrong, it is up to the people to call attention to that wrong." Others expressed the opinion that women religious had no business participating in the civil rights movement. One caller, for instance, had no respect for them, and believed "they should stay in their chapels and churches and do their praying there."[54]

Women religious challenged racism in the institutional church as well as in American society. When Sister Mary Martin de Porres Grey, RSM, a Sister of Mercy, returned from serving as an observer at a meeting of African

Right to left, Sisters John Christine Donnelly (Maryknoll), Madeline Maria Dorsey (Maryknoll), and Eileen Sheey (Sisters of Charity, Leavenworth), in Selma, Alabama, 1965. Courtesy of Maryknoll Mission Archives.

American priests in April 1968, she began to organize an intercongregational gathering of black women religious. Four months later, 155 African American sisters attended the first meeting of what became the National Black Sisters Conference. Representing seventy-five religious communities, the women traveled to Pittsburgh's Carlow College from forty-five American cities and Caribbean and African countries. During the course of the meeting, the sisters "listened to, argued with and affirmed interpretations of black power activists, educators, students, and social workers on the condition of black America."[55] The preamble to the Conference's constitution clearly described its purpose: "Through the power of God, Black religious women, who are in covenant with God to serve His kingdom, do now create an inclusive cooperative organization of Black religious women in the United States of America to confront individual and institutional racism found in society and in the Church, to work unceasingly for the liberation of Black people, and to witness to our unity and mission by being the organ through which we can be with one another in prayer, study, fellowship and cooperative action."[56]

In an effort to educate congregations of women religious, the Conference developed the Institute on Black Sister Formation, a five-day study session designed to introduce leaders of predominantly white communities to "black spiritual, social, cultural, and theological perspectives."[57] Black sisters hoped that the Institute, which was held at least four times between 1971 and 1975, would influence how white women religious viewed blacks, especially black sisters, and help them modify their formation process so that it would benefit African American women seeking entrance into a religious community.[58] The Conference also addressed larger concerns, such as community-controlled schools in the black community. Project DESIGN—Development of Educational Services in the Growing Nation—organized black educators to train teachers and principals, developed curricula, and began programs to increase parental involvement in the educational process.[59]

Changes and Transitions

Women religious responded to the changes taking place in both the Catholic Church and American society during the 1960s in a variety of ways. Some communities, such as the Sisters of Loretto, were involved in the renewal process before Vatican II ended. When the members of that community gathered together at the General Chapter (meeting) in 1964, Sister Mary Luke Tobin announced, "The Sisters of Loretto will go on record as a result of this chapter as supporting the program of Pope Paul VI that the church should seek relevance to the modern world."[60] The community organized a central planning committee and subcommissions to examine four general areas: "theology of religious life, community living, habit, and apostolate."[61] Every aspect of religious life was examined to determine its relevance for sisters engaged with the modern world. Other communities developed similar processes as they responded to the documents of the Second Vatican Council.

The first major "outward" change concerned the clothing traditionally worn by women religious. Although sisters dressed in habits distinctive to their particular congregations, they were all easily recognized as "nuns" by the general public, Catholic and non-Catholic alike. In 1951, Pius XII encouraged women religious to choose clothing that "expresses your interior lack of affectation, simplicity, and religious modesty."[62] The bishops attending the Second Vatican Council seemed to support Pius XII, writing in the Decree on the Appropriate Renewal of Religious Life that "[Religious habits] should meet the requirements of health and be suited to the circumstances of time and place as well as to the services required by those who wear them. *Habits of men and women which do not correspond to these norms are to be changed.*"[63] Statements such as this led women religious to believe that when they adapted their clothing to reflect contemporary life and ministries, they would meet no resistance from church leaders.

Some early modifications in dress responded to the practical needs of women religious working in twentieth-century apostolates. When a Sister of Charity of Convent Station, New Jersey, for instance, died in a car accident because the headpiece that framed her face hindered her ability to see, the community abandoned it.[64] Other groups concluded that the habit "acted as a barrier, placing sisters beyond ordinary life and making their life forbidding and unapproachable," and decided to dress as professional women of the twentieth century in order to be more effective in their ministries.[65]

The Ursulines in Paola, Kansas, were probably the first community to experiment with a modified or simplified habit. The new style of dress did not include the white head binding, known as a guimpe, a wimple (front and shoulder covering), or a floor-length skirt. The two sisters modeling the proposed habit wore a black skirt, white blouse, black weskit or tunic containing the Ursuline insignia, and a white ribbon in their hair. The response was immediate and loud; some approved, but most did not like the "new look." Mother Charles McGrath, OSU, the superior at the time, later reflected that critics viewed changes in wardrobe as representative of all that was wrong with the modern world and the modern church. "[American Catholics]," she later explained, "equated a new dress for religious not only with the habit but with faith, decency, cessation of prayer and sacrifice, the devil and communism, total lack of modesty, hence chastity. Length, style, high heels, nylons, and above all 'a ribbon around the head of an old grey-haired nun' was the height of indecency."[66]

In the end, the Vatican ordered the Ursulines' to cease their experiment with modern dress. The sisters responded by deciding to move more slowly toward a modified habit, but did not stop debating the issue. After a lengthy process that included style shows, correspondence with Rome, and building consensus within the community, the sisters settled on a "black or brown suit—skirt, jacket, blouse—with a short veil." Within ten years, the Ursulines' dress code changed again, and community members were able to choose either a dress from a variety of styles and colors, with or without a veil, or a modified habit. The majority chose not to wear the habit.[67]

The Sisters of Loretto were the first to do away with the habit altogether. During the time Sister Mary Luke Tobin spent as an observer at the Second Vatican Council, she showed Cardinal Antoniutti a picture of a sister dressed in the suit that was replacing the congregation's traditional dress. Sister Mary Luke recalled, "He never looked me straight in the eye. He took the picture, took a pen, and drew the skirt down, the sleeves down, then added a little veil."[68] The community did not follow the cardinal's advice.

The decision of women religious to change the way they had dressed for centuries—whether in modified habits or secular clothing—caused a good deal of consternation both within religious congregations and in the larger society. "No phase of renewal," Sister Mary Bonaventure, OSF, wrote, "has precipitated so much re-examination, appraisal, dialogue and even heated debate as the question of change or adaptation of the religious habit."[69] Both sides agreed those in need were often drawn to women religious because of their distinctive dress, but some people stayed away from them for the same reason. By 1967, the Congregation of the Humility of Mary in Ottumwa, Iowa, were experimenting with different styles of dress. Some altered the traditional habit, while others wore dresses and skirts, sometimes without veils. A member of the community, Sister Jeanne Reidy, CHM, who advocated modern dress for women religious, told the story of a Protestant minister pointing at her during a discussion, saying, "Sister, why must you shout at me that you are a sacred person [by wearing your habit]? It takes me so long to get through to you."[70] Other stories were less dramatic. A young wife and mother told Sister Jeanne that she felt she could converse with her more naturally after seeing her in "ordinary clothes."[71]

A second set of changes involved adapting the rule—which had governed religious communities for centuries—to meet the needs of women involved in active ministries in the contemporary world. Although the particulars of the rule varied from one congregation to another, most women religious were rarely allowed to listen to the radio or watch television. As a result, sisters were often among the last to learn of major news events. One community, for instance, did not hear that the United States had dropped atomic bombs on Hiroshima and Nagasaki until several weeks after the attacks. The Adrian Dominicans were only allowed to watch television to see Bishop Fulton Sheen, the President of the United States, and religious and educational programs. In addition, they were prohibited from exchanging letters with friends, or sitting in the front seat of a car if a man was driving.[72] Most congregations required sisters to ask permission for "virtually every little thing from a pair of shoes to a pen or a dose of aspirin."[73] At times, communities went to great lengths to prevent sisters from interacting with others. Sister Thomas Roach, a Sister of St. Joseph, explained that although members of her congregation, many of whom were involved in health care, attended regional hospital association meetings, they were not allowed to eat lunch with others. Instead, they sat in the limousine hired to drive them to the meeting and "ate the sandwiches we had brought with us, while the driver kept circling the parking lot so he wouldn't block traffic. That was to help us stay away from talking to strangers."[74]

During the 1960s and 1970s, most communities softened these rules of strict enclosure, and sisters began visiting their families, eating in restaurants, and driving cars. As women religious moved away from a world where rules governed every aspect of their lives, they often chafed at being assigned to the traditional "sister occupations" of teaching and nursing; they wanted to make their own decisions regarding where they worked and ministered. Sister Mary Luke Tobin, SL, president of CMSW in 1967, noted that "The Christian today must vitally concern himself with the world of today, it is no longer permitted to avoid it, to ignore it, or merely to tolerate it." Although the world needed those willing to teach and nurse, sisters needed to think about "the ever larger number of Catholics who are not reached by the present commitments of Orders and Congregations."[75]

Changes in the rule of religious communities resulted in some sisters choosing to live outside traditional convents. When three sisters attending graduate school at Milwaukee's Marquette University moved into an apartment in an inner-city neighborhood, a young girl asked them to come and see her mother. When the sisters arrived, they found "a woman not entirely sober [who] told the sisters that she had been deserted and that her fourteen-year-old daughter was being drawn into a dangerous teen-age gang at school."[76] The women arranged for the family to receive financial assistance and found a new school for her daughter. The fact that women religious were willing to assist a family in need did not raise eyebrows, but the young girl could have asked for help at either of the two Catholic convents located in the same neighborhood as the sisters' apartment. Some sisters thought that the neighborhood residents might have viewed women religious living in an apartment as more attuned to the needs of the poor and oppressed than those residing in traditional convents.

As religious communities wrestled with the challenges of the late twentieth century, they began to initiate ministries that moved beyond Catholic schools and hospitals. In 1966, members of the Sisters of Charity of Leavenworth were assigned to secular institutions for the first time. One year later, Sister Mary James Harrington began teaching remedial reading at Emporia State University in Kansas.[77] By the early 1970s some members of the community had moved into more nontraditional ministries such as working with Native Americans on issues of land and participating in an Ecumenical Peace Seminar.[78] In an effort to better serve the poor, other sisters founded new ministries. Along with her teaching responsibilities, Sister Kathryn Flanagan, a Sister of St. Joseph of Springfield, Massachusetts, served as coordinator of a weekly soup kitchen in Pittsfield, Massachusetts, during the late 1980s.[79] Other sisters were called to work with immigrants on the United States' borders, develop programs of prison literacy, and serve as pastoral associates in Catholic parishes.

Religious congregations also began to experiment with different styles of community prayer during the 1960s. Prior to the middle of the twentieth century, the prayer life of women religious was centered on the Divine Office, a set of daily prayers that includes hymns and readings. As communities began to adapt their rule and custom to meet the needs of their members ministering in active apostolates, many of them discovered that the Divine Office did not lead to the building of a strong spiritual community. Some Sisters of Charity of Leavenworth, for instance, hoped for a prayer life that was "based on scripture, practiced in both traditional and new forms, and conducive to community living." They adamantly expressed a desire for prayer, explaining that "no one can stay in religious life and put anything . . . before prayer."[80] Patterns of prayer developed during this era reflected the spiritual needs of women religious in the wake of the Sister Formation Conference and the Second Vatican Council.

Conflicts

Changes approved by communities of women religious during the 1960s caused conflicts between sisters and church leaders. The Sisters of the Immaculate Heart (IHM), founded in 1848 in Spain, arrived in California in 1871. They began teaching at St. Viviana's School in Los Angeles in 1886, and by 1967 staffed or partially staffed fifty-one elementary and eleven secondary schools. The community also administered Los Angeles' Immaculate Heart College.[81] In 1967, in an experiment designed to last several years, the IHMs, under the leadership of Mother Mary Humiliata Caspary (later Anita Caspary), endorsed a series of changes to their rule and life-style, including allowing sisters to choose their own apostolate, reducing maximum class sizes in their schools from forty to thirty-five, and encouraging members of the community to select their style of dress from among several options.[82] Mother Mary Humilitia explained to a reporter that they wanted to be "more open to the world, reaching out into fresh fields, more a part of the world, and more responsible and involved in it."[83] The changes, she continued, were rooted in the mandates of Vatican II asking women religious to heed the "signs of the times."[84]

The community did not notify Los Angeles' Cardinal James McIntyre (1948–1970) of their proposed changes, explaining that they were accountable to the Vatican, not the local bishop.[85] McIntyre was unhappy with the IHM's decisions and asked them to reconsider their planned experiment. He was especially concerned that the archdiocese could be left with an inadequate number of parochial school teachers for the 1968–1969 academic year, because in addition to allowing sisters the freedom to choose their own work, the community planned to withdraw forty-three teachers from their schools and allow them to complete the education needed to receive their teaching credentials.[86] The IHMs had clearly been influenced by the work of the Sister Formation Conference and were willing to implement a number of changes to provide their members with an appropriate education.

In January 1968 the congregation warned that thirty-five schools might close at the end of the current academic year. Archdiocesan officials assured parents that the schools would remain open. Several months later the community learned that the Vatican's Sacred Congregation of Religious had ruled against it, and the sisters were directed to obey the rulings of McIntyre. When a straw vote revealed that many of the women preferred resignation from the community to complying with the church's directives, the sisters decided to appeal directly to Rome, but the Vatican declined to review the case.[87]

A committee consisting of three American bishops and Father Thomas Gallagher recognized the formal internal separation between the two groups of Immaculate Heart sisters on June 6, 1968. About 315 out of 400 sisters organized themselves into a secular or noncanonical community, which means that they did not come under the authority of either the Vatican or American bishops. Anita Caspary, the new community's leader, announced that the women planned to involve themselves in teaching, health care, social service, and the fine arts. They continued to administer

Immaculate Heart College, one high school, a hospital, and a retreat center. The second group of approximately fifty sisters became the California Institute of the Sisters of the Most Holy and Immaculate Heart of Mary.[88]

More than one half of the members of the new group, now called the Immaculate Heart Community, continued to work in education. In 1970, approximately thirty women were teaching in the Los Angeles public schools, and several others taught in a bilingual program administered by the Archdiocese. Seven bishops invited the community to provide teachers for their diocesan schools, and other sisters, including well-known artist Corita Kent, remained on the faculty of Immaculate Heart College.[89] Although many superiors of religious communities backed the sisters in their struggles with McIntyre, the CMSW decided against supporting the IHMs by one vote. In 1995 the Leadership Conference of Women Religious (LCWR), successor to the CMSW, apologized for the decision to remove itself from the controversy.[90] At the beginning of the twenty-first century, the Immaculate Heart Community, which included men and married couples in addition to single women, worked in and supported several diverse ministries in California, including Alverno High School, Citrus Valley Health Partners, and Housing Works, an organization dedicated to assisting families struggling to find permanent housing.[91]

Other communities responded differently from the IHMs when the Vatican or a local bishop disagreed with either the decisions of congregational leaders or proposed changes in lifestyle. The Benedictine sisters at the Mt. St. Angel monastery in Oregon—now Queen of Angels—had to make important choices about their futures when they found themselves under investigation by the Vatican after Mother Gemma Piennett protested Rome's interference in the Sister Formation movement. After conducting a brief examination, the Benedictine priest assigned to the case removed Mother Piennett and the community's entire leadership council, refusing to give a reason for his decision. Although the Benedictines could have responded in a manner similar to the Los Angeles IHMs, the community chose not to contest the ruling. The investigation, however, profoundly impacted the Oregon sisters. Individual members expressed their dissatisfaction with the process in a number of ways. Some sisters left the congregation and others moved away from the monastery to work outside the area.[92]

Even religious communities that were not established until the twentieth century found themselves embroiled in controversies over proposals to modernize their lifestyle. The Glenmary Sisters were founded in 1941 by Father William Howard Bishop "to work for the extension of the Catholic faith and the spiritual advancement of the people in sections of America where there are few or no Catholics by means of Christian education, nursing, and social service."[93] By the 1960s many sisters were ministering in either central Appalachia or urban areas populated by those who moved from rural America in search of work. Their experiences led the community to begin "to transform their mission from being charity-driven to development-oriented, from organizing donation boxes to working for social change."[94] In addition, the sisters' apostolate made it difficult to follow the rules governing women religious prior to the mid-1960s. It was not easy, for example, to abide by their eight o'clock curfew when they needed to attend evening organizing meetings that drew coal miners and their families.[95]

In 1964 several sisters complained to Cincinnati's Archbishop Karl Alter that the community was "interpreting the role of sisters too liberally in the post-Vatican II age."[96] Alter agreed, and issued a number of directives to return the Glenmary Sisters to a more traditional lifestyle, including a ten o'clock bedtime.[97] Like the IHMs and the Oregon Benedictines, the differences among the various factions in the community proved irreconcilable. In this case the women chose one of four options: some stayed in the community, others left religious life; still others left to start a new community; and forty-four formed FOCIS—Federation of Communities in Service—a nonprofit organization dedicated to assisting those living in rural mountain areas.[98]

About 25 percent of religious congregations believed that the changes in the lives of women religious were far too radical and went beyond what was called for by the Second Vatican Council. By 1971, a group of major superiors began to break away from the Conference of Major Superiors of Women and form their own group, Consortium Perfectae Caritatis (CPC).[99] The new organization quickly gained support from church leaders and in 1971 Rome noted its approval and support of CPC. The consortium eventually became the Council of Major Superiors of Women Religious (CMSWR), and along with the LCWR was officially recognized by the Vatican as a legitimate organization composed of congregations of women religious. In 2011 approximately 90 communities were members of the CMSWR, while 292 belonged to the LCWR.[100]

Departures

The statistics concerning the number of women entering religious life between 1948 and 1975 are sobering. Between 1948 and 1957, 34,448 women chose to enter a congregation; that figure dropped to 6,394 between 1966 and 1975, a decrease of 81 percent. At the same time that fewer women were called to religious life, the numbers of sisters leaving began to increase. In 1950, about 381 women religious left their communities; 4,337 sisters left in 1970. Between 1966 and 1981, 31,763 decided that religious life was not for them.[101]

When congregational leaders were asked why they thought women were leaving religious life, they tended to differentiate between those departing before or after making final vows. In 1966 superiors believed that 47 percent of women who left before final vows simply did not have a vocation; that number increased to 65 percent by 1982. The number of women deciding they preferred marriage to religious life rose from 33 percent to 49 percent among those who had not yet taken final vows, but those classified as having a "psychological disturbance" dropped from 41 percent to 8 percent.[102]

The results were somewhat different for those who left after taking final vows. In 1966 superiors responded that only 16 percent were leaving because they did not have a vocation; by 1982 that figure had increased to 33 percent. The major reason for exiting a religious congregation in 1982 was dissatisfaction with community life; this figure increased from 48 percent in 1966 to 61 percent in 1982. The 1966 survey had not included "disenchantment with direction of community," but in 1982 the superiors noted that 33 percent left for that reason.[103] The surveys' administrators claimed the results accurately represented the views of women leaving their community because the respondents personally knew those who had departed.

A 1967 article in *TIME* magazine suggested that many sisters were leaving their communities because religious life was not changing quickly enough for them. One former sister explained the difficulty with her congregation, saying, "There seemed to be such great conservatism and such lack of promise from updating my community that I felt there was no point in waiting for the next fifty years."[104] Several years later, the magazine noted that two of the most prominent advocates for the renewal of religious life, Sisters Jacqueline Grennan and Charles Borromeo (Mary Ellen) Muckinhern, had both left their communities. Sister Jacqueline had married Paul Wexler and was serving as president of New York City's Hunter College.[105] A former Sister of the Holy Cross, Muckinhern was directing the graduate program in theology at St. Xavier College in Chicago. Other women seemed to blend seamlessly into the secular world, finding jobs, marrying, and raising a family.

The ways in which women religious left their communities changed in the years following Vatican II. Prior to the 1960s, a sister simply disappeared. "You'd hear crying in the dormitory the night before and she wouldn't be in class the next day," Sister Mary Jeremy Daigler, RSM, remembered. After the Council, sisters informed the community of their plans to depart in advance. According to Sister Mary Jeremy, "It was healthier. We'd have a farewell party for her; we'd help her get a wardrobe together." Those who stayed still mourned the loss of departed members. "[W]hen she left we didn't know if we'd have any contact with her, so when she did leave, it felt like death."[106]

Political Tensions

When Democratic presidential candidate Walter Mondale chose Representative Geraldine Ferraro (D-NY) as his running mate in 1985, the American Catholic bishops expressed grave concerns about her stance on abortion. In the aftermath of the 1973 Supreme Court decision, *Roe v. Wade*, church leaders began to look closely at political candidates and their stance on abortion. Dissatisfied with the ruling that tied a woman's right to terminate a pregnancy to the trimester of her pregnancy, U.S. bishops entered into a debate over what role religion should play in moral issues, especially abortion. Their collective voice grew louder when Ferraro, a practicing Catholic, who claimed to be personally opposed to abortion but pledged to uphold the law, received the vice presidential nomination.

On October 7, 1984 Catholics for a Free Choice placed an ad defending Ferraro in the *New York Times*. The original draft, entitled "Catholic Statement on Pluralism and Abortion," was written in 1983 by Catholic ethicist Daniel Maguire; his wife, theologian Marjorie Maguire; and Frances Kissling, president of Catholics for a Free Choice. The final copy, "A Diversity of Opinions regarding Abortion Exists among Committed Catholics," signed by twenty-four women religious belonging to fourteen communities, four priests, and sixty-nine lay men and women, immediately received national attention for its claim that American Catholics did not hold a monolithic view on this issue, noting that a survey of Catholics showed that only 11 percent considered themselves against abortion in all circumstances. The signers called for "a candid and respectful discussion on this diversity of opinion within the Church," and took the position that those who disagreed with the church's teachings on this subject should not be penalized.[107]

Cardinal Jean Jerome Hamer of the Vatican Congregation for Religious and Secular Institutes wrote to the presidents of religious communities represented in the ad, and asked them to have the signers retract their endorsement of the prochoice position. Failure to do so, Hamer warned, would lead to possible dismissal from the congregation. By early 1985 all four of the priest signers had followed Hamer's directive and withdrew their endorsement of the statement. The leaders of women's religious communities originally supported their members, believing that to demand a retraction was a step back from the post-Vatican II church that now allowed members of religious congregations to form their own conclusions on contemporary issues. Rome responded by stating that as public members of the church, the signers were "expected to adhere to its teachings in the public arena."[108]

Fourteen of the women religious who signed the document had "clarified" their position by the end of 1986; the Vatican closed their cases.[109] Eight of the ten remaining sisters later resolved their situation after meeting with Archbishop Vincenzo Fagiolo of the Congregation for Religious and Secular Institutes. Sisters of Notre Dame de Namur Barbara Ferraro and Patricia Hussey, who learned of the ad from Dominican Sister Marjorie Tuite, did not retract their signatures, however, and the ensuing battle with both their congregation and the Vatican signaled that, despite major changes that had occurred in religious life during the second half of the twentieth century, American sisters were not expected to contradict church teachings in a public venue.

Barbara Ferraro entered the Sisters of Notre Dame on August 1, 1962. Patricia Hussey joined the community five years later in 1967.[110] The novitiate, as well as the congregation itself, underwent a transformation during those five years, and Hussey's experience as a novice was very different from that of Ferraro. Even the vows each woman spoke were different. Hussey remembered, "The cut-and-dried formula that Barbara had recited five years earlier had been changed. I wrote my own vow, trying to express exactly how I wanted to live my life."[111] The two women did not meet until they were graduate students in Chicago, but quickly became friends. They eventually decided that they "wanted to live a simple life-style, within our means as workers, and to identify and work with working-class people," and "be involved with others engaged in creating more just situations."[112]

The Charleston (West Virginia) Interdenominational Council on Social Concerns hired the women to administer Covenant House, an ecumenical project that included "direct service with 'people who fall between the cracks' and efforts to look at long-term changes required to improve those people's lives."[113] When the doors of Covenant House opened on September 28, 1981, Ferraro and Hussey hoped at least one person would arrive to take advantage of the help they were offering. By 1990, they were seeing about ninety people a day.[114] The sisters' work included making phone calls to various social service offices and helping people procure food, clothing, and bus tickets, but they also set aside time each day for prayer and meditation.[115]

When Ferraro and Hussey saw a copy of the *New York Times* ad, they signed their names almost immediately. According to Hussey, "Barbara and I signed that statement because we had finally realized that we, too, are *women*."[116] Both women—along with other signers—hoped the ad would initiate a dialogue on abortion within the Catholic Church; they also wanted to demonstrate their support for the candidacy of Geraldine Ferraro. In early December 1984 Sister Catherine Hughes, general superior of the community, called from Rome to inform Ferraro and Hussey that she had received a letter from the Vatican explaining that both women were to disassociate themselves from the statement.

After studying the history and development of the church's position on abortion, as well as its stance on issues relating to Catholic women, Ferraro and Hussey devised a strategy to respond to the situation. "We were no longer calling for dialogue," they wrote. "We were publicly, urgently demanding recognition of women's right to choose."[117] On March 22, 1986, the two sisters attended a meeting at Trinity College (Washington, D.C.) with representatives of their community and Archbishops Vincenzo Fagiolo and Pio Laghi, the Papal Nuncio to the United States. At that meeting, Ferraro and Hussey made it clear that they would not recant their statements supporting a woman's right to have an abortion. When it came time to introduce herself, Barbara Ferraro said in part, "In my work in parishes I have been called upon by many women who have had to struggle with the issues of birth control and abortion." Hussey defended the ad, saying, "It was important to state in a public forum that other Catholics and theologians hold different views on the question of abortion."[118]

Congregational leaders expressed displeasure with the sisters' actions, writing, "You [Ferraro and Hussey] have assumed an intransigent position which has consistently blocked attempts at dialogue initiated by the general government, the leadership of your province, and other Sisters of Notre Dame. . . . You have, in practice, placed yourself outside of the life and mission of the Congregation." The women were warned that they might be dismissed from their order early in 1988, but in June that year they were told the congregation had decided not to take such an action. Ferraro and Hussey held a press conference to announce the decision, stating triumphantly, "You can be publicly pro-choice and still be a nun."[119] It was clear, however, that they were no longer "Sisters of Notre Dame in spirit," and as the women themselves explained, the congregation's decision not to dismiss the women allowed them to leave on their own terms. On July 13, 1988, Ferraro and Hussey formally resigned from their community; they were no longer interested in dialoging with either the Catholic Church or the Sisters of Notre Dame de Namur.[120] In addition, they no longer believed it was possible to work with the poor as long as they were members of a religious community, because "one must be in a relationship of equality with them."[121] Some Catholics believed that the entire chain of events leading up to Ferraro's and Hussey's resignations was the direct result of the changes taking place in religious communities during the 1960s and 1970s. James Likoudis of Catholics United for the Faith suggested, for instance, that "This is what happens when you have religious who no longer live in community, no longer wear the religious habit, no longer understand their own vows of religious consecration to Christ. They have forgotten what poverty, chastity and obedience means."[122]

Other women religious were also forced to choose between remaining a member of their communities and keeping a job that the hierarchy claimed supported positions antithetical to Catholic teaching. Sister of Mercy Mary Agnes Mansour, who had been a member of her community for thirty years, chose to leave religious life in 1983 after some Catholics disagreed with her appointment as head of Michigan's Department of Social Services on the grounds that slightly less than 1 percent of the budget was designated for Medicaid abortions. Another Sister of Mercy, Arlene Violet, had to decide whether to resign from her congregation or drop out of the 1984 race for Attorney General of Rhode Island when informed that a new canon law did not allow women religious to hold either elective or appointed civil offices. Violet resigned from her community.[123]

Transformation of American Catholic Sisters

Reflecting on the changes that had taken place among women religious in the second half of the twentieth century, Sisters Lora Ann Quiñonez, CDP, and Mary Daniel Turner, SNDdeN, wrote that the place of sisters "in both church and world has been jarred loose, their communities shaken up. Sisters appear in worldly dress, occupy houses among ordinary folks, work in secular agencies, and participate in grassroots movements."[124] Changes in lifestyle, however, were indicators of a larger shift among women religious relating to the way they viewed religious life. "Traditional formulations of religious life," Sisters Lora Ann and Mary Daniel wrote, "have been revised, even totally recast."[125] Sisters no longer depended on church leaders to define religious life, they defined it for themselves; but the changes had not come without a price. By the early 1990s the number of sisters in the United States had decreased from over 180,000 in 1966 to 128,000; only 1 percent was under thirty years of age.[126] In addition, women religious were no longer working primarily in what Quiñonez and Turner described as "an impressive array of institutions," and most of them did not wear a distinctive habit, live in convents, or embrace uniform spiritual practices.

Declining numbers and a radically different way of manifesting one's commitment to religious life did not change the mission of serving those in need—a mission embraced by American sisters since the arrival of the Ursulines in New Orleans in 1727. The shifting demographics of Catholicism in the United States, changes in the way health care and social services were administered at the national level, and declining numbers of sisters meant that they were not as visible in the classroom, hospital, or settlement house as they had been in the 1950s, but they remained involved in ministries related to teaching, health care, and social service. As the twentieth century drew to a close, women religious were also active in work that enabled them to respond to the "signs of the times," including ministries that led to calls for the abolition of the death penalty, immigration reform, and environmental responsibility.

8

Serving Today

SISTER HELEN PREJEAN did not hesitate when asked if she would write
to an inmate housed on Louisiana State Penitentiary's death row. She later
explained that agreeing to the request seemed to fit with her ministry in St.
Thomas, a New Orleans housing project of mostly poor African American
residents. Sister Helen remembered that she came "to St. Thomas to serve
the poor, and [assumed] that someone occupying a cell on Louisiana's
death row fits that category."[1] She had no way of knowing that her willingness to write to convicted murderer Elmo Patrick Sonnier would cause
her to become one of the best-known American sisters of the twenty-first
century.

Born in 1939 in Baton Rouge, Louisiana, Sister Helen entered the Sisters
of St. Joseph of Medaille, now known as the Congregation of St. Joseph, in
1957. As the community struggled to determine the best way to respond to
the challenges of the late twentieth century, a decision was made to stand
with the poor. Sister Helen was less than enthusiastic about the changing
direction of her congregation. "I didn't want to struggle with politics and
economics," she wrote. "We were nuns, after all, not social workers, and
some realities in life were, for better or worse, rather fixed—like the gap
between rich and poor. Even Jesus Christ himself had said, 'The poor you
will always have with you.'"[2] She reversed her position after attending a
presentation by sociologist Sister Marie Augusta Neal, SNDdeN, a Sister
of Notre Dame de Namur, who was a passionate advocate of the importance of considering the poor when implementing policy and examining
issues of social justice.[3] Sister Marie Augusta seemed to respond directly to
Sister Helen's concerns, contending "that to claim to be apolitical or neu-
tral in the face of such injustices would be, in actuality, to uphold the status
quo—a very political position to take, and on the side of the oppressors."[4]
Sister Helen was especially moved by the way she presented the teachings of Jesus, explaining that he came to preach good news to the poor;
they were not expected to accept their situation, but struggle to claim
that which is rightfully theirs. "Something in me must have been building

toward this moment," she recounted, "because there was a flash and I realized that my spiritual life had been too ethereal, too disconnected. I left the meeting and began seeking out the poor."[5]

Sister Helen agreed to serve as Sonnier's spiritual advisor, and as their friendship developed she learned more about the circumstances surrounding his crime, trial, and sentencing. Convinced that the death penalty was inherently unjust, she embarked on a crusade to abolish capital punishment. *Dead Man Walking: An Eyewitness Account of the Death Penalty in the United States* was published in 1993, and made into a movie starring Susan Sarandon and Sean Penn in 1996. Along with her books, Sister Helen's work with death row inmates and her efforts to eradicate the death penalty captured the attention of American Catholics concerned with issues of social justice.

Like Sister Helen Prejean, other women religious in the twenty-first century have expanded their ministries beyond the traditional network of schools, hospitals, and social service institutions that have characterized the work of women religious since the eighteenth century, working in a variety of settings that were not available to their predecessors. Nineteenth-century sisters may have visited prisoners as a part of their work with the poor, for instance, but they did not advocate for reforms in the criminal justice system. The changes that took place within congregations of women religious during the middle decades of the twentieth century provided future generations of sisters with the opportunity to minister in ways best suited to their talents and interests.

Activists in the Church and Society

By the end of the 1970s, American sisters were speaking out against discrimination at all levels of society, including the way women were viewed by Catholic Church leaders. In 1979, when Pope John Paul II first visited the United States, Sister Theresa Kane, a Sister of Mercy and president of the Leadership Conference of Women Religious (LCWR), confronted him on issues related to women and the church, including its refusal to ordain them to the priesthood. "I urge you, Your Holiness," Sister Theresa said, "to be open to and respond to the voices coming from the women of this country who are desirous of serving in and through the church as fully participating members."[6] About ten months later, Sister Theresa reiterated her message to the pope when she addressed the Leadership Conference of Women Religious. "The Roman Catholic Church," she firmly stated, "must recognize and acknowledge the serious social injustices by which its very system is imposed upon women of the Roman Catholic Church. . . . Until the institutional Catholic Church undertakes a serious, critical examination of its mode of acting toward women, it cannot, it will not, give witness to justice in the world."[7]

While Sister Theresa Kane was calling on church leaders to end institutional discrimination against women, a group of Catholics began to voice their support for ordaining women to the diaconate. Limited to males, these "permanent deacons" serve the church by preaching, baptizing, visiting the sick, and preparing men and women for marriage. In 1974, the Sisters of Mercy formally proposed that women be allowed to enter the diaconate, asking, "When the expanse of the Church's mission is examined, is it feasible to limit the official, public ministry to the male sex alone when fifty-one percent of the persons being ministered to are of the female sex?"[8] The campaign to ordain women to the diaconate was unsuccessful, but women religious continued to lobby for justice for women within the Catholic Church.

When sisters discovered "needs unmet at diocesan levels, many women religious congregations . . . encountered conflict with the local hierarchy when they [sought] to minister to these needs."[9] Sister Jeannine Grammick, a School Sister of Notre Dame, cofounded New Ways Ministry with Father Robert Nugent in 1977 to address the concerns of lesbian and gay Catholics. Their work drew the attention of church officials, and in 1984 they were ordered to disassociate themselves from the organization. They continued to work with and advocate for the inclusion of gays and lesbians in the full life of Catholicism, but after a Vatican investigation concluded that Sister Jeannine and Father Nugent should no longer be involved in this work, the School Sisters of Notre Dame asked her to find another way in which to minister within the church. Several months later, Sister Jeannine was told to stop speaking on the subject of homosexuality and to refrain from criticizing church teachings on this subject.

Unlike Patricia Hussey and Barbara Ferraro, who left religious life altogether over the church's teachings on abortion, Sister Jeannine transferred from her community to the Sisters of Loretto, which supported her ministry to the gay and lesbian community, making her final vows in 2004. When asked to assess her work in this area, Sister Jeannine explained that when the Vatican began to pay attention to New Ways Ministry, "[i]t put homosexuality on the agenda. . . . In 1971 you never saw the word 'homosexual' in any Catholic publication. Now, we have dioceses that have instituted ministries for lesbian and gay people. We have 200 [gay-friendly] parishes in the country. Now it's a drop in the bucket, but that didn't exist [in the 1970s]."[10]

Other women religious challenged Catholics to become involved in the antinuclear movement that gained adherents during the final decades of the twentieth century. On October 6, 2002, Dominican Sisters Carol Gilbert, age 55, Jackie Hudson, age 68, and Ardeth Platte, age 66, cut through fences at a Colorado missile silo, and pounded on it with hammers to symbolize the "beating of swords into plowshares (Isaiah 2:4)." The women were arrested and found guilty of defacing a Minuteman III silo, a felony. To the surprise of many, the sisters were sentenced to prison terms that ranged from two and a half years to three years, five months.[11] The three Dominicans found themselves denounced by a number of people opposing their position on nuclear weapons, including Catholics uncomfortable with women religious engaged in political activism. A 2008 article in the *Washington Times* reported that Sisters Ardeth and Carol had been "branded by Maryland State Police as terrorists and placed on a national watch list."[12]

Martyred for the Poor

In the 1970s, many congregations involved in mission work outside the United States began to emphasize the preferential "option for the poor," and "evangelization, justice and presence among the poor became the touchstones of authenticity, a kind of measuring rod for missionaries."[13] Focusing on the concept of "option for the poor" meant that sister-missionaries began to advocate a "transformation of systems,"[14] which often caused governing officials to view them with suspicion. Advocacy for the poor in other countries sometimes placed sisters in danger and on several occasions cost them their lives.

On December 4, 1980 Maryknoll Sisters received the news that the bodies of Sisters Maura Clarke and Ita Ford, along with those of Maryknoll lay missioner Jean Donovan and Ursuline Sister Dorothy Kazel, had been discovered in a ditch in El Salvador. The four women, who had been ministering among refugees of that country's civil war, had been missing since December 2, when Sisters Maura and Ita were picked up at the airport by Sister Dorothy and Jean Donovan.[15] A subsequent investigation determined that they were tortured and killed shortly after leaving the airport.

Only two of the four women killed that day in El Salvador were Mary-knoll Sisters, but the congregation "became indelibly associated" with the murders and was often linked to the movement to change U.S. policy toward Central American countries governed by repressive military and political dictatorships. Many Catholics had supported Ronald Reagan's campaign for the presidency, and did not hesitate to state their disagreement with the community's political position on Central America. For the first time in Maryknoll's history, the sisters "found themselves publicly reviled from conservative quarters, forced to justify their faith and mission."[16] Sister Melinda Roper, who served as the community's president during these years, insisted that the sisters' stance on U.S. foreign policy was consistent with the history and work of Maryknoll. She maintained and defended this position despite attempts on the part of some of President Reagan's top advisors to suggest that the four women were somehow responsible for their own deaths. In an interview with a reporter, Jeanne Kirkpatrick, who had been nominated as Reagan's Ambassador to the United Nations, claimed that "[t]he nuns were not just nuns, the nuns were also political activists. We ought to be a little more clear about this than we actually are." Several months later, Secretary of State Alexander Haig suggested "that perhaps the vehicle in which the nuns were riding may have tried to run a road block or may have accidentally been perceived to have been doing so and there may have been an exchange of fire."[17]

In the spring of 1983, five Salvadoran National Guardsmen were accused of murdering the four American women. Secretary of State George Schultz commissioned an independent review of the case under the leadership of New York Judge Harold Tyler, Jr. "The Churchwomen Murders: A Report to the Secretary of State" concluded that Sub-Sergeant Colindres Aleman ordered "four National Guardsmen to rape and murder the four churchwomen," but the commission was unable to determine if Aleman had acted on orders from a highly placed government or military official.[18] The trial of Aleman and the four National Guardsmen took place from May 23–24, 1984 in El Salvador and lasted nineteen hours. All five men were sentenced to thirty years in prison.[19] The Maryknoll community felt vindicated in its conviction that the sisters were killed because their ministry, which was consistent with the congregation's model of mission that had developed since Vatican II, "insisted on seeing and defending in the bodies of the poor the living image of God."[20]

Although the Maryknoll Sisters were founded to minister as missionaries to those in other countries, other congregations allocated funds and personnel to projects overseas as a way to emphasize their commitment to the poor. American Adorers of the Blood of Christ began working in Liberia in 1971, when Sisters Bonita Wittenbrink and Alvina Schott opened a mission on the Kru coast and remained in the country until a civil war forced the women to return to the United States in 1990. The congregation resumed its work in Liberia in 1991, and in addition to ministries in education and health care, devoted time to helping the country's citizens recover from trauma suffered during the war. About eighteen months after their return, five sisters were murdered in two separate incidents. Although the exact circumstances surrounding the deaths of Sisters Barbara Ann Muttra, Mary Joel Kolmer, Kathleen McGuire, Agnes Mueller, and Shirley Kolmer are unknown, it is clear that they were somehow related to the civil war. Sisters Barbara Ann and Mary Joel were driving a worker from Gardnersville to Barnersville on October 2, 1992 when they were caught in crossfire. Sisters Kathleen, Agnes, and Shirley were killed three days later when soldiers representing the National Patriotic Front of Liberia lined them up in front of the convent and shot them in cold blood.[21]

No members of the community have worked in Liberia since the five sisters were murdered. The congregation remained supportive of their ministries in this country, however, remembering that the "blood of five U.S. Adorers has mingled with that of the thousands of Liberians killed during the civil war, and the Adorers have shared with the Liberian people the grief of losing loved ones through violence." This shared sorrow has "irrevocably bound the [community] and the people of Liberia in a way that no one could possibly have imagined when the first Adorers were welcomed by the Liberian people."[22] The events surrounding the murders of members of this community remind women religious that a decision to stand with the poor can place them in grave danger, and even lead to their death.

In some instances, sisters from the United States were working in an individual ministry when they were killed by forces hostile to their work with the poor. Dorothy Mae Stang entered the Sisters of Notre Dame de Namur on July 26, 1948, at the age of seventeen. In 1963, when Pope John XXIII asked North American religious communities of women and men to send 10 percent of their members to Latin America, Sister Dorothy enthusiastically volunteered. She arrived in Brazil in August 1966 and immediately began learning the culture of the people she had come to serve.[23]

Sister Dorothy quickly recognized the ways in which rural Brazilians were oppressed by the country's wealthy landowners. In order to

Statue dedicated to the five members of the Adorers of the Blood of Christ killed in Liberia on October 20 and 23, 1992 and to all women who have worked for justice. Courtesy of the Adorers of the Blood of Christ archives.

demonstrate concern for the poor, Sister Dorothy and those with whom she worked decided that when they arrived in a particular area they would stay with the poor farmers rather than in the landowner's house. "They wanted to show the people that their preference was to work with the poor."[24] During the 1970s, 1980s, and 1990s, Sister Dorothy's understanding of the burden government policies placed on poor farmers increased, and she began to advocate for legislation to protect them. Her involvement in disputes between farmers and landowners led to her murder on February 12, 2005.[25] Like the women religious murdered in El Salvador and Liberia, Sister Dorothy's life and death became an important event in her congregation's vision of becoming "Women with Hearts as Wide as the World."[26]

Those women religious who chose to risk their lives in order to stand with the poor engaged in a ministry that was strikingly similar to Sister Helen Prejean's ministry to death row inmates in Louisiana. As these women read the "signs of the times," they concluded that their calling was to meet the needs of the poor and oppressed. Some, such as the Maryknoll Sisters, who dedicated themselves to mission work with the poor, chose to become visible political activists after receiving word that their sisters and a lay missionary had been murdered in El Salvador. The Adorers of the Blood of Christ ministered in a number of countries, including the United States, and established a Liberian mission after agreeing to commit to the poor in that country. Other communities, such as the Sisters of Notre Dame de Namur, supported Sister Dorothy Stang's call to work with the poor in Brazil because they understood that she believed she could be most effective in that ministry. Most sisters did not face death on a daily basis, but those who did believed it was consistent with their calling to serve those in need in ways that change lives.

Recognizing the Needs of the Twenty-First Century: Environmental Responsibility

In a 1989 survey of 139,000 women religious in the United States, more than 80 percent of the respondents reported that social justice was "their primary mission in religious life."[27] They were still working in education, health care, and social service, but recognized that these ministries were connected to larger systemic issues of justice and inequality. Many sisters who worked actively to resolve one or more of the important issues of the twenty-first century placed a special emphasis on protecting the earth and its resources for future generations. "Sisters at work in earth ministries . . . have decided to 'dig in' and reinhabit the structures and traditions of religious life and community according to what they identify as the most pressing needs of the day."[28]

In 1982, Sister Gail Worcelo, CP, entered the Passionist community at St. Gabriel's Monastery in Clarks Summit, Pennsylvania. As a novice, Sister Gail attended classes taught by Thomas Berry, a Passionist priest and a strong advocate of ecospirituality. Under Berry's tutelage, Sister Gail founded a community ministry called "Homecomings: Center for Ecology and Contemplation." Homecomings included teaching and retreat work, the creation of small community gardens, and a focus on sustainability, all of which allowed the sisters to express their understanding of the earth as a "communion of subjects." In 1999, Sister Gail received permission to leave the Passionists and begin a new community of women religious. Along with Sister Bernadette Bostwick, she founded the Green Mountain Monastery in Weston, Vermont.[29]

Although Sister Gail could have chosen otherwise, she decided to request "canonical status," or approval from Rome, for her new community. "[I]t was important to her to work within the framework of the Church and to be recognized by the institutional hierarchy."[30] The Green Mountain Sisters adopted a version of the habit; "[a]n attractive, but modest brushed cotton blue denim dress (short sleeves in the summer, long sleeves in the winter), [became] the . . . community dress."[31] Although this garb proved impractical when cooking, gardening, or performing manual or physical labor, the sisters could wear it when attending Mass and at other public events. According to the community's Rule of Life, the dress was chosen as an "act of resistance against the dominant culture of advertising and its large-scale manipulation of women."[32]

When the Second Vatican Council encouraged women religious to respond to the "signs of the times," many sisters began to read and watch television in order to keep abreast of current events and gain an understanding of the issues facing modern Americans. Yet sisters living in the Green Mountain Monastery, and other communities who shared a concern for stewardship of the earth, tended to retreat from television and many other forms of mass media. At the Green Mountain Monastery the sisters listened to the BBC and National Public Radio, read newspapers or news magazines, and subscribed to Internet news services "where they [could] control what news topics they spend their time on and the medium through which it is delivered."[33]

Other communities of women religious were also influenced by those advocating responsibility for the earth and its resources. The Sisters, Servants of the Immaculate Heart of Mary (IHM) in Monroe, Michigan, for instance, replaced their cars with hybrid vehicles.[34] When the community had to decide on the best way to create a facility that could care for their sick and elderly, they chose not to tear down the motherhouse that had been built in the 1930s, but "set about recycling the valued contents of the building, reusing these materials in new, creative, and environmentally friendly ways."[35] As they began the process of transforming the building, the sisters focused on practicing "ecological sustainability." Wooden windows, doors, trim, and wainscoting were reused; marble found throughout the motherhouse became windowsills and countertops; and light fixtures were made energy efficient. A recycled water system was installed to collect the water from sinks and showers and use it to flush toilets; this reduced the freshwater consumption at the motherhouse by over 50 percent. In addition, an energy-efficient geothermal heating and cooling system—the largest in the United States—was installed to keep the temperature in the motherhouse comfortable during all seasons.[36]

As the IHMs transformed themselves into "Blue Nuns Going Green" (the blue refers to the color of the habits once worn by the Monroe community), they contended that environmental responsibility was consistent with the congregation's mission. According to Sister Janet Ryan, the sisters "have always been committed to social justice and advocacy for the abandoned and the poor. Our founders' call was to respond to the needs of the world. In this century, we have come to understand the Earth is abandoned in many ways."[37] At the end of the twentieth century, approximately 71 percent of the congregation's members were sixty-five or older and about 50 percent were "retired or infirm"; their commitment to ecology and sustainability allowed the community to invest in the future and "keep their community 'moving forward.'"[38]

A number of congregations initiated agricultural ministries as a way to connect their call to serve those in need with ecological responsibility. In 1996, the Sisters of Charity in New York created an organic community garden on property that had been willed to them in 1916, linking "care and concern for creation with their mission to serve those most in need."[39] Sisters Hill Farm, as it is called, allocated part of its harvest to those who would otherwise go hungry by sharing it with needy families or donating it to soup kitchens.[40] The Dominican Alliance, a group of nine Dominican communities that joined together to "live out Catholic social teachings on the care of creation," supported a number of agricultural ministries, including Crown Point Ecology Center (Bath, Ohio), Sophia Garden (Amityville, New York), Heartland Farm (Pawnee Rock, Kansas), and Crystal Spring (Plainville, Massachusetts). Although the sisters who lived and worked on these farms were not directly involved with the poor, the food grown was donated to the hungry, permitting the Dominicans to serve those in need and address issues that—if not corrected—threatened the quality of life of future generations.[41]

Women religious involved in ministries that focused on environmental responsibility believed they were remaining faithful to the vision of the founding members of their communities. Established to meet the needs of earlier eras, such as the education of girls and young women, the care of orphans and children abandoned by their parents, and the need for trained nurses and hospital administrators, religious congregations viewed issues such as global warming, sustainability, and dependence on oil as vital to the future of the United States.

Return to Tradition

Rather than develop new ministries that reflected a concern for contemporary issues as the congregations discussed above chose to do, some communities consciously decided to maintain their traditional lifestyles and work. During the 1960s, as women religious struggled with how best to respond to both the Second Vatican Council and the changes in American society, the leader of the Dominican Sisters of St. Cecilia was Mother Marie William MacGregor, OP, who was instrumental in the founding of Consortium Perfectae Caritatis, a group of major superiors concerned that the changes taking place in religious life were doing more harm than good. Along with emphasizing the importance of prayer, the superior strongly advocated wearing the traditional habit, explaining that it was "a symbol of our life-long dedication. In a crisis of self-identity, it gives you an identity. . . . Wearing it presupposes a tremendous obligation on our part to be genuine witnesses. The habit will enhance this; not detract from it, if it is worn worthily."[42]

The distinctive long white habits with black veils worn by the Dominican Sisters of St. Cecilia identified them as women religious. Young Catholic women considering religious life were attracted to this community with its traditional philosophy and lifestyle. In 2010, according to a National

Public Radio (NPR) report, almost one-third of the community's members were under thirty years of age. Twenty-seven women entered the community that year, and twenty-three postulants were accepted in 2009. Two of the young women interviewed by NPR admitted that the habit was part of what had drawn them to the community. Sister Zandra Man desired to dedicate her life to service and was impressed by "the pleasure [they] appeared to take in their work and in their apparent devotion to serving children." In addition, she was "intrigued by the full, head-to-toe white habits."[43]

The Los Angeles-based Carmelite Sisters of the Most Sacred Heart responded to the changes taking place in religious life by defining themselves "in opposition to an allegedly Americanist church."[44] Founded in Mexico in 1866 by Luisa-Maria de la Peña, whose religious name was Mother Luisa Josefa, the community arrived in Los Angeles in 1927. "In response to Vatican II's call for religious communities to renew their vows in light of their founder's or foundress's charism [the grace that allowed her to perform her work], the sisters . . . discovered in Mother Luisa . . . a model for world renunciation in the modern political context."[45] Members of the community chose to wear a traditional habit that included a crucifix around the neck and a long rosary hanging from the waist. The congregation staffed parochial schools in California, Arizona, Florida, and Colorado; operated several child care centers; and has been involved in a ministry of health care.[46]

The Dominican Sisters of Mary, Mother of the Eucharist were founded in 1997 with four sisters constituting the core group. In the first fourteen years of the congregation's existence, it grew to over one hundred sisters with an average age of twenty-eight. In February 2010, members of the community appeared on the Oprah Winfrey Show to answer questions about their life and work. Like the Dominican Sisters of St. Cecilia, the Sisters of Mary, whose motherhouse is in Michigan, wear a traditional Dominican habit and engage in a ministry of teaching. In August 2011, the community accepted eighteen postulants.[47]

Members of congregations considered traditional sometimes disagreed on the direction in which their community was moving. In 1988, the *New York Times* reported that five Discalced Carmelite nuns were protesting the introduction of television, classical music, and brighter lights in the monastery's chapel. Fearful that they would be evicted from their home, the nuns barricaded themselves in the infirmary until the Vatican agreed to listen to their complaint.[48] The newspaper later reported that the five nuns were also protesting the transfer of a previous superior to France, and expressing their dissatisfaction with the new prioress.[49] The Vatican ruled against the protestors on March 3, 1989.[50]

Perhaps the best-known figure publicly advocating a return to the pre-Vatican II structure of religious communities was Mother Angelica Rizzo. Born Rita Rizzo in 1923, Mother Angelica entered the Poor Clares in 1944 determined to serve the church as a cloistered nun. When the community was granted permission to open a new monastery in the vicinity of Birmingham, Alabama, in 1961, Mother Angelica was chosen to oversee the planning and construction of the building.[51] Prior to moving into their new home, the nuns hosted an open house for residents of the surrounding area; seven thousand visitors toured the monastery during the ten days it was open to the public.[52]

After moving into the monastery, Mother Angelica found herself writing pamphlets and booklets that called Catholics to get excited about their faith and spread the teachings of the church to others. "Every housewife, every businessman can be a missionary," she said. "You plant the seed and then the Spirit will take over."[53] By 1978, after publishing several books and producing a weekly ten-minute radio program in Birmingham, Mother Angelica entered the world of television. Claiming that "[f]or too long the TV tube has been in the hands of the enemy," she began taping a program before a live audience that would "beam the teachings of the Church to the masses."[54] A disagreement in 1978 with the general manager of the local CBS affiliate over its decision to air a miniseries that questioned the divinity of Jesus led her to set up a recording studio in the monastery so that she could tape her own programs. The result was Eternal Word Television Network (EWTN) with a target audience of "the man in the pew, the woman who is suffering from heartache, the child who is lonely."[55]

Despite her growing popularity as a woman religious who did not hesitate to use television to criticize those who went too far in adapting the teachings of the church to the late twentieth century, Mother Angelica remained a cloistered nun. Taping the television show and administering EWTN constituted her work; all other time was spent in the cloister with members of her community. Time at the monastery was devoted to supervising the nuns' spiritual life, teaching a lesson each day, and setting a schedule for everyone. "I think the Lord gave me the grace to concentrate on the network, with all its multitudinous details, and then go back to the monastery and drop everything," Mother Angelica said. "Once there I was not CEO; I was abbess. I had to be what the Lord wanted me to be at that moment."[56]

For many Catholics, Mother Angelica served as the primary representative of church traditionalists. Her role as a leader in the Catholic communications industry, however, drew criticism from bishops, who perhaps agreed with a critic's comment that "Cloistered nuns should stay in their monasteries and not get involved in stuff like this."[57] Such negative feedback did not deter her from continuing her ministry, and in 1983 she launched the very successful "Mother Angelica Live" on EWTN. "Mother Angelica was like no one else on television. She coughed when her asthma acted up, chomped on lozenges, unleashed explosive sneezes that drew tears from her eyes, and regularly collapsed into fits of laughter. This purposely unvarnished approach endeared her to the audience."[58] In 2000, the administration of EWTN was transferred to a lay board, and a year later Mother Angelica suffered a series of strokes that forced her to withdraw from her responsibilities at the network.

Popes, Bishops, and Women Religious

The history of American women religious includes struggles with church leaders over a variety of issues. Many of these conflicts, such as Vincennes Bishop Celestine de la Hailandière's efforts to assume control over Mother Theodore Guerin and her community, or Cardinal James McIntyre's unhappiness with the way in which the IHMs in Los Angeles chose to adapt to the modern world, center on issues of power and authority. In 2010, Sister of Mercy Margaret McBride, a member of the ethics committee at St. Joseph's Hospital in Phoenix, was excommunicated by Bishop Thomas J. Olmsted, which meant that she was unable to receive the sacraments or participate in the life of the church. Sister Margaret allowed a twenty-seven-year-old mother of four diagnosed with pulmonary hypertension to receive an abortion at the hospital because doctors were convinced she would die if the pregnancy was not terminated. Olmsted decided to excommunicate Sister Margaret because she "gave her consent that the abortion was morally good and allowable under church teaching."[59] In this case, a bishop chose to exert his authority and punish a sister because he disagreed with her interpretation of a church teaching. Although she was responsible for a number of important decisions made at St. Joseph's Hospital, Olmsted had the power to remove Sister Margaret from her position and prevent her from participating in the sacramental life of the church.

Church leaders have also faulted the writings of women religious that they believed were inconsistent with traditional Catholic doctrine. Sister Elizabeth Johnson, a Sister of St. Joseph of Brentwood and professor of theology at Fordham University, was criticized by the Committee on Doctrine of the United States Conference of Catholic Bishops because her book, entitled *Quest for the Living God* (2007), contained what they believed to be a "series of 'misrepresentations, ambiguities and errors' and thus [did] not accord with essential Catholic teaching on essential points."[60] Sister Elizabeth's supporters, including members of the Catholic Theological Society of America, immediately rose to her defense and issued a written statement responding to the bishops' critique.[61] Church leaders, however, did not agree, maintaining that Sister Elizabeth Johnson's work did not accurately represent Catholic theological teaching.

The decrease in the number of women religious as well as the implementation of what some Catholics viewed as inappropriate ministries concerned ecclesiastical leaders, who believed these two factors were causing sisters to become more militant in their critique of church teaching. In the 1980s, Pope John Paul II formed the Papal Commission on Religious Life (also known as the Quinn Commission because Archbishop John Quinn was chosen to head the group) to determine the reasons for the decrease in the numbers of women religious. Although the members of the commission concluded that women's religious communities were both stable and providing a great service to the church, some Catholic leaders continued to question the ways in which sisters' lives and work had changed in the aftermath of Vatican II.[62]

In January 2009, the Vatican announced that it planned to conduct an apostolic visitation, or investigation, of women religious in the United States. The motivation behind this decision was unclear, but possible reasons included a desire to gain access to the financial records of religious communities and beginning the process of requiring sisters to return to their pre-Vatican II lifestyle and ministries.[63] Mother Clare Millea, Superior General of the Apostles of the Sacred Heart of Jesus, was appointed "visitator," or official examiner, and charged with collecting data relating to contemporary religious life. The investigation focused only on active religious communities, or sisters; contemplative congregations were exempted from the study because of their "distinctively different lifestyles."[64] Teams of women religious, all of whom had sworn a loyalty oath to Rome, were assigned specific congregations to visit. Mother Clare assumed responsibility for synthesizing the information gathered and preparing a confidential report to be submitted to Rome.[65]

Many sisters strenuously objected to the investigation of their communities by representatives of the Vatican. "Apostolic visitations . . . are not celebratory occasions," Sister Anne Marie Mongoven reflected in an article in the liberal *National Catholic Reporter*. Women religious had done exactly what the documents of Vatican II and the writings of Pope Pius XII had asked, she continued. To respond to the needs of the late twentieth century more effectively, for instance, some sisters had moved out of parochial schools in order to teach adult and religious education, begun programs to educate the poor so that they were able to apply for appropriate social services, and returned to school to complete advanced degrees in theology in order to teach at the university level.[66] Was it possible, Sister Anne Marie asked, that the bishops were unaware that religious communities had simply done what the church had asked of them?[67]

American Catholics supported women religious and were puzzled by the decision to conduct an investigation. "The voices of many Catholics have been strong and consistent in support of the sisters."[68] Many echoed the sentiments of an editorial in the *National Catholic Reporter*, which praised sisters, stating that their "example and encouragement facilitated a culture of participation and increased lay ownership in the church. . . . Women religious continue to lead the way in practicing the primacy of Gospel love."[69]

Mother Clare Millea submitted her findings to Rome at the end of 2011, but the report was not made public. Some women religious continue to worry that church officials will eventually force their communities to revert to a lifestyle they chose to abandon in the wake of the Second Vatican Council. Supporters of the visitation, however, have consistently argued that the decreasing numbers of women choosing to enter religious life indicated that "some reform" was needed.[70]

"If Not Us, Who?"

"If Not Us, Who?" was the Facebook status for the Sisters of Mercy of the Americas, Northeast Community, on September 8, 2011. "Friends" of the group could link to a blog post entitled "What Will It Take?" to read a reflection on the tenth anniversary of the attacks on the World Trade Center and the Pentagon. The post's author, Sister Sheila, asked that on September 11, 2011 readers remember those who lost their lives, and reminded them to pray for the families of those who had died. She also reflected, however, on what needed to occur to bring true peace to the world. Although her words were intended for all readers, they may have especially appealed to members of her religious congregation, and would also have resonated with American women religious of earlier centuries: "The Gospel calls us to a radical way of living—loving our enemies, binding up the wounds of the suffering, feeding the hungry, giving to the poor, sharing all that we have, giving without counting the cost and more."[71]

Benedictine Sister Joan Chittister's reflections on that day also connected the aftermath of September 11 to the history of women religious. Americans need to be careful, Sister Joan explained, to respect differences among peoples. "Having worn the medieval habit once characteristic of European nuns," she wrote, "I remember the catcalls, the frowns, the exclusion and distancing that came with it outside of the Catholic community."[72] Contrasting this experience to that of Muslims in a post-9/11 society, Sister Joan told readers that her religious community, located in Erie, Pennsylvania, had reached out to their neighbors by accompanying Muslim women as they shopped and checking on those worried about their safety. As the Benedictine sisters remembered their own history, they tried to ensure that Americans of Middle Eastern descent did not suffer because of the way they looked or dressed.[73]

American sisters and nuns—those serving as spiritual advisors to inmates on death row and those engaged in ministries of teaching, health care, and social service—have continued the work begun by European and American congregations to meet the needs of the poor and dispossessed. Unlike earlier generations of women religious, many twenty-first-century sisters have attempted to address the structural issues that they believe contribute to inequality and poverty in the United States. "Sisters . . . are still feeding the hungry and clothing the naked, but [they're] also addressing the issues that result in people being hungry and homeless. It's social sin [they're] fighting now."[74] Some congregations engaged in work related to global warming, while others vigorously protested the United States' involvement in wars on foreign soil as they advocated for a society built on justice and peace. Sisters continued to teach, care for the sick, and work with the poor, but remembered that their work must encompass justice as well as charity.

Since the nineteenth century, women religious have been the face of the Catholic Church in the United States for many people. It is hard to imagine the shape of the American church had sisters and nuns not played a role in its growth and development. As Catholic women in the United States founded congregations of women religious and European communities sent members to develop ministries of teaching and nursing, sisters' distinctive habits made them easily recognizable as they established schools and hospitals that were open to people of all religious denominations. The first communities in the United States ministered in New Orleans, Maryland, and Washington, D.C., but by 1829 women religious were serving the church and its people up and down the East Coast and along what was then known as the Kentucky frontier.

The story of women religious helps historians to gain a better understanding of the story of Catholicism in the United States. Mother Philippine Duchesne's struggle to adapt a community grounded in French culture to life in rural Missouri exemplifies the experience of the many immigrants who left European countries for a difficult life in areas that contained few, if any, amenities. When the Irish Sisters of Mercy, who arrived in Pittsburgh in 1843, were asked to send sisters to Chicago, Providence, Hartford, and Washington, D.C., for instance, they followed lay Catholics who had arrived in those cities in numbers large enough to require schools, hospitals, and child care facilities. Bishops and priests could not have created the network of institutions that made the Catholic Church a key player in education, health care, and social services without these religious congregations. Some Americans expressed a good deal of resentment toward nineteenth-century immigrants, and this hostility was sometimes manifested in attacks on women religious and convents. Fear of and hostility toward the role of women religious in educating future wives and mothers eventually led to the burning, in 1834, of the Ursuline convent in Charlestown, Massachusetts, in one of the most virulent expressions of anti-Catholicism in the history of the United States.

Sisters did more than serve as a visible representation of Catholicism, however; they are also a part of the larger story of American history. The development of a Catholic parochial school system is an integral part of the history of education in the United States, for instance, and—although they have often been left out of the story—women religious played a crucial role in the establishment and administration of Catholic elementary and secondary schools. Sister Assisium McEvoy was well aware that the 1884 mandate for parishes to build parochial schools pressured religious congregations to place sister-teachers in the classroom as soon as possible, even if they had not yet finished their undergraduate degrees. In an effort to prevent young Catholic women from attending secular universities, women religious began to administer and staff Catholic women's colleges in the late nineteenth and early twentieth centuries, adding a new dimension to higher education in the United States. These colleges educated young women and encouraged them to be leaders. After Barack Obama's election to the presidency in November 2008, he selected Kathleen Sebelius, a graduate of Trinity College, to be Secretary of Health and Human Services. Another graduate of Trinity, Nancy Pelosi, was elected the first woman speaker of the House of Representatives in 2007.

When the Sisters of Charity agreed to send community members to nurse victims of Philadelphia's cholera epidemic in 1832, residents of the city, Catholic and non-Catholic, could not help but be aware of their presence. The sisters' efforts during epidemics saved many lives and sometimes prevented chaos from erupting in hospitals and almshouses. Thirty years after the sisters' work in Philadelphia, Sister Serena Klimkiewicz was nursing Union soldiers wounded during the Battle of Gettysburg regardless of religious affiliation. The experiences of sister-nurses during the Civil War helped to lay the foundations for the modern profession of nursing and contributed to a better understanding of Catholicism by non-Catholics in the United States. Like other women nursing wounded troops during the conflict, sisters learned a great deal about treating wounds and disease as a result of their work with Union and Confederate soldiers.

As they ministered to Catholics in a variety of settings, sisters demonstrated their ability to adapt to changes in both their church and American society. Although an original ministry of the Felician Sisters involved working with the Polish and Polish American population in Wisconsin, they remained on Milwaukee's South Side long after their constituents had moved to the suburbs, but no longer focused on a particular ethnic group. Their Child Development Center of St. Joseph was founded as a community-based school for preschool and kindergarten age children regardless of religious or ethnic background. Other congregations remained committed to caring for abused, neglected, and troubled children by converting orphanages into residential programs, and working to ensure that their facilities met the standards set by federal and state agencies.

The response of women religious to the mandates of the Second Vatican Council and the societal changes of the 1960s and 1970s deepens our understanding of Catholicism in the United States during this era. As many communities ceased requiring members to wear a distinctive habit, sisters were not as easily recognized on the streets of America's cities and towns as they had once been. In addition, many moved from traditional ministries of teaching, nursing, and social service to more direct advocacy for social justice. They marched for voting rights in Selma, moved into apartments in the inner city, and refused to obey church leaders by retracting a statement calling for a discussion on abortion. During these years, some sisters decided—for a variety of reasons—to leave religious life.

Despite declining numbers and an aging population, sisters have remained the face of Catholicism for many Americans in the twenty-first century. Because Sister Mary Scullion does not wear a traditional habit, she may not be recognized by Philadelphians passing by her on a street, but many of the city's residents are very aware of her ministry to the homeless and mentally ill. Although the Catholic Church officially teaches that capital punishment should only be used as a last resort, Sister Helen Prejean is the person who often comes to mind when considering the role played by religion in attempts to abolish the death penalty in the United States.

"If Not Us, Who?" It is difficult to predict the future of American women religious, but it is clear that they will continue to answer this question by engaging in ministries that are focused on schools, hospitals, and service to the poor, as well as by advocating for social justice and debating issues related to ethics and theology. Women entering religious life in the twenty-first century are called to serve in the same ways that the sisters who established schools and hospitals on the frontier, opened orphan asylums, and marched in Selma responded to the needs facing American Catholics in previous centuries. "Religious life as we have known it," according to the *National Catholic Reporter*, "will continue to do what it has always done: inspire, mentor, serve the poor, challenge power, and if needed, empty itself into the future now being shaped by God and us."[75] As they have since the first religious congregations began ministering among American Catholics, sisters and nuns will continue to serve in ways that reflect the needs of both Catholics in the United States and the larger American society.

Notes

Introduction

1. Jennifer Lin, "Mary of Mercy Homeless Find Hope, Hanging Out with a Nun," *Philadelphia Inquirer*, 18 April 2010. http://articles.philly.com/2010-04-18/news/25212870_1_jon-bon-jovi-everyday-heroes-sister-mary-scullio (6 July 2011).

2. "Time Cites Nun among 100 Most Influential," *National Catholic Reporter*, 2 April 2009. http://ncronline.org/news/people/time-cites-nun-among-100-most-influential (16 September 2011).

3. Lin, "Mary of Mercy."

4. In 1989, Joan Dawson McConnon, a native of Philadelphia who had been volunteering at Mercy Hospice, decided to "begin working with others to find permanent solutions to end homelessness." See "Our Co-Founders," www.projecthome.org, 2006, <http://www.projecthome.org/about/co-founders.php> (20 August 2011).

5. Elizabeth Rapley, *The Lord as Their Portion: The Story of the Religious Orders and How They Shaped Our World* (Grand Rapids: William B. Eerdmans, 2011), 1.

6. See JoAnn Kay McNamara, *Sisters in Arms: Catholic Nuns through Two Millennia* (Cambridge: Harvard University Press, 1996), chapters 2–3; and Rapley, 37.

7. Rapley, 38–41.

8. Elizabeth Kuhns, *The Habit: A History of the Clothing of Catholic Nuns* (New York: Doubleday, 2003), 43.

9. Ibid., 81–89.

10. A convent is a term commonly used to define a residence for women religious. Members of cloistered communities of women religious refer to their residences as monasteries.

11. Rapley, 42.

12. See McNamara, chapters 10–11, for a full discussion of the development of cloister.

13. Rapley, 145.

14. Quoted in ibid., 177.

15. McNamara, 317.

16. Rapley, 178.

17. Ibid., 193.

18. Ibid.

19. Ibid., 190–191.

20. See McNamara, 485. The 1983 Code of Canon Law—the official body of law governing the Catholic Church—abolished any sort of differentiation between vows taken by women religious, but the church's official language continues to distinguish between a nun and a sister. In today's church, nuns are technically cloistered women religious; all others are classified as sisters. Few American Catholics recognize the differences between the two groups and use both terms when referring to women religious. I have tried to use the terms according to their strict definition throughout this book.

21. In this book, I use the words community and congregation interchangeably to mean a specific group of women religious organized around a particular founder and her vision.

22. Kathleen Sprows Cummings, *New Women of the Old Faith: Gender and American Catholicism in the Progressive Era* (Chapel Hill: University of North Carolina Press, 2009), 139.

23. Ibid., 110.

24. See "Frequently Requested Church Statistics," 2011. http://cara.georgetown.edu/CARAServices/requestedchurchstats.html (26 July 2011). For information on CARA Catholic Polls, see http://cara.georgetown.edu/CARAServices/CCP-Methods.html.

25. See "Ordinations and Vocations," 2011. http://cara.georgetown.edu/CARAServices/FRStats/ordvocation.pdf (26 July 2011).

26. Cheryl L. Reed, *Unveiled: The Hidden Lives of Nuns* (New York: Berkley Books, 2004), 107.

Chapter 1

1. [Sister Josephine Barber], "Life of Mrs. Jerusha Barber," in L[ouis] DeGoesbriand, *Catholic Memoirs of Vermont and New Hampshire* (Burlington, Vt.: n.p., 1886), 90.

2. Eleanore C. Sullivan, *Georgetown Visitation since 1799* (Georgetown: Georgetown Visitation, 1975), 64.

3. Ibid.

4. Sister Mary Augustine is sometimes referred to as Sister Mary Austin. According to Sister Mada-anne Gell, VHM, community archivist, Sister Mary Augustine "was shortly gifted with the diminutive Austin, and so she was known throughout her life." Email to author, 11 August 2011.

5. Sullivan, 65. I have drawn heavily on Sullivan for this account.

6. [Sister Josephine Barber], 96.

7. See Emily Clark, *Masterless Mistresses: The New Orleans Ursulines and the Development of a New World Society, 1727–1834* (Chapel Hill: University of North Carolina Press, 2007), 27, 43–53.

8. Ibid., 24–25.

9. McNamara, 470–471.

10. Ibid., 479; Sarah A. Curtis, *Civilizing Habits: Women Missionaries and the Revival of French Empire* (New York: Oxford University Press, 2010), 44.

11. McNamara, 480.

12. Quoted in Clark, 50.

13. McNamara, 480; Clark, 50.

14. Quoted in Clark, 54.

15. Ibid., 54–55.

16. Ibid., 65, 75.

17. Ibid., 187.

18. See James J. Hennesey, SJ, *American Catholics: A History of the Roman Catholic Community in the United States* (New York: Oxford University Press, 1981), 145–146. The phrase, the "peculiar institution," is from Kenneth M. Stampp, *The Peculiar Institution: Slavery in the Antebellum South* (New York: Alfred Knopf, 1956).

19. Annabelle M. Melville, *John Carroll of Baltimore: Founder of the American Catholic Hierarchy* (New York: Charles Scribner's Sons, 1955), 176. Since French colonists first arrived in Louisiana, New Orleans had been under the jurisdiction of the Dioceses of Quebec, Santiago de Cuba, Havana, and Louisiana and the Floridas. Melville, 176.

20. Mary Ewens, *The Role of the Nun in Nineteenth Century America* (Salem, N.H.: Ayer, 1984), 43.

21. Melville, 177.

22. See Clark, 261.

23. Quoted in Hennesey, 72. Franklin's role in Carroll's appointment remains open to debate.

24. Ibid., 73.

25. Ibid.

26. Ibid.

27. Ibid.

28. Ibid., 87.

29. George C. Stewart, Jr., *Marvels of Charity: History of American Sisters and Nuns* (Huntington, Ind.: Our Sunday Visitor, 1994), 47.

30. Charles Warren Currier, *Carmel in America: A Centennial History of the Discalced Carmelites in the United States* (Baltimore: John Murphy, 1890), 51–52.

31. Ibid., 56.

32. Currier, 66; Stewart, 50.

33. Melville, 172.

34. Currier, 70.

35. See McNamara, 493–497.

36. Currier, 99.

37. Barbara Misner, SCSC, *"Highly Respectable and Accomplished Ladies"*:

Catholic Women Religious in America, 1790–1850 (New York: Garland Publishing, 1988), 122.

38. Stewart, 50.

39. Melville, 172.

40. John Carroll to Charles Plowden, 26 May 1788, in Thomas O'Brien Hanley, SJ, ed., *The John Carroll Papers*, Volume 1, 1755–1791 (Notre Dame: University of Notre Dame Press, 1976), 312. Also quoted in Misner, 174.

41. Quoted in Melville, 171.

42. See Misner, 173–174.

43. John Carroll to Leonardo Antonelli, 23 April 1792, in Thomas O'Brien Hanley, SJ, ed., *The John Carroll Papers*, Volume 2, 1792–1806 (Notre Dame: University of Notre Dame Press, 1976), 32.

44. Quoted in Melville, 172.

45. See John Carroll to Bernadine Matthews, 1 March 1793, *The John Carroll Papers*, II, 84–85; Melville, 172.

46. Quoted in Melville, 173.

47. Currier, 183.

48. Ibid., 192–193.

49. Ibid., 197.

50. Sullivan, 48; Gabriel Naughton, OFM, "The Poor Clares in Georgetown: Second Convent of Women in the United States," *Franciscan Studies* 24 (1943): 63–66.

51. McNamara, 307–308.

52. Ibid., 310.

53. Naughton, 69.

54. A coadjutor is essentially an assistant bishop.

55. Naughton, 68.

56. Sullivan, 49–50; Melville, 173; Thomas W. Spalding, *The Premier See: A History of the Archdiocese of Baltimore, 1789–1989* (Baltimore: Johns Hopkins University Press, 1989), 56.

57. Quoted in Sullivan, 50; Melville, 174.

58. McNamara, 465.

59. Ibid., 466–467.

60. Sullivan, 51–52.

61. Ibid., 53.

62. Ibid.

63. Ibid., 54.

64. Ibid.

65. Ibid., 81–83.

66. Quoted in Jenny Franchot, *Roads to Rome: The Antebellum Protestant Encounter with Catholicism* (Berkeley: University of California Press, 1994), 290.

67. Judith Metz, SC, "Elizabeth Bayley Seton: Extending the Role of Caregiver beyond the Family Circle," *American Catholic Studies* 16 (Summer 2005): 19–24.

68. Franchot, 299.

69. Ibid.

70. Melville, 181.

71. Franchot, 300.

72. Judith Metz, SC, "Elizabeth Bayley Seton: Animator of the Early American Catholic Church," *U.S. Catholic Historian* 22 (Winter 2004): 61.

73. Franchot, 300.

74. John Carroll to "His Sisters," 20 April 1809, in Thomas O'Brien Hanley, SJ, *The John Carroll Papers*, Volume 3, 1807–1815 (Notre Dame: University of Notre Dame Press, 1976), 84.

75. Judith Metz, SC, "The Founding Circle of Elizabeth Seton's Sisters of Charity," *U.S. Catholic Historian* 14 (Winter 1996): 23.

76. Quoted in ibid., 27.

77. Metz, "Animator of the Early American Church," 63–65.

78. Misner, 57.

79. Ibid., 128.

80. Ibid., 147. In 1850, the Sisters of Charity of St. Joseph joined with the Daughters of Charity in France and the name of the community was changed. Events prior to 1850 refer to the Sisters of Charity; when writing about events that took place subsequent to that year, I refer to the Emmitsburg community as the Daughters of Charity. This turn of events is further discussed in chapter 3.

81. See Anne M. Boylan, *The Origins of Women's Activism: New York and Boston 1797–1840* (Chapel Hill: University of North Carolina Press, 2002), especially chapter 3, for an excellent discussion of the work performed by Catholic sisters and Protestant laywomen.

82. Joseph G. Mannard, "Maternity . . . of the Spirit: Nuns and Domesticity in Antebellum America," *U.S. Catholic Historian* 5 (Summer/Fall 1986): 309. See also his "Converts in Convents: Protestant Women and the Social Appeal of Catholic Religious Life in Antebellum America," *Records of the American Catholic Historical Society of Philadelphia* 104 (Spring–Winter 1993): 79–90; and "Widows in Convents of the Early Republic: The Archdiocese of Baltimore, 1790–1860," *U. S. Catholic Historian* 26 (Spring 2008): 111–132.

83. Mannard, "Maternity . . . of the Spirit," 311.

84. Ibid., 314.

85. Ibid., 316.

86. Diane Batts Morrow, "Outsiders Within: The Oblate Sisters of Providence in 1830s Church and Society," *U.S. Catholic Historian* 15 (Spring 1997): 37; Cyprian Davis, OSB, "Black Catholics in Nineteenth Century America," *U.S. Catholic Historian* 5 (1986): 1; Diane Batts Morrow, *Persons of Color and Religious at the Same*

Time: The Oblate Sisters of Providence 1828–1860 (Chapel Hill: University of North Carolina Press, 2002), 3.

87. Morrow, *Persons of Color and Religious at the Same Time*, 14–15.

88. Ibid., 16.

89. Thaddeus J. Posey, OFM, Cap., "Praying in the Shadows: The Oblate Sisters of Providence, a Look at Nineteenth-Century Black Catholic Spirituality," *U.S. Catholic Historian* 12 (Winter 1994): 17–18.

90. Ibid., 18. Emphasis in original.

91. M. Reginald Gerdes, "To Educate and Evangelize: Black Catholic Schools of the Oblate Sisters of Providence (1828–1880)," *U.S. Catholic Historian* 7 (Spring–Summer 1988): 188.

92. Ibid., 189.

93. Morrow, *Persons of Color and Religious at the Same Time*, 89.

94. Misner, 46–47.

95. Quoted in Morrow, "Outsiders Within," 46.

96. Quoted in ibid., 51.

97. Ibid., 52.

98. Quoted in Morrow, *Persons of Color and Religious at the Same Time*, 140.

99. Quoted in ibid., 132.

100. Ibid., 127–128.

101. Ibid., 174–175.

102. Ibid., 203.

103. Ibid., 215.

104. Quoted in ibid. Purcell was unusual among American Catholic bishops because in 1862 he argued for the emancipation of slaves. See Hennesey, 147–148.

105. See Clyde F. Crews, *An American Holy Land: A History of the Archdiocese of Louisville* (Wilmington, Del.: Michael Glazier, 1987), 76–80.

106. The community's original name was Friends of Mary at the Foot of the Cross.

107. Crews, 89; Misner, 34. The mission founded by the sisters in Missouri was also called Bethlehem.

108. The Diocese of Bardstown is now the Archdiocese of Louisville.

109. Quoted in Mary Ellen Doyle, SCN, *Pioneer Spirit: Catherine Spalding Sister of Charity of Nazareth* (Lexington: University Press of Kentucky, 2006), 22.

110. Ibid., 33–34.

111. Misner, 38.

112. See Doyle, 71–74, 95–97; Crews, 88; Misner, 38–40. The community would later withdraw from Nashville after a dispute with the bishop over authority. Some of the members chose to remain in Nashville, however, becoming the nucleus for the Sisters of Charity of Leavenworth.

113. McNamara, 312.

114. Stewart, 34–35. Second order refers to the feminine branch of a religious community.

115. Mary Nona McGreal, OP, ed., *Dominicans at Home in a Young Nation 1786–1865* (Strasbourg, France: Editions du Signe, 2001), 97; Ewens, 58; Crews, 90.

116. McGreal, 97; Ewens, *Role of the Nun*, 59.

117. Ewens, *Role of the Nun*, 58–61; Crews, 91; Misner, 41–43.

118. Stewart, 64–65.

119. Quoted in ibid, 73.

120. Quoted in Misner, 50.

121. See Stewart, 73–74.

122. Misner, 50–51.

123. See ibid., 52.

124. I am very grateful to Sister Anne Francis, OLM, archivist for the Sisters of Charity of Our Lady of Mercy for providing additional information on her community.

Chapter 2

1. When the Diocese of Vincennes was established in 1834, it comprised the entire state of Indiana and the eastern third of Illinois. After 1878, the bishop resided in Indianapolis, and in 1898 the name was changed to the Diocese of Indianapolis.

2. Sister Mary Theodosia Mug, ed., *Journals and Letters of Mother Theodore Guérin Foundress of the Sisters of Providence of St. Mary-of-the-Woods Indiana* (St. Mary-of-the-Woods, Ind.: Sisters of Providence, 1942), xx.

3. Ibid., 54.

4. Ibid., 55–56.

5. Ibid., 65.

6. Ibid., 181.

7. Kathleen Sprows Cummings, "Strongly-Willed Sister and Sorin Ally Named Saint," *Notre Dame Magazine* (Winter 2006/2007): 9.

8. Quoted in ibid.

9. Jay P. Dolan, *The American Catholic Experience: A History from Colonial Times to the Present* (Garden City, N.Y.: Doubleday, 1985), 127.

10. Ibid., 128, 130.

11. Suellen Hoy, "The Journey Out: The Recruitment and Emigration of Irish Women Religious to the United States, 1812–1914," *Journal of Women's History* 6/7 (Winter/Spring 1995): 65.

12. Suellen Hoy and Margaret MacCurtain, *From Dublin to New Orleans: The Journey of Nora and Alice* (Dublin: Attic Press, 1994), 96.

13. Curtis, 43.

14. Quoted in L. Keppel, *Rose Philippine Duchesne: Religious of the Sacred Heart and Missioner 1769–1852* (London: Longmans, Green, 1940), 42.

15. Ibid., 45.

16. Quoted in ibid., 38.

17. Ibid., 57.

18. Sister Maria Kostka Logue, *Sisters of St. Joseph of Philadelphia: A Century of Growth and Development 1847–1947* (Westminster, Md.: Newman Press, 1950), 15.

19. Carol Coburn and Martha Smith, *Spirited Lives: How Nuns Shaped Catholic Culture and American Life, 1836–1920* (Chapel Hill: University of North Carolina Press, 1999), 43–44.

20. Ibid., 44. The poor town of Carondolet would become the community's U.S. headquarters.

21. See ibid., 5; and Logue, 13–14.

22. Coburn and Smith, *Spirited Lives,* 49–50.

23. Ibid., 53.

24. See Hoy, "The Journey Out," 164.

25. See Ann M. Harrington, BVM, "Sisters of Charity of the Blessed Virgin Mary, 1833–1843," *U.S. Catholic Historian* 27 (Fall 2009): 17–30. The Diocese of Dubuque was elevated to an archdiocese in 1893.

26. Sister M. Jerome McHale, RSM, *On the Wing: The Story of the Pittsburgh Sisters of Mercy 1843–1968* (New York: Seabury Press, 1980), 25.

27. Hoy, "The Journey Out," 67.

28. See Anne M. Butler, "Adapting the Vision: Caroline in 19th Century America," in *One Vision Many Voices: Lectures Delivered at the Mother Caroline Freiss Centenary Celebrations 1992,* eds. Virgina Geiger, SSND, and Patricia McLaughlin, SSND (Lanham, Md.: University Press of America, 1993), 37.

29. [Sister Dymphna?], *Mother Caroline and the School Sisters of Notre Dame in North America,* Volume I (St. Louis: Woodward & Tiernan, 1928), 29.

30. Quoted in Sister Jerome Frances Woods, CDP, "Congregations of Religious Women in the Old South," in *Catholics in the Old South,* eds. Randall M. Miller and Jon Wakelyn (Macon, Ga.: Mercer University Press, 1999), 104.

31. McHale, 32–36.

32. Ibid., 61.

33. Doyle, 41.

34. Woods, 105.

35. Doyle, 31.

36. McHale, 49.

37. Doyle, 31.

38. See Butler, "Adapting the Vision," 43.

39. Quoted in Ewens, *The Role of the Nun,* 62.

40. Hoy, "The Journey Out, 68.

41. Dymphna, 123.

42. Anne M. Butler, "There Are Exceptions to Every Rule: Adjusting the

Boundaries—Catholic Sisters and the American West," *American Catholic Studies* 116 (Fall 2005): 7.

43. Ewens, *The Role of the Nun*, 87–88.

44. Quoted in ibid., 62–63.

45. Ibid., 63.

46. Quoted in Dolan, 121.

47. Ewens, *The Role of the Nun*, 53.

48. Quoted in ibid., 53–54.

49. Quoted in ibid., 96.

50. Quoted in ibid.

51. Ibid., 288.

52. McHale, 48–49.

53. Ibid., 50.

54. Ibid., 72ff.

55. Mary J. Oates, ed., "'Lowell': An Account of Convent Life in Lowell, Massachusetts, 1852–1890," *New England Quarterly* 61 (March 1988): 102–103.

56. See Doyle, 71–74, 95–97; Crews, 88; Misner, 38–40.

57. Anne M. Butler, "Pioneer Sisters in a Catholic Melting Pot: Juggling Identity in the Pacific Northwest," *American Catholic Studies* 114 (Spring 2003): 27.

58. See ibid., 23.

59. Ibid., 27.

60. Butler, "There Are Exceptions to Every Rule," 7.

61. Quoted in ibid.

62. Dolan, 158.

63. See Dolan, 201–202, for a succinct discussion of the Know-Nothing Party. See also John Higham, *Strangers in the Land: Patterns of American Nativism, 1860–1925* (New York: Atheneum, 1963).

64. Mannard, "Converts in Convents," 80.

65. Mannard, "Maternity . . . of the Spirit," 309–310.

66. Barbara J. Howe, "Pioneers on a Mission for God: The Order of the Visitation of the Blessed Virgin Mary in Wheeling, 1848–1860," *West Virginia History: A Journal of Regional Studies* 4 (Spring 2010): 65.

67. Ibid., 79.

68. $10,000 in 1800 would translate to approximately $126,530 in 2010. See "The Inflation Calculator," http://www.westegg.com/inflation/infl.cgi, 24 September 2011.

69. For the story of the founding of the Ursuline convent in Boston, see Nancy Lusignan Schultz, *Fire and Roses: The Burning of the Charlestown Convent, 1834* (New York: Free Press, 2000), 11–15.

70. Ibid., 15.

71. Ibid., 18.

72. Daniel A. Cohen, "Miss Reed and the Superiors: The Contradictions of

Convent Life in Antebellum America," *Journal of Social History* 30 (Autumn 1996): 156.

73. Ibid., 149.

74. Hennesey, 121.

75. Quoted in Schultz, 157. See Schultz, 154–158 for a more detailed account of Sister Mary John's "escape" from and return to the Ursuline convent in Charlestown.

76. Quoted in ibid., 158.

77. Quoted in ibid., 162.

78. Quoted in ibid., 165. The speech was later published under the title *A Plea for the West.*

79. Ibid., 167.

80. Ibid.; Cohen, 161.

81. Cohen, 164.

82. Oates, "Lowell," 107–108.

83. Mary J. Oates, "The Good Sisters: The Work and Position of Catholic Churchwomen in Boston, 1870–1940," in *Catholic Boston: Studies in Religion and Community, 1870–1940*, eds. Robert E. Sullivan and James M. O'Toole (Boston: Archdiocese of Boston, 1985), 171–172.

84. Spalding, 134. See Joseph G. Mannard, "The 1839 Baltimore Nunnery Riot: An Episode in Jacksonian Nativism and Social Violence," in *Urban American Catholicism: The Culture and Identity of the American Catholic People*, ed. Timothy J. Meagher (New York: Garland Publishing, 1988), 192–206, for a full account of the episode.

85. Mark S. Massa, SJ, *Anti-Catholicism in America: The Last Acceptable Prejudice* (New York: Crossroad, 2003), 22. Monk's book remains in print in the twenty-first century.

86. See Ray Allen Billington, "Maria Monk and Her Influence," *Catholic Historical Review* 22 (October 1936): 286. According to Billington, 300,000 copies of the book were sold before the Civil War, 296.

87. See Stewart, 87, 179; Hennesey, 126. Stewart rightly explains the difficulty involved in arriving at an accurate count of women's religious communities.

88. Doyle, 59.

89. Quoted in ibid., 119–120. Historians should be grateful to Mary Ellen Doyle, SCN, for her willingness to write about the role played by her community in the institution of slavery. Many religious communities are only just beginning to uncover this aspect of their history.

90. Ibid., 122.

91. Ibid., 122–124.

92. Ibid., 124–125.

93. Tracy Fessenden, "The Sisters of the Holy Family and the Veil of Race," *Religion and American Culture: A Journal of Interpretation* 10 (Summer 2000): 191. See

also Edward T. Brett, "Race Issues and Conflict in Nineteenth- and Early Twentieth-Century Religious Life," *U.S. Catholic Historian* 29 (Winter 2011): 114–115.

94. Fessenden, 195.

95. Ibid., 201. Deggs does not specify the specific congregation of Sisters of St. Joseph protesting her community's wearing of the habit.

96. Marita-Constance Supan, IHM, "Dangerous Memory: Mother M. Theresa Maxis Duchemin and the Michigan Congregation of the Sisters, IHM," in Sisters, Servants of the Immaculate Heart of Mary, *Building Sisterhood: A Feminist History of the Sisters, Servants of the Immaculate Heart of Mary* (Syracuse: Syracuse University Press, 1997), 34.

97. Ibid., 37–39.

98. Ibid., 40.

99. Ibid., 43–44.

100. Patricia Byrne, CSJ, "*Sisters of St. Joseph*: The Americanization of a French Tradition," *U.S. Catholic Historian* 5 (Summer/Fall 1986): 256.

101. Marie Hubert Kealy, IHM, "Immigrant Church to University: Growth of the Sisters, Servants of the Immaculate Heart of Mary in Eastern Pennsylvania," *U.S. Catholic Historian* 27 (Fall 2009): 35–38; Supan, 53–55.

102. See Margaret Susan Thompson, "The Context—Part One," in Sisters, Servants of the Immaculate Heart of Mary, Monroe, Michigan, *Building Sisterhood: A Feminist History of the Sisters, Servants of the Immaculate Heart of Mary* (Syracuse: Syracuse University Press, 1997), 26.

103. Margaret Susan Thompson, "Introduction: Concentric Circles of Sisterhood," in Sisters, Servants of the Immaculate Heart of Mary, Monroe, Michigan, *Building Sisterhood: A Feminist History of the Sisters, Servants of the Immaculate Heart of Mary* (Syracuse: Syracuse University Press, 1997), 6.

Chapter 3

1. David Cowan and John Kuenster, *To Sleep with the Angels: The Story of a Fire* (Chicago: Ivan R. Dee, 1996), 23–27.

2. See ibid., 20–36.

3. Ibid., 131.

4. Ibid., 129; Suellen Hoy, "Stunned with Sorrow," *Chicago History* XXXIII (Summer 2004): 14.

5. Hoy, "Stunned with Sorrow," 4.

6. Ibid., 9.

7. Cowan and Kuenster, 273.

8. Ibid., 275.

9. Ibid.

10. Ibid., 8.

11. Quoted in Kathleen Sprows Cummings, "'The Wageless Work of Paradise':

Integrating Women into American Religious History," *Journal of Religion and Society* Supplement 5 (2009): 117. An expanded version of Cummings's article can be found in Kathleen Sprows Cummings, *New Women of the Old Faith.*

12. Quoted in Cummings, "Wageless Work of Paradise," 115.

13. See Ewens, *The Role of the Nun,* 22.

14. Quoted in Clark, 56. See also Eileen Mary Brewer, *Nuns and the Education of American Catholic Women, 1860–1920* (Chicago: Loyola University Press, 1987), 8.

15. Clark, 149.

16. Ibid., 156. Protestant denominations also believed women were responsible for religious education. See, for example, Ann Douglas, *The Feminization of American Culture,* rev. ed. (New York: Farrar, Strauss, and Giroux, 1998).

17. Clark, 56–57.

18. Misner, 26.

19. Quoted in Ellin Kelly and Annabelle Melville, eds., *Elizabeth Seton: Selected Writings* (New York: Paulist Press, 1987), 19.

20. Ibid.

21. Quoted in Metz, "Animator of the Early American Church," 56.

22. Misner, 174.

23. Doyle, 75.

24. Quoted in Misner, 177.

25. Quoted in Mary J. Oates, "Catholic Female Academies on the Frontier," *U.S. Catholic Historian* 12 (Fall 1994): 130.

26. Ibid., 124.

27. Ibid.

28. Quoted in Joseph G. Mannard, "Protestant Mothers and Catholic Sisters: Gender Concerns in Anti-Catholic Conspiracy Theories, 1830–1860," *American Catholic Studies* 111 (Spring–Winter 2000): 1.

29. Quoted in Sister M. Rosalita, IHM, *No Greater Service: The History of the Congregation of the Sisters, Servants of the Immaculate Heart of Mary, 1845–1945* (Detroit: Congregation of the Sisters, Servants of the Immaculate Heart of Mary, Monroe, Michigan, 1948), 85.

30. Ibid., 86. The school year began on the first Monday in October and ended on the last Tuesday in August. Ibid., 66.

31. Jo Ellen McNergney Vinyard, *For Faith and Fortune: The Education of Catholic Immigrants in Detroit, 1805–1925* (Urbana: University of Illinois Press, 1998), 78–79.

32. Ibid., 80.

33. [Sister Dymphna?], 59.

34. Suzanne H. Schrems, *Uncommon Women Unmarked Trails: The Courageous Journey of Catholic Missionary Sisters in Frontier Montana* (Norman, Okla.: Horse Creek Publications, 2003), 13.

35. Ibid., 15.

36. Ibid., 16.

37. Ibid.

38. Mary J. Oates, *The Catholic Philanthropic Tradition in America* (Blooming-ton: Indiana University Press, 1995), 145.

39. See ibid., 148.

40. Quoted in ibid., 147.

41. Dolan, 272.

42. Leslie Woodcock Tentler, *Seasons of Grace: A History of the Catholic Archdio-cese of Detroit* (Detroit: Wayne State University Press, 1990), 230.

43. Cummings, *New Women of the Old Faith*, 112.

44. Cummings, "Wageless Work of Paradise," 117.

45. Cummings, *New Women of the Old Faith*, 104–105.

46. Cummings, "Wageless Work of Paradise," 115–116.

47. Cummings, *New Women of the Old Faith*, 137.

48. See Margaret M. McGuinness, "Americanization and the Schools," *American Catholic Studies* 117 (Summer 2006): 98–102, for a brief account of this controversy.

49. Dolan, 287–288.

50. Quoted in Sarah E. Miller, "'Send Sisters, Send Polish Sisters': American-izing Catholic Immigrant Children in the Early Twentieth Century," *Ohio History* 114 (2007): 48.

51. Quoted in Dolan, 290.

52. Joseph H. Lackner, "Two Italian Parishes in Cleveland," *U.S. Catholic Histor-ian* 6 (Fall 1987): 315–316.

53. Miller, 53–54.

54. Vinyard, 176.

55. See Grace Donovan, "Immigrant Nuns: Their Participation in the Process of Americanization: Massachusetts and Rhode Island, 1880–1920," *Catholic Historical Review* 77 (April 1991): 206–207.

56. See S. M. Liguori, "Polish American Sisterhoods and Schools to 1919," *Polish American Studies* 13 (July–December 1956): 72–76.

57. Marvin Lazerson, "Understanding American Catholic Educational History," *History of Education Quarterly* 17 (Autumn 1977): 308.

58. Ibid., 309.

59. Ibid.

60. Stewart, 285–286; Margherita Marchione, MPF, "Religious Teachers Filip-pini in the United States," *U.S. Catholic Historian* 6 (Fall 1987): 354–359.

61. See Ewens, *Role of the Nun*, 126.

62. Ibid., 125.

63. Donovan, 200.

64. Ibid.

65. Sister Marie de Lourdes Walsh, *The Sisters of Charity of New York 1809–1959*, Volume 1 (New York: Fordham University Press, 1960), 127.

66. Ibid., 130–134.

67. See Judith Metz, SC, "By What Authority: The Founding of the Sisters of Charity of Cincinnati," *Vincentian Heritage Journal*: Volume 20: Iss. 1, Article 4 (1999) http://via.library.depaul.edu/vhj/vol20/iss1/4 (13 August 2011).

68. Quoted in Tentler, 242.

69. Quoted in ibid., 243.

70. Theresa A. Rector, "Black Nuns as Educators," *Journal of Negro Education* 51 (Summer 1982): 250–251. The law was never passed. See also Cecilia A. Moore, "Keeping Harlem Catholic: African-American Catholics and Harlem, 1920–1960," *American Catholic Studies* 114 (Fall 2003): 1–21.

71. Rector, 251.

72. Quoted in Karl Markus Kries, ed., *Lakotas, Black Robes, and Holy Women: German Reports from the Indian Missions in South Dakota, 1886–1900* (Lincoln: University of Nebraska Press, 2007), 123.

73. Mary J. Oates, CSJ, "The Development of Catholic Colleges for Women, 1895–1960," *U.S. Catholic Historian* 7 (Fall 1988): 413.

74. See Cummings, *New Women of the Old Faith*, 61ff.

75. See ibid., 61–62.

76. Quoted in Kathleen Mahoney, "American Catholic Colleges for Women: Historical Origins," in *Catholic Women's Colleges in America*, eds. Tracy Schier and Cynthia Russett (Baltimore: Johns Hopkins University Press, 2002), 51.

77. Karen M. Kennelly, CSJ, "Faculties and What They Taught," in *Catholic Women's Colleges in America*, eds. Tracy Schier and Cynthia Russett (Baltimore: Johns Hopkins University Press, 2002), 104.

78. Ibid., 105.

79. Quoted in Mary J. Oates, "Sisterhoods and Catholic Higher Education, 1890–1960," in *Catholic Women's Colleges in America*, ed. Tracy Schier and Cynthia Russett (Baltimore: Johns Hopkins University Press, 2002), 176.

80. Tracy Schier and Cynthia Russett, eds., *Catholic Women's Colleges in America* (Baltimore: Johns Hopkins University Press, 2002), 5. See also Fernanda Perrone, "'A Well-Balanced Education': Catholic Women's Colleges in New Jersey, 1900–1970," *American Catholic Studies* 117 (Summer 2006): 1–31.

81. See Perrone, "'A Well-Balanced Education,'" 23–24. A number of Catholic colleges founded by women religious were originally intended to educate members of the community.

82. Suellen Hoy, *Good Hearts: Catholic Sisters in Chicago's Past* (Urbana: University of Illinois Press, 2006), 89. The community's original name was the Sisters of the Blessed Sacrament for Indians and Colored People. For a biography of Katharine Drexel, see Lou Baldwin, *Saint Katharine Drexel: Apostle to the Oppressed* (Philadelphia: Catholic Standard and Times, 2000).

83. Oates, "Sisterhoods and Catholic Higher Education," 166. In order to protect his daughters from unscrupulous suitors, however, Drexel's will only allowed them to receive the income generated from the $14 million; they could not give

away or spend anything other than their current income. In addition, if all three children died childless, the money would be distributed among the charities to which Francis Drexel had bequeathed a portion of his estate. See Baldwin, 52–53.

84. Mary Linehan, "'Nazareth College Leads the Way': Catholicism, Democracy, and Racial Justice at a Southern College, 1920–1955," *U.S. Catholic Historian* 19 (Winter 2001): 72.

85. Ibid., 72–76.

86. R. Bentley Anderson, *Black, White, and Catholic: New Orleans Interracialism, 1947–1956* (Nashville: Vanderbilt University Press, 2005), 193–194.

87. Ibid., 169.

88. Jill Ker Conway, "Faith, Knowledge, and Gender," in *Catholic Women's Colleges in America*, eds. Tracy Schier and Cynthia Russett (Baltimore: Johns Hopkins University Press, 2002), 14. Women religious also founded a number of junior colleges throughout the United States. For a discussion of two-year Catholic colleges for women in New Jersey, see Fernanda Perrone, "Gone and Forgotten? New Jersey's Catholic Junior Colleges," *American Catholic Studies* 121 (Summer 2010): 31–64.

89. For one story of a male university deciding to admit women, see Susan Poulson, "From Single-Sex to Coeducation: The Advent of Coeducation at Georgetown, 1965–1975," *U.S. Catholic Historian* 13 (Fall 1995): 117–137. More remains to be written on the movement toward coeducation by Catholic men's colleges from the perspective of their sister institutions.

90. See Conway, 14–15. Some schools deliberately chose not to merge with their male counterparts. Examples of this include College of Notre Dame in Baltimore (Loyola) and St. Mary's College, South Bend (University of Notre Dame).

91. See Harold A. Buetow, *Of Singular Benefit: The Story of Catholic Education in the United States* (New York: Macmillan, 1970), 285–286.

92. Stewart, 460–463.

93. See Margaret Mary McGuinness and Margaret Mary Reher, "From St. Edward's School to Providence Center: A Story of Commitment," *Records of the American Catholic Historical Society of Philadelphia* 107 (Spring–Summer 1996): 101–122, for the story of the Sisters of the Holy Child Jesus and St. Edward's.

94. Ibid., 111.

95. Ibid., 119.

96. Ibid.

97. Quoted in ibid., 120.

Chapter 4

1. William Watson, "The Sisters of Charity, the 1832 Cholera Epidemic in Philadelphia and Duffy's Cut," *U.S. Catholic Historian* 27 (Fall 2009): 5. A classic book on cholera is Charles E. Rosenberg, *The Cholera Years* (Chicago: University of Chicago Press, 1962).

2. Watson, "The Sisters of Charity," 11.

3. Ibid.

4. Ibid.

5. Ibid., 12–13.

6. Ibid.

7. Rosenberg, 64.

8. Quoted in Watson, "The Sisters of Charity," 15.

9. William E. Watson, J. Francis Watson, John H. Ahtes III, and Earl H. Schandelmeier III, *The Ghosts of Duffy's Cut: The Irish Who Died Building America's Most Dangerous Stretch of Railroad* (Westport, Conn.: Praeger, 2006), 89. The story of the Sisters of Charity and Philadelphia's cholera epidemic is found in this book as well as in the article quoted above.

10. Coburn and Smith, *Spirited Lives*, 191.

11. Quoted in Ann Doyle, RN, "Nursing by Religious Orders in the United States Part I, 1809–1840," *American Journal of Nursing* 29 (July 1929): 775.

12. Quoted in Bernadette McCauley, *Who Shall Take Care of Our Sick? Roman Catholic Sisters and the Development of Catholic Hospitals in New York City* (Baltimore: Johns Hopkins University Press, 2005), 17.

13. Quoted in Christopher J. Kauffman, *Ministry and Meaning: A Religious History of Catholic Health Care in the United States* (New York, Crossroad, 1995), 34.

14. Baltimore's St. Agnes Hospital traces its beginnings to the Baltimore Infirmary.

15. Kauffman, 39.

16. Ibid., 40.

17. See Carlan Kraman, OSF, "Women Religious in Health Care: The Early Years," in *Pioneer Healers: The History of Women Religious in American Health Care*, eds. Ursula Stepsis, CSA, and Dolores Liptak, RSM (New York: Crossroad, 1989), 27.

18. Kauffman, 51–52.

19. Kraman, 32. Mercy Hospital is now UPMC Mercy (University of Pittsburgh Medical Center).

20. Ibid.

21. Ibid., 34–35.

22. McCauley, 18–19.

23. Ibid., 47.

24. Kauffman, 54.

25. See Morrow, *Persons of Color and Religious at the Same Time*, 70–72.

26. Ibid., 148. It is not clear what motivated Joubert to stipulate that the Oblates be separated from the Sisters of Charity. Morrow suggests that he may have either been attempting to prevent any outbreaks of racial hostility or ensuring the Oblates would be caring for African Americans. See Morrow, *Persons of Color and Religious at the Same Time*, 148–149.

27. Ibid., 147.

28. Kauffman, 60, 76; McHale, 65.

29. Coburn and Smith, *Spirited Lives*, 191–192.

30. Kauffman, 85.

31. Judith Metz, SC, "In Times of War," in *Pioneer Healers: The History of Women Religious in American Health Care*, eds. Ursula Stepsis, CSA, and Dolores Liptak, RSM (New York: Crossroad, 1989), 42. A total of 617 sisters from 21 religious communities served either the Union or the Confederacy during the Civil War.

32. Ibid., 42–43. See also Sister Mary Denis Maher, *To Bind Up the Wounds: Catholic Sister Nurses in the U.S. Civil War* (New York: Greenwood Press, 1989), 232.

33. Maher, 71–72. See also Sister M. Liguori, HFN, "Polish Sisters in the Civil War," *Polish American Studies* VII (January–June 1950): 1.

34. Quoted in Maher, 86.

35. Quoted in ibid., 88.

36. Quoted in Kauffman, 88.

37. Quoted in Metz, "In Times of War," 44.

38. Sister Mary Paulinus Oakes, RSM, ed., *Angels of Mercy: An Eyewitness Account of Civil War and Yellow Fever by a Sister of Mercy. A Primary Source by Sr. Ignatius Sumner, RSM* (Baltimore: Cathedral Foundation Press, 1998), 18.

39. Maher, 87.

40. Quoted in Metz, "In Times of War," 44.

41. Quoted in Maher, 76.

42. Ibid., 101.

43. Quoted in Liguori, "Polish Sisters in the Civil War," 5–6.

44. John Brinton, *Personal Memoirs of John H. Brinton, Major and Surgeon U.S.V., 1861–1865* (New York: Neale, 1914), 44–45.

45. Barbra Mann Wall, "Grace under Pressure: The Nursing Sisters of the Holy Cross, 1861–1865," *Nursing History Review* 1 (1993): 71–87.

46. Coburn and Smith, *Spirited Lives*, 193.

47. Ibid., 192. The plan almost backfired. "Firing began before the Confederates recognized the sisters, and flying bullets narrowly missed Mother Monica Pugh." See ibid.

48. Oakes, 14.

49. See George Barton, *Angels of the Battlefield: A History of the Labors of the Catholic Sisterhoods in the Late Civil War* (Philadelphia: Catholic Art Publishing, 1898), 243.

50. Quoted in Maher, 116–117.

51. See also John Fialka, *Sisters: Catholic Nuns and the Making of America* (New York: St. Martin's Press, 2003), 69–70.

52. Byrne, *"Sisters of St. Joseph,"* 263.

53. Quoted in Maher, 127.

54. Quoted in Ann Doyle, "Nursing by Religious Orders in the United States: Part II: 1841–1870," *American Journal of Nursing* 29 (August 1929): 966.

55. Sister Margaret Patrice Slattery, CCVI, *Promises to Keep: A History of the Sisters of Charity of the Incarnate Word, San Antonio, Texas*, Volume 2 (San Antonio, Tex.: Private Printing, 1995); and Sioban Nelson, *Say Little, Do Much: Nurses, Nuns, and Hospitals in the Nineteenth Century* (Philadelphia: University of Pennsylvania Press, 2001), 102.

56. Barbra Mann Wall, *Unlikely Entrepreneurs: Catholic Sisters and the Hospital Marketplace, 1865–1925* (Columbus: Ohio State University Press, 2005), 134.

57. Nelson, 104.

58. Gail Farr Casterline, "St. Joseph's and St. Mary's: The Origins of Catholic Hospitals in Philadelphia," *Pennsylvania Magazine of History and Biography* 108 (July 1984): 305.

59. Ibid., 307.

60. Ibid., 309.

61. Ibid., 309–310.

62. Judith G. Cetina, "In Times of Immigration," in *Pioneer Healers: The History of Women Religious in American Health Care*, eds. Ursula Stepsis, CSA, and Dolores Liptak, RSM (New York: Crossroad, 1989), 103.

63. Quoted in Mary Louise Sullivan, MSC, *Mother Cabrini: "Italian Immigrant of the Century"* (Staten Island, N.Y.: Center for Migration Studies, 1992), 45.

64. Quoted in ibid., 62.

65. Ibid., 103. St. Frances Cabrini's work with immigrants will be discussed in chapter 5.

66. Mary Louise Sullivan, MSC, "Mother Cabrini: Missionary to Italian Immigrants," *U.S. Catholic Historian* 6 (Fall 1987): 270.

67. Ibid.

68. Wall, *Unlikely Entrepreneurs*, 4.

69. Quoted in John Scanlon, "The Yellow Fever Epidemic of 1878 in the Diocese of Natchez," *Catholic Historical Review* 40 (April 1954): 30.

70. Ibid.

71. Oakes, 41.

72. Scanlon, 35.

73. Quoted in Margaret M. McGuinness, *Neighbors and Missionaries: A History of the Sisters of Our Lady of Christian Doctrine* (New York: Fordham University Press, 2012), 66.

74. Kauffman, 153.

75. Quoted in Todd L. Savitt and Janice Willms, "Sisters' Hospital: The Sisters of Providence and St. Patrick Hospital, Missoula, Montana, 1873–1890," *Montana: The Magazine of Western History* 53 (Spring 2003): 32–33.

76. Ibid., 34.

77. Ibid., 35.

78. Edna Marie LeRoux, RSM, "In Times of Socioeconomic Crisis," in *Pioneer Healers: The History of Women Religious in American Health Care,* eds. Ursula Stepsis, CSA, and Dolores Liptak, RSM (New York: Crossroad, 1989), 119.

79. Carol Coburn and Martha Smith, "'Pray for Your Wanderers': Women Religious on the Colorado Mining Frontier, 1877–1917," *Frontiers: A Journal of Women's Studies* 15 (1995): 35–36.

80. Ibid., 43.

81. LeRoux, 124.

82. Quoted in Kauffman, 162.

83. Ibid., 165.

84. Kathleen M. Joyce, "The Evil of Abortion and the Greater Good of the Faith: Negotiating Catholic Survival in the Twentieth-Century American Health Care System," *Religion and American Culture: A Journal of Interpretation* 12 (Winter 2002): 94.

85. Kauffman, 165.

86. Ibid.

87. Ibid., 167.

88. Joyce, 101–102. The CHA was the result of a discussion between Moulinier and fourteen Sisters of St. Joseph of Carondelet–all of whom worked in health care—who deferred to the Jesuit's leadership. See Kauffman, 168–169.

89. Kauffman, 170.

90. Ibid., 171.

91. Ibid., 259; and Angelyn Dries, OSF, *The Missionary Movement in American Catholic History* (Maryknoll, N.Y.: Orbis Books, 1998), 104–106.

92. Kauffman, 259; and Margaret Mary Reher, "Denis J. Dougherty and Anna M. Dengel: The Missionary Alliance," *Records of the American Catholic Historical Society of Philadelphia* 101 (Spring 1990): 24. Dougherty claimed the new community was his idea, but according to Reher, Dengel and Father Michael A. Mathis, CSC, were the first to realize the need for such a community. Reher, 23.

93. Reher, 24; Wall, *Unlikely Entrepreneurs,* 184.

94. Kauffman, 259–260.

95. Ibid., 200.

96. Susan Karina Dickey, OP, "Dominican Sisters Encounter Jim Crow: The Desegregation of a Catholic Hospital in Mississippi," *American Catholic Studies* 116 (Spring 2005): 44–45.

97. Ibid., 46–47.

98. Ibid., 47.

99. See ibid., 49–50.

100. Ibid., 55.

101. Ibid., 56–57.

102. See Barbra Mann Wall, "Catholic Sister Nurses in Selma, Alabama, 1940–1972," *Advances in Nursing Sciences* 32 (January–March 2009): 91–102, for a full discussion of the mission of the Sisters of St. Joseph in Alabama.

103. Ibid, 92–93.

104. Ibid., 94.

105. See Amy L. Koehlinger, *The New Nuns: Racial Justice and Religious Reform in the 1960s* (Cambridge: Harvard University Press, 2007), 149–151.

106. Wall, "Catholic Sister Nurses," 96.

107. Koehlinger, *The New Nuns*, 172.

108. Quoted in ibid., 178.

109. Quoted in ibid., 172.

110. See Wall, "Catholic Sister Nurses," 99–100. Good Samaritan hospital closed in 1983.

111. Joyce, 111.

112. Oates, *The Catholic Philanthropic Tradition in America*, 88.

113. Kauffman, 281.

114. Quoted in ibid.

115. Ibid., 283.

116. See "Network," www.networklobby.org/about-us/history (18 June 2010).

117. Quoted in "Nuns: Vote for Health Bill Would Be 'Life-Affirming,'" *National Catholic Reporter*, 18 March 2010. http://ncronline.org/news/politics/nuns-vote-health-bill-would-be-life-affirming (18 June 2010).

118. Dennis Coady, "Thousands of Catholic Sisters Support Health Care Reform," *National Catholic Reporter*, 17 March 2010. http://ncronline.org/blogs/ncr-today/thousands-catholic-sisters-support-health-care-reform (18 June 2010).

119. Quoted in Helene Cooper, "Nuns Back Bill Amid Broad Rift Over Whether It Limits Abortion Enough," *New York Times*, 19 March 2010. http://www.nytimes.com/2010/03/20/health/policy/20abortion.html (18 June 2010).

121. Kevin Sack, "Nuns, a 'Dying Breed,' Fade from Leadership Roles at Catholic Hospitals," *New York Times*, 21 August 2011, 11. The focus of the article was SSM Health Care, a network of Catholic hospitals with over 22,000 employees.

122. Ibid.

Chapter 5

1. Clement M. Thuente, OP, "America's Pioneer Catholic Settlement House," *Rosary Magazine* LXIII (October 1923): 3. The article's title is misleading. The first Catholic social settlement, Cincinnati's Santa Maria Institute, was founded in 1897. St. Rose's was established in 1898.

2. Ibid., 2.

3. "Institute of Our Lady of Christian Doctrine," *Church Progress*, 16 July 1908.

4. McGuinness, *Neighbors and Missionaries*, 41.

5. Elizabeth McKeown and Dorothy M. Brown, *The Poor Belong to Us: Catholic Charities and American Welfare* (Cambridge: Harvard University Press, 1997), 1.

6. Ibid., 3.

7. Oates, *The Catholic Philanthropic Tradition in America*, 5–6.

8. Quoted in ibid., 6.

9. Ibid.

10. Ibid.

11. Judith Metz, SC, "150 Years of Caring: The Sisters of Charity of Cincinnati," *Cincinnati Historical Society Bulletin* 37 (Fall 1979): 152–153. The "him" referred to by Fenwick was Rev. Louis Deluol, SS, who was the ultimate authority over the community during this time.

12. Oates, *The Catholic Philanthropic Tradition in America*, 30.

13. Marian J. Morton, "The Transformation of Catholic Orphanages: Cleveland, 1851–1996," *Catholic Historical Review* 88 (January 2002): 65. Known originally as the Orphan Asylum of the Immaculate Conception, the name was later changed to St. Vincent's Orphan Asylum. See Donald Philip Gavin, *In All Things Charity: History of the Sisters of Charity of St. Augustine Cleveland, Ohio, 1851–1954* (Milwaukee, Wis.: Bruce Publishing, 1955), 2–22, for the early history of the Sisters of Charity of St. Augustine in Cleveland.

14. Sister Mary Loyola Hegarty, CCVI, *Serving with Gladness: The Origin and History of the Congregation of the Sisters of Charity of the Incarnate Word Houston, Texas* ([Houston]: Bruce Publishing, in cooperation with the Sisters of Charity of the Incarnate Word Houston Texas, 1967), 230–233.

15. Ibid., 328–330. To remember those who perished in the storm, members of the community sing "Queen of the Waves" every year on September 8.

16. Coburn and Smith, *Spirited Lives*, 54.

17. Ibid., 101–102.

18. Kathleen Healy, *Frances Warde: American Founder of the Sisters of Mercy* (New York: Seabury Press, 1973), 313–314.

19. Morton, 69.

20. Ibid., 70. Both orphanages were administered by the Ladies of the Sacred Heart.

21. Maureen Fitzgerald, "The Perils of 'Passion and Poverty': Women Religious and the Care of Single Women in New York City, 1845–1890," *U.S. Catholic Historian* 10 (1991/1992): 52.

22. Maureen Fitzgerald, *Habits of Compassion: Irish Catholic Nuns and the Origins of New York's Welfare System, 1830–1920* (Urbana: University of Illinois Press, 2006), 225.

23. Elizabeth McKeown and Dorothy M. Brown, "Saving New York's Children," *US Catholic Historian* 13 (Summer 1995): 88; Fitzgerald, *Habits of Compassion*, 227.

24. Linda Gordon, *The Great Arizona Orphan Abduction* (Cambridge: Harvard University Press, 1999), 65. Gordon's book provides a detailed account of this series of events.

25. Ibid., 42. The sisters later claimed that they were worried that the adoptive mothers did not seem "as fair as we had hoped for." Ibid., 65.

26. McKeown and Brown, "Saving New York's Children," 89–90.

27. Quoted in Gordon, 294.

28. McKeown and Brown, "Saving New York's Children," 90–91.

29. Morton, 79–80.

30. Ibid., 82–83.

31. Ibid., 65.

32. Fitzgerald, "The Perils of 'Passion and Poverty,'" 53.

33. Fitzgerald, *Habits of Compassion,* 225; "The Perils of 'Passion and Poverty,'" 53.

34. Fitzgerald, "The Perils of 'Passion and Poverty,'" 53.

35. Ibid., 48.

36. Ibid., 49.

37. Hoy, *Good Hearts,* 48.

38. Ibid., 55; Fitzgerald, *Habits of Compassion,* 75.

39. Hoy, *Good Hearts,* 53–54.

40. Ibid., 60.

41. Ibid., 50, 60.

42. Ibid., 61.

43. Fitzgerald, "The Perils of 'Passion and Poverty,'" 49–50.

44. Fitzgerald, *Habits of Compassion,* 74.

45. Hennesey, 173–174.

46. Margaret M. McGuinness, "Urban Settlement Houses and Rural Parishes: The Ministry of the Sisters of Christian Doctrine, 1910–1986," *U.S. Catholic Historian* 26 (Winter 2008): 25.

47. Ibid., 26.

48. Quoted in Margaret M. McGuinness, "Body and Soul: Catholic Social Settlements and Immigration," *U.S. Catholic Historian* 13 (Summer 1995): 66.

49. Ibid.

50. See M. Christine Anderson, "Catholic Nuns and the Invention of Social Work: The Sisters of the Santa Maria Institute of Cincinnati, Ohio, 1897 through the 1920s," *Journal of Women's History* 12 (Spring 2000): 68.

51. Quoted in McGuinness, "Body and Soul," 66.

52. Ibid., 67.

53. Quoted in Anderson, 70.

54. Ibid.

55. Sullivan, *Mother Cabrini: "Italian Immigrant of the Century,"* 73.

56. Ibid., 74.

57. Ibid., 80–81.

58. Sister Mary Janice Ziolkowski, CSSF, *The Felician Sisters of Livonia, Michigan: First Province in America* (Livonia, Mich.: Felician Sisters, OSF, Livonia, Michigan, 1984), 83–85.

59. See ibid., 333–344.

60. Roberto R. Treviño, "Facing Jim Crow: Catholic Sisters and the 'Mexican Problem' in Texas," *Western Historical Quarterly* 34 (Summer 2003): 144.

61. Ibid., 143.

62. Ibid., 146–147.

63. Ibid., 148.

64. Ibid., 151.

65. Ibid., 150–153.

66. See Gerald McKevitt, *Brokers of Culture: Italian Jesuits in the American West, 1848–1919* (Stanford: Stanford University Press, 2007), 162.

67. See Susan C. Peterson, "Doing 'Women's Work': The Grey Nuns at Fort Totten Indian Reservation, 1874–1900," *North Dakota History* 52 (Spring 1985): 19.

68. Ibid., 18–25.

69. Ibid., 20.

70. Ibid., 20–21.

71. Ibid., 22–25.

72. Dries, 35–36.

73. See Susan Carol Peterson and Courtney Ann Vaughn-Robertson, *Women with Vision: The Presentation Sisters of South Dakota, 1880–1985* (Urbana: University of Illinois Press, 1988), 59–60.

74. Ibid., 60–61.

75. See Susan C. Peterson, "A Widening Horizon: Catholic Sisterhoods on the Northern Plains, 1874–1910," *Great Plains Quarterly* 5 (Spring 1985): 125–132.

76. Thomas W. Foley, "Father Francis M. Craft and the Indian Sisters," *U.S. Catholic Historian* 16 (Spring 1998): 45–48.

77. Ibid., 49–50, 54.

78. Quoted in Baldwin, 71.

79. Ibid., 101–102.

80. Anne M. Butler, "Mother Katharine Drexel: Spiritual Visionary for the West," in *By Grit and Grace: Eleven Women Who Shaped the American West,* eds. Glenda Riley and Richard W. Etulain (Golden, Colo.: Fulcrum Publishing, 1997), 202. See also Carol Berg, OSB, "Agents of Cultural Change: The Benedictines at White Earth," *Minnesota History* 48 (1982): 158–170.

81. See Hoy, *Good Hearts,* 87–88.

82. Butler, "Mother Katharine Drexel," 215.

83. See Baldwin, 109–110; and Butler, "Katharine Drexel," 211–213, for Drexel's work in the western United States. See Baldwin, 118–119; and Hoy, *Good Hearts,* 88, for her ministry in Chicago.

84. Hoy, *Good Hearts,* 88–89.

85. Margaret Susan Thompson, "Philemon's Dilemma: Nuns and the Black Community in Nineteenth-Century America: Some Findings," in *The American Catholic Religious Life,* ed. Joseph M. White (New York: Garland Publishing, 1988), 88. In 2001, the Franciscan Sisters of Baltimore merged with the Sisters of

St. Francis of Assisi, headquartered in St. Francis, Wisconsin. See "Sisters of St. Francis of Assisi," http://www.lakeosfs.org/who_we_are/history.asp (10 March 2011).

86. Thompson, "Philemon's Dilemma," 10.

87. Ibid., 11.

88. Dries, 51.

89. Quoted in ibid., 47.

90. Ibid., 51–52.

91. Ibid. 54.

92. Paul R. Rivera, "'Field Found!' Establishing the Maryknoll Mission Enterprise in the United States and China, 1918–1928," *Catholic Historical Review* 84 (July 1998): 483–484.

93. Dries, 77. For a history of the Maryknoll Sisters, see Penny Lernoux, *Hearts on Fire: The Story of the Maryknoll Sisters* (Maryknoll, N.Y.: Orbis Books, 1993).

94. See Lernoux, 50–55.

95. Quoted in Dries, 122.

96. Quoted in ibid.

97. Lernoux, 112.

98. Ibid., 119.

99. See McGuinness, *Neighbors and Missionaries*, 94–95.

100. Dries, 26.

101. See chapters 7 and 8 for further discussion of these ministries in the late twentieth century.

Chapter 6

1. Kristin Ohlson, *Stalking the Divine: Contemplating Faith with the Poor Clares* (New York: Hyperion, 2003), 22. Although they are often used interchangeably, the terms contemplative and cloistered do not have the same meaning. Contemplative nuns refer to those women religious whose apostolate is focused on prayer. Cloistered nuns live within an enclosed area, and do not leave unless necessary. Reasons for leaving the cloistered environment include visits to doctors and dentists, and family funerals. Contemplative nuns are cloistered, but there are some cloistered communities that are engaged in a ministry of teaching; their schools are located within the enclosure.

2. Ibid., 16.

3. Ibid., 21.

4. Ibid., 22.

5. Ibid.

6. Ibid., 23.

7. Ibid., 24.

8. Ibid., 16.

9. Ibid., 49.

10. Ibid., 44.

11. See "Personal Sacrifices for Faith," 2007. http://abcnews.go.com/2020/story?id=3160621&page=1 (4 May 2011).

12. Mary Jo Weaver, *Cloister and Community: Life within a Carmelite Monastery* (Bloomington: Indiana University Press, 2002), 84.

13. See ibid., 11–14, for a full discussion of the development of the Carmelites.

14. Peter Thomas Rohrbach, OCD, *Journey to Carith: The Sources and Story of the Discalced Carmelites* (Washington, D.C.: ICS Publications, 1966), 126.

15. Ibid., 128.

16. Weaver, 14.

17. Ibid.

18. Ibid., 15.

19. Currier, 71.

20. Quoted in Joseph P. Chinnici, OFM, "Culture and Prayer: Towards a History of Contemplation in the Catholic Community in the United States," *U.S. Catholic Historian* 15 (Fall 1997), 10.

21. Ibid., 10–11.

22. Each Carmelite monastery is limited to a maximum of about twenty members. This has kept the number of Carmelites relatively small compared to other communities of women religious.

23. Sister Mary Christina Sullivan, SUCS, "Some Non-Permanent Foundations of Religious Orders and Congregations of Women in the United States (1793–1850)," *Historical Records and Studies* XXXI (1940): 11–118.

24. Sister Mary Camilla Koester, PCC, *Into This Land: A Centennial History of the Cleveland Poor Clare Monastery of the Blessed Sacrament* (Cleveland: Robert J. Liederbach, 1980), 10–11.

25. Eileen Flanagan, "Establishment of the Poor Clares in the United States: Ecclesiastical Conflicts—Vocational Challenges," *American Catholic Studies* 121 (Spring 2010): 51–68.

26. Eileen Flanagan, "Poor Clare Life Incompatible with American Lifestyle 1876–1888: Mother Maddalena Bentivoglio Challenges the Perception," *U.S. Catholic Historian* 20 (Winter 2011): 100–101.

27. Ibid.

28. Flanagan, "Establishment of the Poor Clares," 57–62.

29. Flanagan, "Poor Clare Life," 96.

30. Koester, 12–14. It is unclear whether Janknecht asked or ordered the Poor Clares to leave New Orleans. See Flanagan, "Poor Clare Life," 105, n.26.

31. Koester, 19–25.

32. Ibid., 26.

33. Flanagan, "Poor Clare Life," 105.

34. See Koester, chapter 12, for a full discussion of the Cleveland Poor Clares and their practice of Perpetual Adoration.

35. Ibid., 84–86.

36. Ibid., 90.

37. Ibid., 99.

38. Ibid., 103.

39. Ibid., 104.

40. Ibid., 104–105.

41. See McNamara, 399; and the website of the Benedictine Sisters of Elk County, http://www.benedictinesistersofelkcounty.org/history/history.cfm.

42. See Sister Dolores Dowling, OSB, *In Your Midst: The Story of the Benedictine Sisters of Perpetual Adoration* (n.p.: Congregation of Benedictine Sisters of Perpetual Adoration, 1988), chapters 1 and 2.

43. Ibid., 12.

44. Ibid., 19.

45. Ibid., 18.

46. Ibid., 75.

47. Ibid., 76.

48. Weaver, 15–16, 24.

49. Ibid., 32.

50. Ibid., 25.

51. Ibid., 33.

52. Ibid., 44.

53. Ibid., 44–45.

54. Ibid., 69.

55. Quoted in Margaret M. McGuinness, "Let Us Go to the Altar: American Catholics and the Eucharist, 1926–1976," in *Habits of Devotion: Catholic Religious Practice in Twentieth-Century America*, ed. James M. O'Toole (Ithaca, N.Y.: Cornell University Press, 2004), 205.

56. Koester, 123.

57. Flanagan, "Establishment of the Poor Clares," 60.

58. Karl Müller, SVD, *Contemplation and Mission: Sister-Servants of the Holy Spirit of Perpetual Adoration, 1896–1966* (Rome: Apud Collegium Verbi Divini, 1998), 133.

59. Ibid., 147.

60. Ibid., 149.

61. Ibid., 272.

62. Ibid., 292.

63. Ibid., 346–348.

64. Koester, 116–117.

65. Müller, 295.

66. Weaver, 85.

67. Ibid., 82–83.

68. Ohlson, 105–106.

Chapter 7

1. Lernoux, 126.

2. Ibid., 127.

3. Sister Maria Del Rey, *Bernie Becomes a Nun* (New York: Farrar, Straus & Cudahy, 1956), 4.

4. Ibid., 10.

5. Kenneth A. Briggs, *Double Crossed: Uncovering the Catholic Church's Betrayal of American Nuns* (New York: Doubleday, 2006), 28.

6. Lernoux, 129.

7. Ibid.

8. Sister Maria del Rey, 81–82.

9. Ibid., 118.

10. Ibid., 136.

11. See Helen Rose Fuchs Ebaugh, *Women in the Vanishing Cloister: Organizational Decline in Catholic Religious Orders in the United States* (New Brunswick, N.J.: Rutgers University Press, 1993), 98.

12. Lucy Kaylin, *For the Love of God: The Faith and Future of the American Nun* (New York: William Morrow, 2000), 22.

13. See, for example, Lernoux, 130.

14. Karen M. Kennelly, CSJ, *The Religious Formation Conference, 1954–2004* (Silver Spring, Md.: Religious Formation Conference, 2009), 8.

15. Sister Judith Ann Eby, "'A Little Squabble among Nuns'?: The Sister Formation Crisis and the Patterns of Authority and Obedience among American Women Religious, 1954–1971" (Ph.D. dissertation, St. Louis University, 2000), 40.

16. Marjorie Noterman Beane, *From Framework to Freedom: A History of the Sister Formation Conference* (Lanham, Md.: University Press of America, 1993), 5.

17. Ibid., 7.

18. Quoted in ibid., 7–8.

19. Kennelly, *The Religious Formation Conference*, 9.

20. Karen Kennelly, CSJ, "Women Religious, the Intellectual Life, and Anti-Intellectualism: History and Present Situation," in *Women Religious and the Intellectual Life: The North American Achievement*, ed. Bridget Puzon, OSU (San Francisco: International Scholars Publication, 1996), 46.

21. Kennelly, *The Religious Formation Conference*, 9.

22. Margaret Fitzer, SSL, "Foreword," in Beane, n.p.

23. Ibid., 14.

24. Kennelly, *The Religious Formation Conference*, 30.

25. Ibid., 31.

26. "Teachers: Nuns for the Twenty-First Century," *TIME*, 17 July 1964, http://www.time.com/time/magazine/article/0,9171,875964,00.html (1 August 2011).

27. Briggs, 53; Edward Wakin, "West Point for Nuns," in *Convent Life: Roman*

Catholic Religious Orders for Women in North America, ed. Joan M. Lexau (New York: Dial Press, 1964), 199.

28. Wakin, 99. Marillac College also admitted laywomen. It closed in 1974.

29. Kennelly, *The Religious Formation Conference,* 62–69.

30. Léon Joseph Suenens, *The Nun and the Modern World: Religious and the Apostolate* (Westminster, Md.: Newman Press, 1963), 33.

31. Beane, 46.

32. Koehlinger, *The New Nuns,* 65.

33. Beane, 49–50.

34. Kennelly, *The Religious Formation Conference,* 72.

35. Koehlinger, *The New Nuns,* 67.

36. Ibid.

37. See Eby, 243; and Regina Siegfried, ASC, "Religious Formation Conference: 'Education for Deepening Relationships: Theological/Communal/Societal/Cultural/Ecological,'" *American Catholic Studies* 120 (Spring 2009): 55–71.

38. Briggs, 70.

39. Ibid., 71–72.

40. Quoted in ibid., 72.

41. Ibid., 73–74.

42. See McGuinness, *Neighbors and Missionaries,* 149.

43. Koehlinger, *The New Nuns,* 69.

44. See ibid., 103–107; and Patricia Lefevere, "Margaret Traxler Lived Her Passion for Justice," *National Catholic Reporter,* 1 March 2002, 13.

45. Hoy, *Good Hearts,* 139.

46. See Barbra Mann Wall, "Catholic Nursing Sisters and Brothers and Racial Justice in Mid-20th Century America," *Advances in Nursing Science* 32 (April–June 2009): E90.

47. Quoted in Hoy, *Good Hearts,* 125.

48. Wall, "Catholic Nursing Sisters and Brothers and Racial Justice in Mid-20th Century America," E90.

49. Cornelia F. Sexauer, "A Well-Behaved Woman Who Made History: Sister Mary Antona's Journey to Selma," *American Catholic Studies* 115 (Winter 2004): 38.

50. Ibid., 44.

51. Ibid., 48–49.

52. Ibid., 49.

53. Ibid., 51.

54. Quoted in ibid., 54.

55. M. Shawn Copeland, "A Cadre of Women Religious Committed to Black Liberation: The National Black Sisters Conference," *U. S. Catholic Historian* 14 (Winter 1996): 129.

56. Quoted in ibid., 133.

57. Ibid., 140.

58. Ibid., 140–141.

59. Ibid., 139.

60. Carmel Elizabeth McEnroy, *Guests in Their Own House: The Women of Vatican II* (New York: Crossroad, 1996), 188.

61. Ibid.

62. Quoted in Kuhns, 139.

63. Quoted in Mark S. Massa, SJ, *Catholics and American Culture: Fulton Sheen, Dorothy Day, and the Notre Dame Football Team* (New York: Crossroad, 1999), 184.

64. Sister Jeanne Reidy, CHM, "Nuns in Ordinary Clothes," in *The New Nuns*, ed. Sister M. Charles Borromeo, CSC (New York: New American Library, 1967), 93.

65. Ibid., 91.

66. Briggs, 86.

67. Ibid., 87–88.

68. Ibid., 71.

69. Quoted in ibid, 89.

70. Reidy, 53.

71. Ibid.

72. See Briggs, 31; and Mary Ewens, OP, "The Double Standard of the American Sister," in *An American Church: Essays on the Americanization of the Catholic Church*, ed. David J. Alvarez (Moraga, Calif.: St. Mary's College of California, 1979), 23–34.

73. Briggs, 32.

74. Quoted in ibid., 33–34.

75. Quoted in Patricia Byrne, "In the Parish but Not of It: Sisters," in Jay P. Dolan, R. Scott Appleby, Patricia Byrne, and Debra Campbell, *Transforming Parish Ministry: The Changing Roles of Catholic Clergy, Laity, and Women Religious* (New York: Crossroad, 1989), 166–167.

76. Michael Novak, "The New Nuns," in *The New Nuns*, ed. Sister M. Charles Borromeo, CSC (New York: New American Library, 1967), 14.

77. Marie Brinkman, SCL, *Emerging Frontiers: Renewal in the Life of Women Religious, The Sisters of Charity of Leavenworth, 1955–2005* (New York: Paulist Press, 2008), 38.

78. Ibid., 165.

79. Kathleen C. Keating, SSJ, *Uncommon Trust in God: The Recent History of the Sisters of Saint Joseph of Springfield* (Holyoke, Mass.: Sisters of Saint Joseph of Springfield, 2009), 32–33.

80. Brinkman, 106; see also Ewens, "The Double Standard of the American Sister," 24–25.

81. See Anita M. Caspary, *Witness to Integrity: the Crisis of the Immaculate Heart Community of California* (Collegeville, Minn.: Liturgical Press, 2003): 15–19, for the early history of the Immaculate Heart Sisters in the United States.

82. Massa, *Catholics and American Culture*, 172–173.

83. Ibid., 172.

84. Ibid., 173.

85. "California Nuns Fight for a Modern Way of Life," *New York Times*, 14 November 1967, 32.

86. Ibid.; Massa, *Catholics and American Culture*, 175.

87. Massa, *Catholics and American Culture*, 176.

88. See Steven V. Roberts, "Coast Nuns Plan a Secular Order," *New York Times*, 3 February 1970, 1, 40.

89. Massa, *Catholics and American Culture*, 189.

90. Briggs, 114–115.

91. See the community's website: "Immaculate Heart Community https://www. immaculateheartcommunity.org/collaborative-ministries.html (16 June 2011).

92. Briggs, 124–125.

93. Quoted in Helen M. Lewis and Monica Appleby, *Mountain Sisters: From Convent to Community in Appalachia* (Lexington: University Press of Kentucky, 2003), 8.

94. Ibid., 34.

95. See ibid., 48.

96. Ibid., 53.

97. Ibid., 59.

98. Ibid., 71.

99. Briggs, 187.

100. Judy Roberts, "Where Have All the Nuns Gone?" *National Catholic Register*, 7 August 2006. http://www.ncregister.com/site/article/where_have_all_ the_nuns_gone (22 August 2011).

101. Marie Augusta Neal, SND de Namur, *Catholic Sisters in Transition from the 1960s to the 1980s* (Wilmington, Del.: Michael Glazier, 1984), 21. The survey from which these figures are taken "laid the groundwork for the Sisters' Survey," which involved 139,000 individual sisters. The initial report included 437 "respondent congregations and accounted for 158,917 sisters through administrative records and opinions," 10.

102. Ibid., 22.

103. Ibid.

104. "Roman Catholics: The Restive Nuns," *TIME*, 13 January 1967. http:// www.time.com/time/magazine/article/0,9171,843279,00.html (1 August 2011).

105. "Priests and Nuns: Going Their Way," *TIME*, 23 February 1970. http:// www.time.com/time/magazine/article/0,9171,876637,00.html (1 August 2011).

106. Quoted in Briggs, 119.

107. The ad appears verbatim in Mary E. Hunt and Frances Kissling, "The *New York Times* Ad: A Case Study in Religious Feminism," *Journal of Feminist Studies in Religion* 3 (Spring 1987): 115–116.

108. Ibid., 119.

109. Ibid., 121.

110. Barbara Ferraro and Patricia Hussey, with Jane O'Reilly, *No Turning Back: Two Nuns' Battle with the Vatican over Women's Right to Choose* (New York: Poseidon Press, 1990), 18; Debra Campbell, *Graceful Exits: Catholic Women and the Art of Departure* (Bloomington: Indiana University Press, 2003), 137. Barbara Ferraro is not related to Geraldine Ferraro.

111. Ferraro and Hussey, 67.

112. Ibid., 179.

113. Ibid., 180.

114. Ibid., 191.

115. Ibid., 194–195.

116. Ibid., 204.

117. Ibid., 250.

118. Ibid., 295–296.

119. Ibid, 320.

120. Ibid., 320–323.

121. Ibid., 323.

122. Quoted in Ari L. Goldman, "Ideas and Trends: 'Pro-Choice Nuns'; Another Challenge to Rome by Liberal Catholics in U.S.," *New York Times*, 12 June 1988, A28.

123. See Chester Gillis, *Roman Catholicism in America* (New York: Columbia University Press, 1999), 100; Ferraro and Hussey, 212, 234.

124. Lora Ann Quiñonez, CDP, and Mary Daniel Turner, SNDdeN, *The Transformation of American Catholic Sisters* (Philadelphia: Temple University Press, 1992), 31.

125. Ibid.

126. Ibid., 141.

Chapter 8

1. Sister Helen Prejean, *Dead Man Walking: An Eyewitness Account of the Death Penalty in the United States* (New York: Vintage Books, 1994), 3.

2. Ibid., 5.

3. See Jane Redmont, "Marie Augusta Neale, Teacher, Author, Researcher, Dead at 82," *National Catholic Reporter*, 16 April 2004. http://www.natcath.org/NCR_Online/archives2/2004b/041604/041604l.php (2 August 2011).

4. Prejean, 5–6.

5. Ibid., 6.

6. Gillis, 99.

7. Ibid., 100.

8. Ibid., 101.

9. Jeannine Grammick, "From Good Sisters to Prophetic Women," in *Midwives of the Future: American Sisters Tell Their Story*, ed. Ann Patrick Ware (Kansas City, Mo.: Leaven Press, 1985), 235.

10. Carole Garibaldi Rogers, *Habits of Change: An Oral History of American Nuns* (New York: Oxford University Press, 2011), 146.

11. Kyle Henley, "Nuns Sentenced for Anti-War Protest/Judge Gives 3 Dominican Sisters Lighter Sentences Despite 'Dangerously Irresponsible' Nuclear Missile Silo Break-In," *The Gazette* [Colorado Springs, Colo.], 26 July 2003, Metro 1.

12. Tom LoBianco, "Protesting Nuns Branded Terrorists," *Washington Times*, 10 October 2008, http://www.washingtontimes.com/news/2008/oct/10/protesting-nuns-branded-terrorists/?page=all (21 January 2012).

13. Dries, 242.

14. Ibid., 243.

15. Lernoux, 241.

16. Ibid., 244–245.

17. Ibid., 247.

18. Phyllis Zagano, *Ita Ford: Missionary Martyr* (New York: Paulist Press, 1996), 47–48.

19. Ibid., 48–49.

20. Lernoux, 248.

21. See the community's website, "ACS Martyrs of Charity," Adorers of the Blood of Christ, http://www.adorers.org/ourfivemartyrs.html (3 August 2011).

22. See "Beginnings and Endings," Adorers of the Blood of Christ, http://www.adorers.org/ascpresenceinliberia.html (5 August 2011).

23. See Roseanne Murphy, *Martyr of the Amazon: The Life of Sister Dorothy Stang* (Maryknoll, N.Y.: Orbis, 2007), chapters 1 to 3, for a discussion of Stang's life and work prior to beginning her ministry in Brazil.

24. Ibid., 32.

25. Ibid., chapter 11.

26. Ibid., 153.

27. Sarah McFarland Taylor, *Green Sisters: A Spiritual Ecology* (Cambridge: Harvard University Press, 2007), 60.

28. Ibid., 63.

29. See Green Mountain Monastery, http://www.greenmountainmonastery.org, for more information on the programs and philosophy of Green Mountain Monastery.

30. Taylor, 50.

31. Ibid., 103.

32. Ibid.

33. Ibid., 105.

34. See ibid., 106ff.

35. Ibid., 79.

36. Ibid., 80.

37. Quoted in ibid., 81.

38. Ibid., 83.

39. Ibid., 189.

40. Ibid.

41. Ibid., 190.

42. See the community's website, specifically "Years of the Second Vatican Council," Dominican Sisters of St. Cecilia, http://nashvilledominican.org/Charism/Congregation_History/Years_of_the_Second_Vatican_Council (4 September 2011), for a summary of this period in the sisters' history.

43. See "Young Catholic Women Get into the Habit," 11 January 2010, http://www.voanews.com/english/news/usa/people/Younger-Catholic-Women-Get-into-the-Habit-113267249.html (4 September 2011), for a discussion of young women entering religious life.

44. Darryl V. Caterine, *Conservative Catholicism and the Carmelites: Identity, Ethnicity, and Tradition in the Modern Church* (Bloomington: Indiana University Press, 2001), xxii.

45. Ibid., xxiv.

46. See the community's website, Carmelite Sisters of the Most Sacred Heart of Los Angeles, http://www.carmelitesistersocd.com/index.asp, for more information about their particular ministries.

47. See the community's website, Dominican Sisters of Mary, Mother of the Eucharist, http://www.sistersofmary.org/index.php, for further information on the Dominican Sisters of Mary. Clips for the sisters' appearance on the Oprah Winfrey Show are available on a number of websites, including: "The American Catholic," http://the-american-catholic.com/2010/02/12/the-dominican-sisters-on-the-oprah-winfrey-show/.

48. Robert Hanley, "5 Nuns in New Jersey Break Away over Break with Tradition," *New York Times*, 8 October 1988, 1, 30.

49. Ari L. Goldman, "Nuns' Protest Illuminates a Cloistered Order," *New York Times*, 21 October 1988, A1.

50. Robert Hanley, "Vatican Orders Nuns in New Jersey to End Protest," *New York Times*, 4 March 1989, 1, 32.

51. See Raymond Arroyo, *Mother Angelica: The Remarkable Story of a Nun, Her Nerve, and a Network of Miracles* (New York: Doubleday, 2005), 91–103.

52. Ibid., 106.

53. Ibid., 134.

54. Ibid., 142.

55. Ibid., 149–150.

56. Ibid., 166.

57. Ibid., 169.

58. Ibid., 192.

59. Tom Roberts, "Ethicists Fault Bishop's Action in Phoenix Abortion Case," *National Catholic Reporter*, 8 June 2010. <http://ncronline.org/news/ethicists-fault-bishop%E2%80%99s-action-phoenix-abortion-case> (9 October 2011).

60. John L. Allen, Jr., "U.S. Bishops Blast Book by Feminist Theologian," *National Catholic Reporter*, 30 March 2011. http://ncronline.org/news/spirituality/us-bishops-blast-book-feminist-theologian (9 October 2011).

61. See "Response of the Board of Directors of the Catholic Theological Society of America to the Statement on 'Quest for the Living God: Mapping Frontiers in the Theology of God,' by Sister Elizabeth A. Johnson Issued by the Committee on Doctrine, United States Conference of Catholic Bishops, March 24, 2011," http://www.ctsa-online.org/johnson.html (9 October 2011).

62. Sandra M. Schneiders, IHM, *Prophets in Their Own Country: Women Religious Bearing Witness to the Gospel in a Troubled Church* (Maryknoll, N.Y.: Orbis, 2011), 4; and Ann Cary, *Sisters in Crisis: The Tragic Unveiling of Women's Religious Communities* (Huntington, Ind.: Our Sunday Visitor, 1997), 211.

63. Schneiders, 40–41.

64. Tom Fox, "Vatican Begins Study of US Women Religious," 30 January 2009. http://ncronline.org/news/women/vatican-begins-study-us-women-religious (1 October 2011).

65. Schneiders, 38–39.

66. Sister Anne Marie Mongoven, "'We Did What the Church Asked Us to Do," *National Catholic Reporter*, 7 August 2009. http://ncronline.org/news/women/we-did-what-church-asked-us-do (1 October 2011).

67. Ibid.

68. Ibid.

69. "Sisters Delivered the Church Vatican II Promised," *National Catholic Reporter*, 8 June 2009. http://ncronline.org/news/women/sisters-delivered-church-vatican-ii-promised (2 October 2011).

70. "Apostolic Visitation of U.S. Religious Concludes," *Women of Grace*, 11 March 2011, http://womenofgrace.com/breaking_news/?p=7390 (2 October 2011).

71. See "Connect with Mercy," http://www.sistersofmercy.org/index.php?option=com_content&task=view&id=3434&Itemid=331 (8 October 2011).

72. Sister Joan Chittister, OSB, "Beyond 9/11 to a Broader View of the World," *Huffington Post*, 7 September 2011. http://www.huffingtonpost.com/sister-joan-chittister-osb/911-interfaith_b_942026.html (8 October 2011).

73. Ibid.

74. Mary Jo Weaver, *New Catholic Women: A Contemporary Challenge to Traditional Religious Authority* (San Francisco: Harper & Row, 1985), 100.

75. "Insights on the Good News of Religious Life," *National Catholic Reporter*, 10 October 2011, http://ncronline.org/news/women-religious/insights-good-news-religious-life (14 October 2011).

Select Bibliography

Alvarez, David J., ed. *An American Church: Essays on the Americanization of the Catholic Church.* Moraga, Calif.: St. Mary's College of California, 1979.

An Ursuline of the Roman Union [Sister Clotilde Angela]. *Ursulines of the West.* [Everett, WA]: n.p., 1936.

Anderson, M. Christine. "Catholic Nuns and the Invention of Social Work: The Sisters of the Santa Maria Institute of Cincinnati, Ohio, 1897 through the 1920s." *Journal of Women's History* 12 (Spring 2000): 61–88.

Anderson, R. Bentley. *Black, White, and Catholic: New Orleans Interracialism, 1947–1956.* Nashville: Vanderbilt University Press, 2005.

Arroyo, Raymond. *Mother Angelica: The Remarkable Story of a Nun, Her Nerve, and a Network of Miracles.* New York: Doubleday, 2005.

Augenstein, John, Christopher Kauffman, and Robert J. Wister, eds. *One Hundred Years of Catholic Education: Historical Essays in Honor of the National Catholic Educational Association.* Washington, D.C.: National Catholic Education Association, 2003.

Baldwin, Lou. *St. Katharine Drexel: Apostle to the Oppressed.* Philadelphia: Catholic Standard and Times, 2000.

[Barber, Sister Josephine]. "Life of Mrs. Jerusha Barber." In *Catholic Memoirs of Vermont and New Hampshire,* edited by L[ouis] DeGoesbriand. Burlington, Vt.: n.p., 1886.

Barton, George. *Angels of the Battlefield: A History of the Labors of Catholic Sisterhoods in the Late Civil War.* Philadelphia: Catholic Art Publishing, 1898.

Beane, Marjorie Noterman. *From Framework to Freedom: A History of the Sister Formation Conference.* Lanham, Md.: University Press of America, 1993.

Berg, Carol, OSB. "Agents of Cultural Change: The Benedictines at White Earth." *Minnesota History* 48 (1982): 158–170.

Billington, Ray Allen. "Maria Monk and Her Influence." *Catholic Historical Review* 22 (October 1936): 283–296.

Borromeo, Sister M. Charles, CSC, ed. *The New Nuns.* New York: New American Library, 1967.

Boylan, Anne M. *The Origins of Women's Activism: New York and Boston 1797–1840.* Chapel Hill: University of North Carolina Press, 2002.

Brett, Edward T. "Race Issues and Conflict in Nineteenth- and Early Twentieth-Century Religious Life." *U.S. Catholic Historian* 29 (Winter 2011): 113–127.

Brewer, Eileen Mary. *Nuns and the Education of American Catholic Women, 1860–1920.* Chicago: Loyola University Press, 1987.

Briggs, Kenneth. *Double Crossed: Uncovering the Catholic Church's Betrayal of American Nuns.* New York: Doubleday, 2006.

Brinkman, Marie, SCL. *Emerging Frontiers: Renewal in the Life of Women Religious, The Sisters of Charity of Leavenworth, 1955–2005.* New York: Paulist Press, 2008.

Brinton, John. *Personal Memoirs of John H. Brinton Major and Surgeon U.S.V., 1861–1865.* New York: Neale, 1914.

Brosnan, Kathleen A. "Public Presence, Public Silence: Nuns, Bishops, and the Gendered Space of Early Chicago." *Catholic Historical Review* 90 (July 2004): 473–496.

Buetow, Harold A. *Of Singular Benefit: The Story of Catholic Education in the United States.* New York: Macmillan, 1970.

Butler, Anne M. "Adapting the Vision: Caroline in 19th-Century America." In *One Vision Many Voices: Lectures Delivered at the Mother Caroline Freiss Centenary Celebrations 1992,* edited by Virgina Geiger, SSND, and Patricia McLaughlin, SSND. Lanham, Md.: University Press of America, 1993.

———. "Mother Katherine Drexel: Spiritual Visionary for the West," In *By Grit and Grace: Eleven Women Who Shaped the American West,* edited by Glenda Riley and Richard W. Etulain. Golden, Colo.: Fulcrum Publishing, 1997.

———. "Pioneer Sisters in a Catholic Melting Pot: Juggling Identity in the Pacific Northwest." *American Catholic Studies* 114 (Spring 2003): 21–39.

———. "There Are Exceptions to Every Rule: Adjusting the Boundaries—Catholic Sisters and the American West." *American Catholic Studies* 116 (Fall 2005): 1–22.

Byrne, Patricia, CSJ. "A Tradition of Educating Women: The Religious of the Sacred Heart and Higher Education." *U.S. Catholic Historian* 13 (Fall 1995): 49–79.

———. "In the Parish but Not of It: Sisters." In Jay P. Dolan, R. Scott Appleby, Patricia Byrne, and Debra Campbell, *Transforming Parish Ministry: The Changing Roles of Catholic Clergy, Laity, and Women Religious.* New York: Crossroad, 1989.

———. "*Sisters of St. Joseph*: The Americanization of a French Tradition." *U.S. Catholic Historian* 5 (Summer/Fall 1986): 241–272.

"California Nuns Fight for a Modern Way of Life," *New York Times* (14 November 1967), 32.

Campbell, Debra. *Graceful Exits: Catholic Women and the Art of Departure.* Bloomington: Indiana University Press, 2003.

Cary, Ann. *Sisters in Crisis: The Tragic Unveiling of Women's Religious Communities.* Huntington, Ind.: Our Sunday Visitor, 1997.

Caspary, Anita M. *Witness to Integrity: The Crisis of the Immaculate Heart Community of California.* Collegeville, Minn.: Liturgical Press, 2003.

Casterline, Gail Farr. "St. Joseph's and St. Mary's: The Origins of Catholic Hospitals in Philadelphia." *Pennsylvania Magazine of History and Biography*, 108 (July 1984): 289–314.

Caterine, Darryl V. *Conservative Catholicism and the Carmelites: Identity, Ethnicity, and Tradition in the Modern Church*. Bloomington: Indiana University Press, 2001.

Cetina, Judith G. "In Times of Immigration." In *Pioneer Healers: The History of Women Religious in American Health Care*, edited by Ursula Stepsis, CSA, and Dolores Liptak, RSM. New York: Crossroad, 1989.

Chinnici, Joseph P., OFM. "Broadening the Horizons: The Historian in Search of the Spirit." *U.S. Catholic Historian* 8 (Winter/Spring 1989): 1–13.

———. "Culture and Prayer: Towards a History of Contemplation in the Catholic Community in the United States." *U.S. Catholic Historian* 15 (Fall 1997): 1–16.

———. "Religious Life in the Twentieth Century: Interpreting the Languages." *U.S. Catholic Historian* 22 (Winter 2004): 24–47.

———. "Rewriting the Master Narrative: Religious Life and the Study of American Catholicism." *American Catholic Studies* 117 (Spring 2006): 1–20.

Clark, Emily. *Masterless Mistresses: The New Orleans Ursulines and the Development of a New World Society, 1727–1834*. Chapel Hill: University of North Carolina Press, 2007.

Clark, Emily, and Virginia Meachem Gould. "The Feminine Face of Afro-Catholicism in New Orleans, 1727–1852." *William and Mary Quarterly* 59 (April 2002): 409–448.

Coburn, Carol K., and Martha Smith. "'Pray for Your Wanderers': Women Religious on the Colorado Mining Frontier, 1877–1917." *Frontiers: A Journal of Women's Studies* 15 (1995): 27–52.

———. *Spirited Lives: How Nuns Shaped Catholic Culture and American Life, 1836–1920*. Chapel Hill: University of North Carolina Press, 1999.

Cohen, Daniel A. "Miss Reed and the Superiors: The Contradictions of Convent Life in Antebellum America." *Journal of Social History* 30 (Autumn 1996): 149–184.

———. "Passing the Torch: Boston Firemen, 'Tea Party' Patriots, and the Burning of the Charlestown Convent." *Journal of the Early Republic* 24 (Winter 2004): 527–586.

———. "The Respectability of Rebecca Reed: Genteel Womanhood and Sectarian Conflict in Antebellum America." *Journal of the Early Republic* 16 (Autumn 1996): 419–461.

Conway, Jill Ker. "Faith, Knowledge, and Gender." In *Catholic Women's Colleges in America*, edited by Tracy Schier and Cynthia Russett. Baltimore: Johns Hopkins University Press, 2002.

Cooney, Kathleen, OSU. "Reasons for Staying in a Religious Community: The Views of Women Entrants, 1945–1975." *U.S. Catholic Historian* 10 (1991/1992): 93–99.

Copeland, Shawn M. "A Cadre of Women Religious Committed to Black Liberation: The National Black Sisters' Conference." *U.S. Catholic Historian* 14 (Winter 1996): 123–144.

Costin, Sister M. Georgia, CSC. *Priceless Spirit: A History of the Sisters of the Holy Cross, 1841–1893*. Notre Dame, Ind.: University of Notre Dame Press, 1994.

Cowan, David, and John Kuenster. *To Sleep with the Angels: The Story of a Fire*. Chicago: Ivan R. Dee, 1996.

Crews, Clyde F. *An American Holy Land: A History of the Archdiocese of Louisville*. Wilmington, Del.: Michael Glazier, 1987.

Cummings, Kathleen Sprows. *New Women of the Old Faith: Gender and American Catholicism in the Progressive Era*. Chapel Hill: University of North Carolina Press, 2009.

———. "Strongly-Willed Sister and Sorin Ally Named Saint," *Notre Dame Magazine* (Winter 2006/2007), 9.

———. "'The Wageless Work of Paradise': Integrating Women into American Religious History." *Journal of Religion and Society* Supplement 5 (2009): 114–128.

———. "'We Owe It to Our Sex as Well as Our Religion': The Sisters of Notre Dame de Namur, the Ladies Auxiliary, and the Founding of Trinity College for Catholic Women, Washington, D.C." *American Catholic Studies* 115 (Winter 2004): 21–36.

Currier, Charles Warren. *Carmel in America: A Centennial History of the Discalced Carmelites in the United States*. Baltimore: John Murphy, 1890.

Curtis, Sarah A. *Civilizing Habits: Women Missionaries and the Revival of French Empire*. New York: Oxford University Press, 2010.

Davis, Cyprian, OSB. "Black Catholics in Nineteenth Century America." *U.S. Catholic Historian* 5 (1986): 1–17.

DeFrees, Madeleine. "Requiem for the Outfitter to the Sisterhood." *Massachusetts Review* 25 (Autumn 1984): 477–488.

DeGoesbriand, Louis. *Catholic Memoirs of Vermont and New Hampshire*. Burlington, Vt.: n.p., 1886.

Del Rey, Sister Maria. *Bernie Becomes a Nun*. New York: Farrar, Straus, & Cudahy, 1956.

Dickey, Susan Karina, OP. "Dominican Sisters Encounter Jim Crow: The Desegregation of a Catholic Hospital in Mississippi." *American Catholic Studies* 116 (Spring 2005): 43–58.

DiGiovanni, Stephen Michael. "Mother Cabrini: Early Years in New York." *Catholic Historical Review* 77 (January 1991): 56–77.

Dolan, Jay P. *The American Catholic Experience: A History from Colonial Times to the Present*. Garden City, N.Y.: Doubleday, 1985.

———, ed. *The American Catholic Parish: A History from 1850 to the Present, Volume I*. New York: Paulist Press, 1987.

Dolan, Jay P., R. Scott Appleby, Patricia Byrne, and Debra Campbell. *Transforming Parish Ministry: The Changing Roles of Catholic Clergy, Laity, and Women Religious.* New York: Crossroad, 1989.

Donovan, Grace. "Immigrant Nuns: Their Participation in the Process of Americanization: Massachusetts and Rhode Island, 1880–1920." *Catholic Historical Review* 77 (April 1991): 194–208.

Douglas, Ann. *The Feminization of American Culture*, rev. ed. New York: Farrar, Strauss, and Giroux, 1998.

Dowling, Dolores, OSB. *In Your Midst: The Story of the Benedictine Sisters of Perpetual Adoration.* n.p.: Congregation of Benedictine Sisters of Perpetual Adoration, 1988.

Doyle, Ann, RN. "Nursing by Religious Orders in the United States: Part I, 1809–1840." *American Journal of Nursing* 29 (July 1929): 764, 775–786.

———. "Nursing by Religious Orders in the United States: Part II, 1841–1870." *American Journal of Nursing* 29 (August 1929): 959–969.

Doyle, Mary Ellen, SCN. *Pioneer Spirit: Catherine Spalding Sister of Charity of Nazareth.* Lexington: University Press of Kentucky, 2006.

Dries, Angelyn, OSF. "Living in Ambiguity: A Paradigm Shift Experienced by the Sister Formation Movement." *Catholic Historical Review* 79 (July 1993): 478–487.

———. *The Missionary Movement in American Catholic History.* Maryknoll, N.Y.: Orbis Books, 1998.

Ebaugh, Helen Rose. "Patriarchal Bargains and Latent Avenues of Social Mobility: Nuns in the Roman Catholic Church." *Gender and Society* 7 (September 1993): 400–414.

Ebaugh, Helen Rose Fuchs. *Women in the Vanishing Cloister: Organizational Decline in Catholic Religious Orders in the United States.* New Brunswick, N.J.: Rutgers University Press, 1993.

Ebaugh, Helen Rose, Jon Lawrence, and Janet Saltzman Chafetz. "The Growth and Decline of the Population of Catholic Nuns Cross-Nationally, 1960–1990: A Case of Secularization as Social Structural Change." *Journal for the Scientific Study of Religion* 35 (June 1996): 171–183.

Eby, Sister Judith Ann. "'A Little Squabble among Nuns'? The Sister Formation Crisis and the Patterns of Authority and Obedience among American Women Religious, 1954–1971." Ph.D. dissertation, St. Louis University, 2000.

Ewens, Mary, OP. "The Double Standard of the American Sister." In *An American Church: Essays on the Americanization of the Catholic Church*, edited by David J. Alvarez. Moraga, Calif.: St. Mary's College of California, 1979.

———. *The Role of the Nun in Nineteenth Century America.* Salem, N.H.: Ayer, 1984.

Fanning, Charles, ed. *New Perspectives on the Irish Diaspora.* Carbondale, Ill.: Southern Illinois University Press, 2000.

Ferraro, Barbara, and Patricia Hussey, with Jane O'Reilly. *No Turning Back: Two Nuns' Battle with the Vatican over Women's Right to Choose.* New York: Poseidon Press, 1990.

Fessenden, Tracy. "The Convent, the Brothel, and the Protestant Woman's Sphere." *Signs* 25 (Winter 2000): 451–478.

———. "The Sisters of the Holy Family and the Veil of Race." *Religion and American Culture: A Journal of Interpretation* 10 (Summer 2000): 187–224.

Fialka, John. *Sisters: Catholic Nuns and the Making of America.* New York: St. Martin's Press, 2003.

Fitzgerald, Maureen. *Habits of Compassion: Irish Catholic Nuns and the Origins of New York's Welfare System,1830–1920.* Urbana: University of Illinois Press, 2006.

———. "The Perils of 'Passion and Poverty': Women Religious and the Care of Single Women in New York City, 1845–1890." *U.S. Catholic Historian* 10 (1991/1992): 45–58.

Flanagan, Eileen. "Establishment of the Poor Clares in the United States: Ecclesiastical Conflicts—Vocational Challenges." *American Catholic Studies* 121 (Spring 2010): 51–68.

———. "Poor Clare Life Incompatible with American Lifestyle 1876–1888: Mother Maddalena Bentivoglio Challenges the Perception." *U.S. Catholic Historian* 20 (Winter 2011): 95–111.

Foley, Thomas W. "Father Francis M. Craft and the Indian Sisters." *U.S. Catholic Historian* 16 (Spring 1998): 41–55.

Franchot, Jenny. *Roads to Rome: The Antebellum Protestant Encounter with Catholicism.* Berkeley: University of California Press, 1994.

Fraser, Mary Beth. "'Devoted to the Interest of the Italians': The Sisters of Charity and the Santa Maria Institute in Cincinnati, Ohio, 1890–1930." Ph.D. dissertation, Catholic University of America, 2006.

Gavin, Donald Philip. *In All Things Charity: History of the Sisters of Charity of St. Augustine Cleveland, Ohio, 1851–1954.* Milwaukee, Wis.: Bruce Publishing, 1955.

Gaynor, Constance, FSP. *Peacemaking Our Journey: A History of the Franciscan Sisters of Peace.* Haverstraw, N.Y.: Franciscan Sisters of Peace, 2006.

Geiger, Virgina, SSND, and Patricia McLaughlin, SSND, eds. *One Vision Many Voices: Lectures Delivered at the Mother Caroline Freiss Centenary Celebrations 1992.* Lanham, Md.: University Press of America, 1993.

Gerdes, M. Reginald. "To Educate and Evangelize: Black Catholic Schools of the Oblate Sisters of Providence (1828–1880)." *U.S. Catholic Historian* 7 (Spring–Summer 1988): 183–199.

Gillis, Chester. *Roman Catholicism in America.* New York: Columbia University Press, 1999.

Goldman, Ari L. "Ideas and Trends: 'Pro-Choice Nuns'; Another Challenge to Rome by Liberal Catholics in U.S.," *New York Times* (12 June 1988), A28.

———. "Nuns' Protest Illuminates a Cloistered Order," *New York Times* (21 October 1988), A1.

———. "2 Nuns Quit Order in Battle with Vatican on Abortion," *New York Times* (22 July 1988), A8.

Gordon, Linda. *The Great Arizona Orphan Abduction*. Cambridge: Harvard University Press, 1999.

Grammick, Jeannine. "From Good Sisters to Prophetic Women." In *Midwives of the Future: American Sisters Tell Their Story*, edited by Ann Patrick Ware. Kansas City, Mo.: Leaven Press, 1985.

Griffin, Martin I. J. "St Joseph's Orphan Asylum, Philadelphia." *American Catholic Historical Researches* 14 (1897): 9–12.

———. "The Sisters of Charity and the Cholera in Baltimore and Philadelphia, 1832." *American Catholic Historical Researches* 14 (July 1897): 113–116.

Griffin, Susan M. *Anti-Catholicism and Nineteenth-Century Fiction*. Cambridge: Cambridge University Press, 2004.

Hamilton, Jeanne, OSU. "The Nunnery as Menace: The Burning of the Charlestown Convent, 1834." *U.S. Catholic Historian* 14 (Winter 1996): 35–65.

Hanley, Robert. "5 Nuns in New Jersey Break Away over Break with Tradition," *New York Times* (8 October 1988), 1, 30.

———. "Vatican Orders Nuns in New Jersey to End Protest," *New York Times* (4 March 1989), 1, 32.

Hanley, Thomas O'Brien, SJ, ed. *The John Carroll Papers*. 3 volumes. Notre Dame: University of Notre Dame Press, 1976.

Harrington, Ann M., BVM. "Sisters of Charity of the Blessed Virgin Mary, 1833–1843." *U.S. Catholic Historian* 27 (Fall 2009): 17–30.

Healy, Kathleen. *Frances Warde: American Founder of the Sisters of Mercy*. New York: Seabury Press, 1973.

Hegarty, Sister Mary Loyola, CCVI. *Serving with Gladness: The Origin and History of the Congregation of the Sisters of Charity of the Incarnate Word Houston, Texas.* [Houston]: Bruce Publishing, in cooperation with the Sisters of Charity of the Incarnate Word Houston, Texas, 1967.

Henley, Kyle."Nuns Sentenced for Anti-War Protest/Judge Gives 3 Dominican Sisters Lighter Sentences Despite 'Dangerously Irresponsible' Nuclear Missile Silo Break-In," *The Gazette* [Colorado Springs, Colo.] (26 July 2003), Metro 1.

Hennesey, James J., SJ. *American Catholics: A History of the Roman Catholic Community in the United States*. New York: Oxford University Press, 1981.

Higham, John. *Strangers in the Land: Patterns of American Nativism, 1860–1925*. New York: Atheneum, 1963.

Howe, Barbara J. "Pioneers on a Mission for God: The Order of the Visitation of the Blessed Virgin Mary in Wheeling, 1848–1860." *West Virginia History: A Journal of Regional Studies* 4 (Spring 2010): 59–92.

Hoy, Suellen. *Good Hearts: Catholic Sisters in Chicago's Past.* Urbana: University of Illinois Press, 2006.

———. "Stunned with Sorrow." *Chicago History* XXXIII (Summer 2004): 4–25.

———. "The Journey Out: The Recruitment and Emigration of Irish Women Religious to the United States, 1812–1914." *Journal of Women's History* 6/7 (Winter/Spring 1995): 64–98.

Hoy, Suellen, and Margaret MacCurtain. *From Dublin to New Orleans: The Journey of Nora and Alice.* Dublin: Attic Press, 1994.

Hunt, Mary E., and Frances Kissling. "The *New York Times* Ad: A Case Study in Religious Feminism." *Journal of Feminist Studies in Religion* 3 (Spring 1987): 115–127.

"Institute of Our Lady of Christian Doctrine," *Church Progress*, 16 July 1908.

Jolly, Ellen Ryan. *Nuns of the Battlefield.* Providence: Providence Visitor Press, 1930.

Joyce, Kathleen M. "The Evil of Abortion and the Greater Good of the Faith: Negotiating Catholic Survival in the Twentieth-Century American Health Care System." *Religion and American Culture: A Journal of Interpretation* 12 (Winter 2002): 91–121.

Kauffman, Christopher J. *Ministry and Meaning: A Religious History of Catholic Health Care in the United States.* New York: Crossroad, 1995.

Kaylin, Lucy. *For the Love of God: The Faith and Future of the American Nun.* New York: William Morrow, 2000.

Kealy, Marie Hubert, IHM. "Immigrant Church to University: Growth of the Sisters, Servants of the Immaculate Heart of Mary in Eastern Pennsylvania." *U.S. Catholic Historian* 27 (Fall 2009): 31–43.

Keating, Kathleen C., SSJ. *Uncommon Trust in God: The Recent History of the Sisters of Saint Joseph of Springfield.* Holyoke, Mass.: Sisters of Saint Joseph of Springfield, 2009.

Kelly, Ellin, and Annabelle Melville, eds. *Elizabeth Seton: Selected Writings.* New York: Paulist   Press, 1987.

Kennelly, Karen M., CSJ. "Faculties and What They Taught." In *Catholic Women's Colleges in America,* edited by Tracy Schier and Cynthia Russett. Baltimore: Johns Hopkins University Press, 2002.

———. *The Religious Formation Conference 1954–2004.* Silver Spring, Md.: Religious Formation Conference, 2009.

———. "Women Religious, the Intellectual Life, and Anti-Intellectualism: History and Present Situation." In *Women Religious and the Intellectual Life: The North American Achievement,* edited by Bridget Puzon, OSU. San Francisco: International Scholars Publication, 1996.

Keppel, L. *Rose Philippine Duchesne: Religious of the Sacred Heart and Missioner 1769–1852.* London: Longmans, Green, 1940.

Koehlinger, Amy L. "'Race Relations Needs the Nun:' Sources of Continuity and Change in the Racial Apostolate of the 1960s." *U.S. Catholic Historian* 23 (Fall 2005): 39–59.

———. *The New Nuns: Racial Justice and Religious Reform in the 1960s.* Cambridge: Harvard University Press, 2007.

Koester, Sister Mary Camilla, PCC. *Into This Land: A Centennial History of the Cleveland Poor Clare Monastery of the Blessed Sacrament.* Cleveland: Robert J. Liederbach, 1980.

Kolmer, Elizabeth, ASC. *Religious Women in the United States: A Survey of the Influential Literature from 1950–1983.* Wilmington, Del.: Michael Glazier, 1984.

Kraman, Carlan, OSF. "Women Religious in Health Care: The Early Years." In *Pioneer Healers: The History of Women Religious in American Health Care,* edited by Ursula Stepsis, CSA, and Dolores Liptak, RSM. New York: Crossroad, 1989.

Kreis, Karl Marcus, ed. *Lakotas, Black Robes, and Holy Women: German Reports from the Indian Missions in South Dakota, 1886–1900.* Lincoln: University of Nebraska Press, 2007.

Kuhns, Elizabeth. *The Habit: A History of the Clothing of Catholic Nuns.* New York: Doubleday, 2003.

Lackner, Joseph H. "Two Italian Parishes in Cleveland." *U.S. Catholic Historian* 6 (Fall 1987): 315–324.

Lazerson, Marvin. "Understanding American Catholic Educational History." *History of Education Quarterly* 17 (Autumn 1977): 297–317.

Lefevere, Patricia. "Margaret Traxler Lived Her Passion for Justice," *National Catholic Reporter* (1 March 2002), 13.

Lernoux, Penny. *Hearts on Fire: The Story of the Maryknoll Sisters.* Maryknoll, N.Y.: Orbis Books, 1993.

LeRoux, Edna M., RSM. "In Times of Socioeconomic Crisis." In *Pioneer Healers: The History of Women Religious in American Health Care,* edited by Ursula Stepsis, CSA, and Dolores Liptak, RSM. New York: Crossroad, 1989.

Lewis, Helen M., and Monica Appleby. *Mountain Sisters: From Convent to Community in Appalachia.* Lexington: University Press of Kentucky, 2003.

Lexau, Joan, ed. *Convent Life: Roman Catholic Religious Orders for Women in North America.* New York: Dial Press, 1964.

Liedel, Leslie. "Property and Power: Women Religious Defend Their Rights in Nineteenth-Century Cleveland." *Ohio History* 112 (Summer–Autumn 2003): 68–86.

Liguori, Sister S. M. "Polish American Sisterhoods and Schools to 1919." *Polish American Studies* 13 (July–December 1956): 72–76.

———. "Polish Sisters in the Civil War." *Polish American Studies* 7 (January–June 1950): 1–7.

Linehan, Mary. "'Nazareth College Leads the Way': Catholicism, Democracy, and Racial Justice at a Southern College, 1920–1955." *U.S. Catholic Historian* 19 (Winter 2001): 65–77.

Logue, Sister Maria Kostka. *Sisters of St. Joseph of Philadelphia: A Century of Growth and Development 1847–1947*. Westminster, Md.: Newman Press, 1950.

Lux-Sterritt, Laurence. *Redefining Religious Life: French Ursulines and English Ladies in Seventeenth-Century Catholicism*. Hants, England: Ashgate Publishing, 2005.

Maher, Sister Mary Denis. *To Bind Up the Wounds: Catholic Sister Nurses in the U.S. Civil War*. New York: Greenwood Press, 1989.

Mahoney, Kathleen. "American Catholic Colleges for Women: Historical Origins." In *Catholic Women's Colleges in America*, edited by Tracy Schier and Cynthia Russett. Baltimore: Johns Hopkins University Press, 2002.

Mannard, Joseph G. "Converts in Convents: Protestant Women and the Social Appeal of Catholic Religious Life in Antebellum America." *Records of the American Catholic Historical Society of Philadelphia* 104 (Spring–Winter 1993): 79–90.

———. "Maternity . . . of the Spirit: Nuns and Domesticity in Antebellum America." *U.S. Catholic Historian* 5 (Summer/Fall 1986): 305–324.

———. "Protestant Mothers and Catholic Sisters: Gender Concerns in Anti-Catholic Conspiracy Theories, 1830–1860." *American Catholic Studies* 111 (Spring–Winter 2000): 1–21.

———. "'Supported Principally by the Funds of Protestants': Wheeling Female Academy and the Making of the Catholic Community in Antebellum West Virginia." *American Catholic Studies* 114 (Spring 2003): 41–79.

———. "The 1830 Baltimore Nunnery Riot: An Episode in Jacksonian Nativism and Social Violence." In *Urban American Catholicism: The Culture and Identity of the American Catholic People*, edited by Timothy J. Meagher. New York: Garland Publishing, 1988.

———. "Widows in Convents of the Early Republic: The Archdiocese of Baltimore, 1790–1860." *U.S. Catholic Historian* 26 (Spring 2008): 111–132.

Manning, Diane T., and Perry Rogers. "Desegregation of the New Orleans Parochial Schools." *Journal of Negro Education* 71 (Winter/Spring 2002): 31–42.

Marchione, Margherita, MPF. "Religious Teachers Filippini in the United States." *U.S. Catholic Historian* 6 (Fall 1987): 351–372.

Massa, Mark S., SJ. *Anti-Catholicism in America: The Last Acceptable Prejudice*. New York: Crossroad, 2003.

———. *Catholics and American Culture: Fulton Sheen, Dorothy Day, and the Notre Dame Football Team*. New York: Crossroad, 1999.

———. *The American Catholic Revolution: How the '60s Changed the Church Forever*. New York: Oxford University Press, 2010.

McCauley, Bernadette. *Who Shall Take Care of Our Sick? Roman Catholic Sisters and the Development of Catholic Hospitals in New York City*. Baltimore: Johns Hopkins University Press, 2005.

McDonald, Sister Grace. "Pioneer Teachers: The Benedictine Sisters of St. Cloud." *Minnesota History* 35 (June 1957): 263–271.

McEnroy, Carmel Elizabeth. *Guests in Their Own House: The Women of Vatican II.* New York: Crossroad, 1996.

McGreal, Mary Nona, OP, ed. *Dominicans at Home in a Young Nation, 1786–1865, Volume I of the Order of Preachers in the United States: A Family History.* Strasbourg, France: Editions du Signe, 2001.

McGuinness, Margaret. "Americanization and the Schools." *American Catholic Studies* 117 (Summer 2006): 98–102.

———. "Body and Soul: Catholic Social Settlements and Immigration." *U.S. Catholic Historian* 13 (Summer 1995): 63–75.

———. "Let Us Go to the Altar: American Catholics and the Eucharist, 1926–1976." In *Habits of Devotion: Catholic Religious Practice in Twentieth-Century America,* edited by James M. O'Toole. Ithaca: N.Y.: Cornell University Press, 2004.

———. *Neighbors and Missionaries: A History of the Sisters of Our Lady of Christian Doctrine.* New York: Fordham University Press, 2012.

———. "Urban Settlement Houses and Rural Parishes: The Ministry of the Sisters of Christian Doctrine, 1910–1986." *U.S. Catholic Historian* 26 (Winter 2008): 23–42.

McGuinness, Margaret Mary, and Margaret Mary Reher. "From St. Edward's School to Providence Center: A Story of Commitment." *Records of the American Catholic Historical Society of Philadelphia* 107 (Spring–Summer 1996): 101–122.

McHale, M. Jerome, RSM. *On the Wing: The Story of the Pittsburgh Sisters of Mercy, 1843–1968.* New York: Seabury Press, 1980.

McKeown, Elizabeth, and Dorothy M. Brown. "Saving New York's Children." *U.S. Catholic Historian* 13 (Summer 1995): 77–95.

———. *The Poor Belong to Us: Catholic Charities and American Welfare.* Cambridge: Harvard University Press, 1997.

McKevitt, Gerald. *Brokers of Culture: Italian Jesuits in the American West.* Stanford: Stanford University Press, 2007.

McNamara, Jo Ann Kay. *Sisters in Arms: Catholic Nuns through Two Millennia.* Cambridge: Harvard University Press, 1996.

Meagher, Timothy J., ed. *Urban American Catholicism: The Culture and Identity of the American Catholic People.* New York: Garland Publishing, 1988.

Melville, Annabelle M. *John Carroll of Baltimore: Founder of the American Catholic Hierarchy.* New York: Charles Scribner's Sons, 1955.

Metz, Judith, SC. "By What Authority: The Founding of the Sisters of Charity of Cincinnati," *Vincentian Heritage Journal* 20 (1999). Available at: http://via.library.depaul/vhj/vol20/iss1/4.

————. "Elizabeth Bayley Seton: Animator of the Early American Church." *U.S. Catholic Historian* 22 (Winter 2004): 49–65.

————. "Elizabeth Bayley Seton: Extending the Role of Caregiver beyond the Family Circle." *American Catholic Studies* 16 (Summer 2005): 19–38.

————. "In Times of War." In *Pioneer Healers: The History of Women Religious in American Health Care*, edited by Ursula Stepsis, CSA, and Dolores Liptak, RSM. New York: Crossroad, 1989.

————. "150 Years of Caring: The Sisters of Charity of Cincinnati." *Cincinnati Historical Society Bulletin* 37 (Fall 1979): 150–174.

————. "The Founding Circle of Elizabeth Seton's Sisters of Charity." *U.S. Catholic Historian* 14 (Winter 1996): 19–33.

Miller, Randall M., and Jon Wakelyn, eds. *Catholics in the Old South.* Macon, Ga.: Mercer University Press, 1999.

Miller, Sarah E. "'Send Sisters, Send Polish Sisters': Americanizing Catholic Immigrant Children in the Early Twentieth Century." *Ohio History* 114 (2007): 46–56.

Misner, Barbara, SCSC. *"Highly Respectable and Accomplished Ladies": Catholic Women Religious in America, 1790–1850.* New York: Garland Publishing, 1988.

Moore, Cecilia A. "Keeping Harlem Catholic: African-American Catholics and Harlem, 1920–1960." *American Catholic Studies* 114 (Fall 2003): 1–21.

Morrow, Diane Batts. "Outsiders Within: The Oblate Sisters of Providence in 1830s Church and Society." *U.S. Catholic Historian* 15 (Spring 1997): 35–54.

————. *Persons of Color and Religious at the Same Time: The Oblate Sisters of Providence, 1828–1860.* Chapel Hill: University of North Carolina Press, 2002.

Morton, Marian J. "The Transformation of Catholic Orphanages: Cleveland, 1851–1996," *Catholic Historical Review* 88 (January 2002): 65–89.

Mug, Sister Mary Theodosia, ed. *Journals and Letters of Mother Theodore Guérin Foundress of the Sisters of Providence of St. Mary-of-the-Woods Indiana.* St. Mary-of-the-Woods, Ind.: Sisters of Providence, 1942.

Müller, Karl, SVD. *Contemplation and Mission: Sister-Servants of the Holy Spirit of Perpetual Adoration, 1896–1966.* Rome: Apud Collegium Verbi Divini, 1998.

Murphy, Roseanne. *Martyr of the Amazon: The Life of Sister Dorothy Stang.* Maryknoll, N.Y.: Orbis Books, 2007.

Naughton, Gabriel, OFM. "The Poor Clares in Georgetown: Second Convent of Women in the United States." *Franciscan Studies* 24 (1943): 63–72.

Neal, Marie Augusta, SND de Namur. *Catholic Sisters in Transition from the 1960s to the 1980s.* Wilmington, Del.: Michael Glazier, 1984.

Nelson, Sioban. *Say Little, Do Much: Nurses, Nuns, and Hospitals in the Nineteenth Century.* Philadelphia: University of Pennsylvania Press, 2001.

Noffke, Suzanne, OP. *Embrace the Swelling Wave: The Dominicans of Racine, Wisconsin, Volume One.* Bloomington, Ind.: Authorhouse, 2004.

Novak, Michael. "The New Nuns." In *The New Nuns*, edited by Sister M. Charles Borromeo, CSC. New York: New American Library, 1967.

Oakes, Sister Mary Paulinus, RSM, ed. *Angels of Mercy: An Eyewitness Account of Civil War and Yellow Fever by a Sister of Mercy. A Primary Source by Sr. Ignatius Sumner, RSM*. Baltimore: Cathedral Foundation Press, 1998.

Oates, Mary J. "Catholic Female Academies on the Frontier." *U.S. Catholic Historian* 12 (Fall 1994): 121–136.

———, ed. "'Lowell': An Account of Convent Life in Lowell, Massachusetts, 1852–1890." *New England Quarterly* 61 (March 1988): 101–118.

———. "Organized Voluntarism: The Catholic Sisters in Massachusetts, 1870–1940." *American Quarterly* 30 (Winter 1978): 652–680.

———. "Sisterhoods and Catholic Higher Education, 1890–1960." In *Catholic Women's Colleges in America*, edited by Tracy Schier and Cynthia Russett. Baltimore: Johns Hopkins University Press, 2002.

———. *The Catholic Philanthropic Tradition in America*. Bloomington: Indiana University Press, 1995.

———. "The Development of Catholic Colleges for Women, 1865–1960." *U.S. Catholic Historian* 7 (Fall 1988): 413–428.

———. "The Good Sisters: The Work and Position of Catholic Churchwomen in Boston, 1870–1940." In *Catholic Boston: Studies in Religion and Community, 1870–1940*, edited by Robert E. Sullivan and James M. O'Toole. Boston: Archdiocese of Boston, 1985.

Ohlson, Kristin. *Stalking the Divine: Contemplating Faith with the Poor Clares*. New York: Hyperion, 2003.

Owens, M. Lilliana, SL. "Loretto Foundations in Louisiana and Arkansas." *Louisiana History: The Journal of the Louisiana Historical Association* 2 (Spring 1961): 202–229.

Perko, F. Michael, SJ, ed. *Enlightening the Next Generation: Catholics and Their Schools, 1830–1980*. New York: Garland Publishing, 1988.

Perrone, Fernanda. "'A Well-Balanced Education': Catholic Women's Colleges in New Jersey, 1900–1970," *American Catholic Studies* 117 (Summer 2006): 1–31.

———. "Gone and Forgotten? New Jersey's Catholic Junior Colleges." *American Catholic Studies* 121 (Summer 2010): 31–64.

Peterson, Susan C. "A Widening Horizon: Catholic Sisterhoods on the Northern Plains, 1874–1910." *Great Plains Quarterly* 5 (Spring 1985): 125–132.

———. "Doing 'Women's Work': The Grey Nuns at Fort Totten Indian Reservation, 1874–1900." *North Dakota History* 52 (Spring 1985): 18–25.

Peterson, Susan Carol, and Courtney Ann Vaughn-Robertson. *Women with Vision: The Presentation Sisters of South Dakota, 1880–1985*. Urbana: University of Illinois Press, 1988.

Posey, Thaddeus J., OFM, Cap. "Praying in the Shadows: The Oblate Sisters of Providence, a Look at Nineteenth-Century Black Catholic Spirituality." *U.S. Catholic Historian* 12 (Winter 1994): 11–30.

Poulson, Susan. "From Single-Sex to Coeducation: The Advent of Coeducation at Georgetown, 1965–1975." *U.S. Catholic Historian* 13 (Fall 1995): 113–137.

Praszalowicz, Dorota. "Polish American Sisterhood: The Americanization Process." *U.S. Catholic Historian* 27 (Summer 2009): 45–57.

Prejean, Sister Helen. *Dead Man Walking: An Eyewitness Account of the Death Penalty in the United States*. New York: Vintage Books, 1994.

Puzon, Bridget, OSU, ed. *Women Religious and the Intellectual Life: The North American Achievement*. San Francisco: International Scholars Publication, 1996.

Quiñonez, Lora Ann, CDP, and Mary Daniel Turner, SNDdeN. *The Transformation of American Catholic Sisters*. Philadelphia: Temple University Press, 1992.

Rapley, Elizabeth. *The Lord as Their Portion: The Story of the Religious Orders and How They Shaped Our World*. Grand Rapids: William B. Eerdmans, 2011.

Rector, Theresa A. "Black Nuns as Educators." *Journal of Negro Education* 51 (Summer 1982): 238–253.

Reed, Cheryl L. *Unveiled: The Hidden Lives of Nuns*. New York: Berkley Books, 2004.

Reher, Margaret Mary. "Denis J. Dougherty and Anna M. Dengel: The Missionary Alliance." *Records of the American Catholic Historical Society of Philadelphia* 101 (Spring 1990): 21–34.

Reidy, Sister Jeanne, CHM. "Nuns in Ordinary Clothes." In *The New Nuns*, edited by Sister M. Charles Borromeo, CSC. New York: New American Library, 1967.

Riley, Glenda, and Richard W. Etulain, eds. *By Grit and Grace: Eleven Women Who Shaped the American West*. Golden, Colo.: Fulcrum Publishing, 1997.

Rivera, Paul R. "'Field Found!' Establishing the Maryknoll Mission Enterprise in the United States and China, 1918–1928." *Catholic Historical Review* 83 (July 1998): 477–517.

Roberts, Steven V. "Coast Nuns Plan a Secular Order," *New York Times* (3 February 1970), 1, 40.

Rogers, Carole Garibaldi. *Habits of Change: An Oral History of American Nuns*. New York: Oxford University Press, 2011.

Rohrbach, Peter Thomas, OCD. *Journey to Carith: The Sources and Story of the Discalced Carmelites*. Washington, D.C.: ICS Publications, 1966.

Rosalita, Sister M., IHM. *No Greater Service: The History of the Congregation of the Sisters, Servants of the Immaculate Heart of Mary, 1845–1945*. Detroit: Congregation of the Sisters, Servants of the Immaculate Heart of Mary, Monroe, Michigan, 1948.

Rosenberg, Charles E. *The Cholera Years*. Chicago: University of Chicago Press, 1962.

Ryan, Ann Marie. "Meeting Multiple Demands: Catholic Higher Education for Women in Chicago, 1911–1939." *American Catholic Studies* 120 (Spring 2009): 1–26.

Sack, Kevin. "Nuns, a 'Dying Breed,' Fade from Leadership Roles at Catholic Hospitals," *New York Times* (21 August 2011), 11, 16.

Savitt, Todd L., and Janice Willms. "Sisters' Hospital: The Sisters of Providence and St. Patrick Hospital, Missoula, Montana, 1873–1890." *Montana: The Magazine of Western History* 53 (Spring 2003): 28–43.

Scanlon, John. "The Yellow Fever Epidemic of 1878 in the Diocese of Natchez," *Catholic Historical Review* 40 (April 1954): 27–45.

Schier, Tracy, and Cynthia Russett, eds. *Catholic Women's Colleges in America*. Baltimore: Johns Hopkins University Press, 2002.

Schneiders, Sandra M., IHM. *Prophets in Their Own Country: Women Religious Bearing Witness to the Gospel in a Troubled Church*. Maryknoll, N.Y.: Orbis, 2011.

Schrems, Suzanne H. *Uncommon Women Unmarked Trails: The Courageous Journey of Catholic Missionary Sisters in Frontier Montana*. Norman, Okla.: Horse Creek Publications, 2003.

Schultz, Nancy Lusignan. *Fire and Roses: The Burning of the Charlestown Convent, 1834*. New York: Free Press, 2000.

Schweickert, Jeanne, SSSF. *Who's Entering Religious Life? An NCRVD National Study*. Chicago: National Conference of Religious Vocation Directors, 1987.

Sexauer, Cornelia F. "A Well-Behaved Woman Who Made History: Sister Mary Antona's Journey to Selma." *American Catholic Studies* 115 (Winter 2004): 1–20.

Siegfried, Regina, ASC. "Religious Formation Conference: 'Educating for Deepening Relationships: Theological/Communal/Societal/Cultural/Ecological." *American Catholic Studies* 120 (Spring 2009): 55–71.

[Sister Dymphna]. *Mother Caroline and the School Sisters of Notre Dame in North America*. St. Louis: Woodward & Tiernan, 1928.

Sisters, Servants of the Immaculate Heart of Mary Monroe, Michigan. *Building Sisterhood: A Feminist History of the Sisters, Servants of the Immaculate Heart of Mary*. Syracuse: Syracuse University Press, 1997.

Slattery, Sister Margaret Patrice, CCVI. *Promises to Keep: A History of the Sisters of Charity of the Incarnate Word, San Antonio, Texas*. Volume 2. San Antonio, Tex.: Private Printing, 1995.

Spalding, Thomas W. *The Premier See: A History of the Archdiocese of Baltimore, 1789–1989*. Baltimore: Johns Hopkins University Press, 1989.

Specht, Anita. "The Power of Ethnicity in a Community of Women Religious: The Poor Handmaids of Jesus Christ in the United States." *U.S. Catholic Historian* 19 (Winter 2001): 53–64.

Stampp, Kenneth M. *The Peculiar Institution: Slavery in the Antebellum South*. New York: Alfred Knopf, 1956.

Starke, Rodney, and Roger Finke. "Catholic Religious Vocations: Decline and Revival." *Review of Religious Research* 42 (December 2000): 125–145.

Stepsis, Ursula, CSA, and Dolores Liptak, RSM, eds. *Pioneer Healers: The History of Women Religious in American Health Care*. New York: Crossroad, 1989.

Stewart, George C., Jr. *Marvels of Charity: History of American Sisters and Nuns.* Huntington, Ind.: Our Sunday Visitor, 1994.

Suenens, Léon Joseph. *The Nun and the Modern World: Religious and the Apostolate.* Westminster, Md.: Newman Press, 1963.

Sullivan, Eleanore C. *Georgetown Visitation since 1799.* Georgetown: Georgetown Visitation, 1975.

Sullivan, Mary Louise, MSC. *Mother Cabrini: "Italian Immigrant of the Century."* Staten Island, N.Y.: Center for Migration Studies, 1992.

———. "Mother Cabrini: Missionary to Italian Immigrants." *U.S. Catholic Historian* 6 (Fall 1987): 265–279.

Sullivan, Robert E., and James M. O'Toole, eds. *Catholic Boston: Studies in Religion and Community, 1870–1940.* Boston: Archdiocese of Boston, 1985.

Sullivan, Sister Mary Christina, SUSC. "Some Non-Permanent Foundations of Religious Orders and Congregations of Women in the United States (1793–1850)." *Historical Records and Studies* XXXI (1940): 11–118.

Supan, Marita-Constance, IHM. "Dangerous Memory: Mother M. Theresa Maxis Duchemin and the Michigan Congregation of the Sisters, IHM." In *Building Sisterhood: A Feminist History of the Sisters, Servants of the Immaculate Heart of Mary.* Syracuse: Syracuse University Press, 1997.

Taylor, Sarah McFarland. *Green Sisters: A Spiritual Ecology.* Cambridge: Harvard University Press, 2007.

Tentler, Leslie Woodcock. *Seasons of Grace: A History of the Catholic Archdiocese of Detroit.* Detroit: Wayne State University Press, 1990.

Thompson, Margaret Susan. "Cultural Conundrum: Sisters, Ethnicity, and the Adaptation of American Catholicism." *Mid-America* 74 (October 1992): 205–230.

———. "Discovering Foremothers: Sisters, Society, and the American Catholic Experience." *U.S. Catholic Historian* 5 (Summer/Fall 1986): 273–290.

———. "Introduction: Concentric Circles of Sisterhood." In *Building Sisterhood: A Feminist History of the Sisters, Servants of the Immaculate Heart of Mary.* Syracuse: Syracuse University Press, 1997.

———. "Philemon's Dilemma: Nuns and the Black Community in Nineteenth-Century America: Some Findings." In *The American Catholic Religious Life,* edited by Joseph M. White. New York: Garland Publishing, 1988.

———. "The Context—Part One." In *Building Sisterhood: A Feminist History of the Sisters, Servants of the Immaculate Heart of Mary.* Syracuse: Syracuse University Press, 1997.

Thuente, Clement M. OP. "America's Pioneer Catholic Settlement House," *Rosary Magazine* LXIII (October 1923): 1–5.

Treviño, Roberto R. "Facing Jim Crow: Catholic Sisters and the 'Mexican Problem' in Texas." *Western Historical Quarterly* 34 (Summer 2003): 139–164.

Vález, Maria Luisa, CCV. "The Pilgrimage of Hispanics in the Sisters of Charity of the Incarnate Word." *U.S. Catholic Historian* 9 (Winter/Spring 1990): 181–194.

Vinyard, Jo Ellen McNergney. *For Faith and Fortune: The Education of Catholic Immigrants in Detroit, 1805–1925.* Urbana: University of Illinois Press, 1998.

Wakin, Edward. "West Point for Nuns." In *Convent Life: Roman Catholic Religious Orders for Women in North America,* edited by Joan M. Lexau. New York: Dial Press, 1964.

Waldron, Florence Mae. "Re-Evaluating the Role of 'National' Identities in the American Catholic Church at the Turn of the Twentieth Century: The Case of Les Petites Franciscaines de Marie (PFM). *Catholic Historical Review* XCV (July 2009): 515–545.

Wall, Barbra Mann. "Catholic Nursing Sisters and Brothers and Racial Justice in Mid-20th-Century America." *Advances in Nursing Science* 32 (April–June 2009): E81–E93.

———. "Catholic Sister Nurses in Selma, Alabama, 1940–1972." *Advances in Nursing Science* 32 (January–March 2009): 91–102.

———. "Grace under Pressure: The Nursing Sisters of the Holy Cross, 1861–1865." *Nursing History Review* 1 (1993): 71–87.

———. *Unlikely Entrepreneurs: Catholic Sisters and the Hospital Marketplace, 1865–1925.* Columbus: Ohio State University Press, 2005.

Walsh, Sister Marie de Lourdes. *The Sisters of Charity of New York 1809–1959.* Volume 1. New York: Fordham University Press, 1960.

Ware, Ann Patrick, ed. *Midwives of the Future: American Sisters Tell Their Story.* Kansas City, Mo.: Leaven Press, 1985.

Watson, William. "The Sisters of Charity, the 1832 Cholera Epidemic in Philadelphia and Duffy's Cut." *U.S. Catholic Historian* 27 (Fall 2009): 1–16.

Watson, William E., J. Francis Watson, John H. Ahtes III, and Earl H. Schandelmeier III. *The Ghosts of Duffy's Cut: The Irish Who Died Building America's Most Dangerous Stretch of Railroad.* Westport, Conn.: Praeger, 2006.

Weaver, Mary Jo. *Cloister and Community: Life within a Carmelite Monastery.* Bloomington: Indiana University Press, 2002.

———. *New Catholic Women: A Contemporary Challenge to Traditional Religious Authority.* San Francisco: Harper & Row, 1985.

White, Joseph M., ed. *The American Catholic Religious Life.* New York: Garland Publishing, 1988.

Wittberg, Patricia. "Non-Ordained Workers in the Catholic Church: Power and Mobility among American Nuns." *Journal for the Scientific Study of Religion* 28 (June 1989): 148–161.

Woidat, Caroline M. "Captivity, Freedom, and the New World Convent: The Spiritual Autobiography of Marie de l'Incarnation Guyart." *Legacy: A Journal of American Women Writers* 25 (2008): 1–22.

Woods, Jerome Frances, CDP. "Congregations of Religious Women in the Old South." In *Catholics in the Old South,* edited by Randall M. Miller and Jon Wakelyn. Macon, Ga.: Mercer University Press, 1999.

Zagano, Phyllis. *Ita Ford: Missionary Martyr.* New York: Paulist Press, 1996.

Ziolkowski, Sister Mary Janice, CSSF. *The Felician Sisters of Livonia, Michigan: First Province in America.* Livonia, Mich.: Felician Sisters, OSF, Livonia, Michigan, 1984.

Index

About the Author

MARGARET M. MCGUINNESS is Professor of Religion and Executive Director of the Office of Mission Integration at La Salle University, Philadelphia. She served as coeditor of *American Catholic Studies* from 2001 until 2013. Previous publications include *A Catholic Studies Reader* and *Neighbors and Missionaries: A History of the Sisters of Our Lady of Christian Doctrine*.